D1603289

HOME AND HOMELAND

HOME AND HOMELAND

THE DIALOGICS OF TRIBAL
AND NATIONAL IDENTITIES IN JORDAN

Linda L. Layne

PRINCETON UNIVERSITY PRESS   PRINCETON, NEW JERSEY

Library of Congress Cataloging-in-Publication Data
Layne, Linda L.
Home and homeland : the dialogics of tribal and national
identities in Jordan / Linda L. Layne.
p. cm
Includes bibliographical references and index.
ISBN 0-691-09478-0
1. Bedouins—Jordan—Ethnic identity.
2. Jordan—Social life and customs. I. Title.
DS153.55.B43L39 1993
956.95′004927—dc20 93-23878

This book has been composed in Adobe Galliard

The maps on pages 24 and 39 are used by permission of
the cartographer, © Lars Wåhlin, Näsbydalsvägen 4,
IX, S–183 31 Täby, Sweden

Princeton University Press books are printed
on acid-free paper and meet the guidelines
for permanence and durability of the Committee
on Production Guidelines for Book Longevity
of the Council on Library Resources

Printed in the United States of America

1 3 5 7 9 10 8 6 4 2

To the people of Jordan

Contents

List of Figures and Table   ix

Preface   xi

A Note on Transliteration   xvii

Chapter 1. Rethinking Collective Identity   3

Chapter 2. A Generation of Change   38

Chapter 3. *ʿArab* Architectonics   52

Chapter 4. Capitalism and the Politics of Domestic Space 79

Chapter 5. National Representations: The Tribalism Debate 96

Chapter 6. The Election of Identity   108

Chapter 7. Constructing Culture and Tradition in the Valley 128

Chapter 8. Monarchal Posture   143

References   161

Index   179

Figures and Table

FIGURES

Figure 1   A mosaic map of Jerusalem   5

Figure 2   The classical form of a politically segmenting
            genealogy   5

Figure 3   Map of Jordan   24

Figure 4   Map of the East Jordan Valley   39

Figure 5   Vernacular house plans   57

Figure 6   The al-Ṭālib tent   83

Figure 7   The al-Ṭālib house   87

Figure 8   A Jordanian dinar bill   154

TABLE

Table 1   New Dwellings—Deir ʿAlla Subdistrict 1950–1978   44

THIS BOOK has been a long time in the making, and over the many years that Jordan has been a part of my life (as the subject of scholarly research and as a second home) there have been important changes in Jordan and in anthropology; changes that intersect in and inform this work.

When I first went to Jordan in 1977 for a year of Arabic at the University of Jordan in Amman, Jordan was enjoying a period of prosperity. The country was celebrating the King's Silver Jubilee with a year of special events commemorating his twenty-five years on the throne and there was, at least to my young and sheltered eyes, a widespread feeling of well-being. These were, after all, the boom years. Oil prices had risen dramatically in 1973; and although Jordan did not possess substantial oil reserves, the new affluence of the region was also felt in Jordan. So many Jordanians were working in the Gulf that Jordan was experiencing a labor shortage, and there was an effort on the part of the government to get Jordanian women to fill part of the gap, especially the white-collar jobs. The impact of remittances from the Gulf was perhaps most visible in Jordan's thriving construction industry. New luxury hotels and beautiful houses were being built at such a rate that people wondered whether there would soon be a glut. In the meantime, fortunes were being made in land speculation. Jordan, well aware of its limited natural resources, hoped to become a new service-industry center in the region, replacing the still war-torn Beirut as a banking center.

At that point I still had not had any formal training in anthropology. My field research in Algeria as an undergraduate had been of the seat-of-the-pants variety, although with the help of Sally Falk Moore I managed to write up a passable network analysis upon my return to the States. My formal training began in 1978 when I joined what would be the first M.Phil. class in social anthropology at Cambridge. Much like Michael Gilsenan's (1990) experience at Oxford in the early 1960s, I was struck by the absence of the Middle East from the canon. Ethnographic material came mostly from sub-Saharan Africa and New Guinea; theoretically, structural Marxism was the rage. I took an Althusserian framework (and what I considered to be an overly detailed scholarly acquaintance with pigs and taro) with me to Princeton, and this framework influenced both my choice of field site (the Jordan Valley) and field topic (public education) (Layne 1986).

In the 1970s the Jordan Valley had been the site of an extensive "integrated rural development" project (another manifestation of the nation's new prosperity), and so it provided an especially rich opportunity for studying the conjuncture of state- and local-level forces and structures. As a by-product of these projects there existed a wealth of statistical data on the area. During the summer of 1980 while in Amman for another course in Arabic I collected an impressive stack of government and agency reports full of figures on the number, ages, educational levels, landholdings, crops, livestock, and dwellings, et cetera, of the "beneficiaries." The following summer, with the support of a Fulbright-Hays grant and the Wenner-Gren Foundation, I returned to Jordan to begin my research. I reestablished contact with Najwa Shasha, one of the factory owners I had interviewed in 1979 while doing research for the M.Phil. Najwa's family also owned extensive agricultural holdings in the Jordan Valley and a lovely villa (complete with rose garden and swimming pool) overlooking the village of Muʿaddi, and she invited me to stay in the family villa while finding a place to live.

Through Najwa I met Hussein Rashrāsh, an enterprising young man who owned a local shop and did odd jobs for the Shasha family. During the academic year 1981–82 I rented a part of his house in the government housing project in Muʿaddi. (He had recently completed a large addition to the original unit which he and his newly married wife occupied.) I became close friends with wife, Nada Abu Ghunmi, who was a schoolteacher in the local high school for girls. Most mornings I spent at Nada's school observing classes, interviewing teachers, socializing in the teachers' lounge, and sitting in the headmistress's office gossiping, looking at school records, and listening to the parents who visited. From time to time this routine was broken by school trips and visits to the other schools in the area.

In the afternoons Nada and I normally visited her natal family in their home in Muthalath al-ʿArda, just three kilometers to the south. Her father was not well, and he spent a large portion of each day installed on a mattress on the veranda smoking and chatting with old cronies from the neighborhood. Nada's mother and her oldest sister, Nura, busied themselves with household chores. Nada's oldest brother, Muhammad, was married and lived in the town of Salt, but he worked at the central marketing center in the Valley and so stopped by frequently. He often left his three-year-old son in the care of his mother and sisters for several days at a time. Ahmad, the youngest of Nada's siblings, was an aspiring young artist. He did not spend much time at home but would sometimes join us for a brief chat and show us his latest work. Nada's two other sisters were schoolteachers like her. (A fourth sister, the eldest, who died prematurely of cancer, had been the first woman from the Valley to become a teacher.) We "working women" usually spent a few hours every afternoon relaxing—napping, chatting, drinking tea, play-ing with their nephew, enjoying their lovely flower garden.

Nada's sisters, especially Nura and Munīra, also undertook the task of educating me. Nura and her mother spent hours recording old songs and proverbs on my tape recorder, and Nura, a skilled embroiderer, ex-plained her craft to me (chapter 7). (Nura embroidered the two lovely dresses that served as my uniform while in the Valley). They also planned a series of outings for me—several trips to local healers, a visit to a local exhibition of tribal artifacts (chapter 7), and a trip to the National Broadcast Service in Amman to meet the people in charge of the tribal music programs and to admire their archives of "traditional music." Each of these trips and their tape recordings were their suggestion. As evidenced from our first encounter when Munira took my notebook and drew a goat-hair tent filled with "typical" people and artifacts, they had definite ideas about what I, as an anthropologist, ought to know about them. The corpus of knowledge that they selected as appropriate consisted of the "traditional" or "folkloric" aspects of their culture. Although I agreed with them on the suitability of these topics, my atten-tion that first year was focused on how unlike the image I had of Bed-ouin they were (an image based both on scholarly texts and Hollywood movies) and how bracketed off from the rest of their lives much of what they taught me seemed to be.

In addition to this relatively passive mode of research, I also engaged in a number of the standard, more structured forms of anthropological investigation. I made a series of kinship charts for the Abu Ghonmi fam-ily and each of the sections of the Ghānānim tribe. I also conducted a household survey, beginning with the government housing project, which I had learned from a number of people in Amman had been one of the most controversial aspects of the development projects (Layne 1984b). I found these more formal, structured activities helped me to feel "professional" and reduced my anxiety about whether I was actually getting the makings of a dissertation (cf. Joseph 1988). They also helped me get to know the entire community, for in the end I visited nearly every household in Mu ʿaddi.

During the summer of 1982 I was a guest of the al-Ṭālib family, a Mu ʿaddi-based ʿAbbādi family, in their goat-hair tent in the foothill region of al-ʿArda (chapters 3–4). It was not until that summer that I became aware of some of the many other dimensions of "tribal" life—practices like the organization and use of space in their homes which were still vital aspects of their daily lives. As a result, the household sur-vey I conducted that summer in al-ʿArda (of both tents and houses) in-cluded more detail on the organization of domestic space. At the end of the summer I returned to the Valley and now saw the concrete and cinder-block houses that had seemed ugly, plain, and certainly not very "Bedouin" in a different light.

That second year I moved from Muʿaddi to live with members of the Mashalkhah tribe in the village of Diyyat. I had become intrigued by the way in which many ʿAbbādis spoke of the Ghawarneh, tribespeople considered to be the original inhabitants of the Valley, and I hoped that by living among them I would come to understand the relationship between tribespeople like the ʿAbbād considered to be noble (aṣīl) and those not so, like the Ghawarneh. I ultimately regretted this decision. The move created what I now view as needless distress for my previous hosts because they "could not protect my honor" there and because they feared my move might be interpreted as a sign of dissatisfaction with the hospitality they had so kindly offered me. In addition, the scholarly goals that had prompted the move proved elusive. Nevertheless, the experience did broaden my understanding of life in the Valley. I was a frequent guest in the meeting room in the house of Sheikh Sālah al-Naʿīm of the Mashalkhah tribe and was able to observe the comings and goings of the wide variety of individuals who visited him there. Abu Naif, one of the sheikh's sidekicks and the owner of my lodgings—a mud-brick one-room, two-storied structure—often invited me to accompany him on errands (many of which were on behalf of the sheikh on behalf of others) to the various state and local government offices. I also sometimes accompanied the local young women who worked as paid laborers in the fields. The summer I had spent with the al-Ṭālibs had been idyllic, and the following year was colored by my new romanticism about tribal life. Nevertheless, the year spent in Diyyat was crucial in shaping my understanding of the way that the change in their mode of production and their changing relationship with the state had altered their way of life.

In 1984 I returned to Jordan for eight weeks to organize an international symposium, Anthropology in Jordan. Following the symposium, I spent several weeks in the Valley studying the participation of the residents of the Deir ʿAlla Subdistrict in the national parliamentary by-elections. It was during this visit that I became aware that there was a national debate on tribalism under way. The question I was by that point focusing on—"What does it mean to be a member of a tribe in contemporary Jordan?"—was, at least at that time, one of national importance.

I returned to Jordan again in 1988 for two weeks as an escort for a group of Mallone Fellows from the National Council on U.S.-Arab Relations. The program included a number of official briefings by state officials including Jordan's Crown Prince Hassan. Two not-unrelated issues dominated the briefings: the continuing Iraq/Iran war and the worsening state of the Jordanian economy. Lower oil prices and a regional recession meant an influx of returning migrants and rising unemployment. The Gulf War, then in its seventh year, entailed the continuing commitment and expenditure of valuable resources, not only by the two combatants but by the other Gulf states as well (Khalaf 1987), countries that had been important sources of financial support for Jordan in the seventies and early eighties. Within months of our visit, King Hussein announced Jordan's disengagement from the West Bank, a decision that entailed additional financial burdens (Layne 1990a) and that contributed, along with the Gulf War, to a shift in Jordanian collective identity making from issues of tribalism to discussion of the place that Jordan holds or should hold in a divided Arab nation. I have not been back to Jordan since, but a number of reports from the area suggest that Islam now plays a more prominent role in discussions of what kind of a country Jordan is and ought to be. (The Muslim Brotherhood won a third of the eighty seats in parliament in the 1989 elections.)

A good portion of the ethnographic material presented here was first grappled with in the doctoral dissertation I completed in 1986 at Princeton under the supervision of Hildred Geertz, Lawrence Rosen, Gananath Obeyeskere, and Rena Lederman. (The many people both in Jordan and at home who assisted me with the dissertation are acknowledged there.) I had by that time abandoned the structural Marxist framework but had found no adequate alternative. That same year George Marcus and Michael Fischer's call for anthropological research to "take account of larger systems" was published, and in the years since anthropology has on the whole moved in that direction (see Foster 1991).

The Department of Science and Technology Studies at Rensselaer Polytechnic Institute has proved to be an intellectual haven that has provided both the security and stimulation I needed to complete this project. I am particularly grateful to my chair, Shirley Gorenstein, for her unwavering confidence and unerring advice and to John Schumacher for sharing his insights with me about the ramifications of human posture.

Dale Eickelman has been an important source of counsel, criticism, and encouragement over the years. His comments on various portions and versions of the manuscript have always been prompt, thorough, and constructive. Michael Herzfeld's work on the complex interrelationships between national- and local-level discourses of collective identity in Greece provided a valuable model for me, and his interest, support, and detailed comments on this book's many iterations have been much appreciated.

Two anonymous reviewers provided astute feedback on the manu-script for this book. The book is a better one as a result of their prod-ding. Dick Antoun, Riccardo Bocco, Seteny Shami, Lars Wahlin, and Mary Wilson have regularly shared their special knowledge of Jordan with me. In addition, Lars Whalin prepared the maps, Linda Shumaker George kindly attempted to systematize my Arabic transliteration, and Lars Wahlin assisted with the transliteration of place and proper names. I am also grateful to my editors at Princeton University Press. Working with them was one of the more pleasurable aspects of writing this book.

My loyal readers and dear friends Mary Huber, Linda Jacobs, Betsy Shally, and Bernard Wilson read and listened to more versions of this book than they probably care to remember. Their suggestions and sup-port over the long haul were invaluable to me.

During the many years I have worked in Jordan, Ahmad Sharkas and his family helped me in countless ways. I cannot think of Jordan without thinking of them with gratitude and fondness.

I would probably never have gone to Jordan had it not been for the generous scholarship provided by His Majesty King Hussein. In subse-quent years, the support I received from both their Majesties greatly fa-cilitated my work and added an important dimension to my understand-ing and appreciation of Jordan.

Finally, I want to thank the people of Jordan. It is to them that this book is dedicated.

A Note on Transliteration

I HAVE on the whole followed the *International Journal of Middle Eastern Studies* system of transliteration. I have chosen, however, to keep some well-known place and proper names in their more common English forms; so, for example, I refer to King Hussein, rather than King Hussayn, and to Jerash rather than Jarash. I have also tried to represent the *ʿarab* colloquial pronunciation of terms as accurately as possible. Hence, the *q* of classical Arabic appears as a *g* in the context of local usage.

HOME AND HOMELAND

CHAPTER 1

Rethinking Collective Identity

IN 1988 ON A TRIP TO JORDAN as "scholar escort" for a study tour of American college professors, most of whom had little prior knowledge of the Middle East, I was struck by the frequency and uniformity of a particular genre of question, one that I consistently found difficult to answer adequately. These questions involved requests for me to identify and categorize people they were seeing into meaningful social groups, often on the basis of physical appearance alone. "Linda, tell me, that woman over there in the embroidered dress, is she Palestinian or Jordanian?" or "Tell me, who wears the red *kufiyya* and who wears the black ones?" or "Those dark-skinned people over there, who would they be?" Or the question might be about the speaker they had heard in the morning, often people I knew quite well, and although in these cases I was able to offer a more substantive answer, the answer was never a simple one. "Well, he is a Palestinian but his family moved to Jordan and established themselves here before Israel was created in 1948." Or, "He is a Circassian whose family lived in Palestine for three generations before fleeing to Jordan in 1948." Time and time and time again, I, their local expert, was unable to order the new world they were confronting into the framework that they had brought to the encounter. I could sympathize with their efforts, for I recalled my sense of progress when during the first or second month of research in the Jordan Valley I made an entry in my field notes titled "Important Social Groups"; and then, how for the better part of that first year, I struggled with limited success to come to some understanding of who fit into each of those groups and what that meant. This book is an exploration of the problem I encountered first as an ethnographer, later as a culture broker for Americans visiting the Middle East, and most recently as an author attempting to discuss "identity" in nonessentializing ways.

The topic of collective identity has been a central one in the anthropology of the Middle East. The assumption that Arabs belong to easily recognizable corporate social groups is one that has dogged Middle Eastern ethnography throughout its history. Two images—the mosaic and the segmentary triangle—have represented the two most pervasive approaches to collective identity in the region. These approaches, although normally utilized to describe different aspects of Middle Eastern society (the cosmopolitan Ottoman Empire on the one hand and Bedouin tribes on the other), share a number of important characteristics.

The image of the Middle East as a mosaic portrays the region as made up of distinct peoples (each represented by a single, clearly demarcated, colored stone). According to this model, these discrete, static, clearly bounded groups keep their unique identities and cultures while contributing to a larger structure. There is no room for overlap, for gradations, for change. Because this metaphor provides a model of social organization that posits equilibrium, it has been associated with the structural functional approach in anthropology. As Dale F. Eickelman pointed out, although the metaphor of the mosaic was "useful for conveying some of the bare geographical and ethnographic facts concerning the Middle East . . . [like structural functionalism] it is less adequate in explaining the interrelations among these elements or their known historical transformations" (Eickelman 1989:49). In other words, the mosaic metaphor has typically been used by anthropologists and others to portray a timeless Middle East made up of distinct, clearly bounded social groups.

The metaphor of a mosaic became popular following the publication of Carleton Coon's *Caravan* in 1951 and although in recent years it has been largely abandoned by anthropologists of the Middle East, this representation still retains remarkable currency in other scholarly and popular arenas. For example, a respected American political scientist recently asserted that "Jordan is much more of a communal mosaic than most analyses portray it to be" (Brand 1988:180).[1] The mosaic metaphor also appears both explicitly and in the organization of the handbooks and guides to Jordan written from the 1940s through the 1980s (Layne 1990a). Kaplan (1980), author of the chapter "The Society and Its Environment" for the "country study" on Jordan produced by the Foreign Area Studies of the American University as part of their Area Handbook Program begins his piece by stating that "although many Middle Eastern societies have been described as mosaics of distinct and often conflicting groups, the East Bank situation is probably more fragmented than most because of the uprooting that so many of its citizens have endured" (1980:53).[2] This pervasive image of Middle Eastern society probably, at least implicitly, informed the questions posed to me by the educated American tourists whom I escorted.

The other core image of collective identity in Middle Eastern ethnography has been the triangle (sometimes also tellingly referred to as a pyramid) used to represent segmentary lineage systems. The theory of segmentary lineage systems was developed by Evans-Pritchard to explain the social organization of an African tribe, the Nuer. E. E. Evans-Pritchard was influenced by Robertson Smith's work on Arab kinship

FIG. 1 A mosaic map of Jerusalem located in Jordan (reprinted with permission from the Ministry of Tourism, Hashemite Kingdom of Jordan)

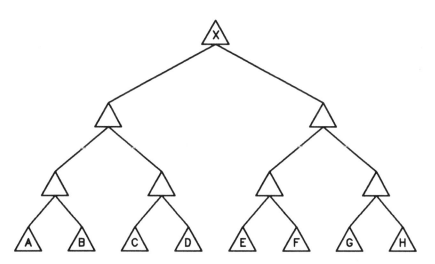

FIG. 2 The classical form of a politically segmenting genealogy (reprinted from Meener [1979] with permission from Cambridge University Press)

(D. Eickelman 1989:132) and thus it is not surprising that this theory has been so widely accepted as representative of the means by which Middle Eastern tribes governed themselves in a stateless society. The theory is based on the idea that "solidary groups form, and then combine or conflict, in predictable ways within a system sustained by a balance of power between its elements" (Dresch 1986:309). Although Evans-Pritchard specified that segmentation did not refer to "social masses" but to "relations among relations", as Dresch (1986:309) observed "arguments about segmentation in the Middle Eastern context still turn on the presence or absence of solidary groups."[3]

Not only do the mosaic and segmentary models tend to posit collective identity in terms of social masses, they also do so in essentialist terms. One's birth defines one's identity permanently as a member of a clearly bounded, easily identifiable group (and in the segmentary model as a member of a series of nesting subgroups). At least in Earnest Gellner's version of segmentary theory, birth also defines the relationships that one will have with members of other groups as well.[4] These approaches share another characteristic: The images of the mosaic and the segmentary triangle each assume and require the presence of an observer located outside the system in order to see the pattern.[5] In these respects the models of a communal mosaic and segmentary lineage system resemble the pigeonhole-style models of collective identity that troubled me as a tour guide and rookie ethnographer. A pigeonhole model of identity is in many ways a distinctively modern Western one whose roots can be traced to the scientific revolution.[6] Newton (1642–1727), sometimes referred to as the "great genius of the scientific revolution," developed a model of matter that was atomistic and essentialistic: the basic units or building blocks of his physics were material particles which were small, solid, indestructible, and homogeneous, "the inner constitution of the particles being independent of their mutual interaction" (Capra 1982:65). According to Fritjof Capra (1982:65), "Newton saw both the particles and the force of gravity as created by God and thus not subject to further analysis." These particles moved mechanistically through space, which he thought of as "absolute," as "an empty container" independent of any physical phenomena occurring in it (Capra 1982:65). Newton described changes in the physical world in terms of time, "which again was absolute, having no connection with the material world and flowing smoothly from the past through the present to the future" (Capra 1982:65). Building on the work of Galileo and Bacon, Newton made it possible for scientists to describe nature mathematically and for science to henceforth restrict itself to the study of "the essential properties of material bodies . . . which could be measured and quantified" (Capra 1982:55).

The scientific revolution resulted not only in a dramatically new way of approaching the natural world but also in new forms of social control. Michel Foucault describes the emergence in the seventeenth century of a system of power, the principles of which parallel those of Newtonian physics. According to Foucault, disciplinary power "separates, analyses, differentiates . . . to the point of necessary and sufficient single units . . . —small, separate cells, organic autonomies, genetic identities" (1979:170). From and through these new forms of discipline emerged what Foucault describes as the power of the Norm. "The marks that once indicated status, privilege and affiliation were increasingly re-placed—or at least supplemented—by a whole range of degrees of nor-mality indicating membership of a homogeneous social body but also playing a part in classification, hierarchization and the distribution of rank" (1979:184).

This modern scientific way of understanding and organizing the world was instrumental in the colonial domination of the Middle East. Michael Gilsenan (1982:150) (following Bourdieu and Sayad 1964) de-scribes the application of the principles of "rationality, linearity, order, visibility, uniformity" by the French in Algeria. Cadastral surveys, land registration, and the resettlement of a massive proportion of the rural population were all part of the French attempt "to fix, to group, to pin down in space" elusive Algerian subjects (Gilsenan 1982:142). Accord-ing to one colonial officer, the most important task was "to gather into groups this people which is everywhere and nowhere; the essential thing is to make them something we can seize hold of" (quoted in Bourdieu and Sayad 1964; translated by Gilsenan 1982:142). Timothy Mitchell (1988) describes similar processes in nineteenth-century Egypt. A mod-ern army was established, agriculture rationalized, and model villages built in an effort to establish "order." Each of these projects utilized "a method of dividing up and containing, as in the construction of barracks or the rebuilding of villages, which operates by conjuring up a neutral surface or volume called 'space'. . . . a series of inert frames or contain-ers" (1988:44–45). According to Mitchell, these practices served to produce "a framework that seem[ed] to precede and exist apart from the actual individuals or objects ordered" (1988:176).

Practices like these that seek to "enframe" actual individuals in the physical world have parallels in cognitive frameworks. The pigeonhole models of collective identity (mosaic, segmentary triangle, and the frameworks that the tourists and I initially attempted to use to frame and order conceptually our first experience of Jordan) begin with a series of inert frames that precede and exist apart from actual individuals. This explains in large part why Eickelman and James Piscatori (1990:16) found, despite "an almost infinitely diverse literature on the concept of identities," that most current approaches to identity "predicate the formulation of identity upon a reality that appears abstract and somehow independent of those persons or groups who perceive and participate in it" (Eickelman and Piscatori 1990:17).

One consequence of a pigeonhole approach is that the units in question are always formally comparable. This applies as much to nations as it does to those forms of collective identity (lineages, tribes, ethnic groups) more commonly considered in the Middle Eastern context. One of the most important characteristics of nations, a distinctively modern form of collectivity, is their "modularity" (B. Anderson 1983:14). As Anderson so astutely observed, nations are always imagined as "limited," having finite boundaries "beyond which lie other nations" (B. Anderson 1983:16). The same could be said of ethnic groups or tribal lineages. Another characteristic of these approaches is their totality. Such frameworks leave no empty social space. Everyone, it is assumed, fits unambiguously into one or another of the frames. In the case of segmentary systems, the principle of complementary opposition means that context will determine at any point the level at which groups coalesce. Once a level has been determined, however, the frames are comparable and every individual is in theory accounted for. Anderson has noted this characteristic with regard to nations: As a cultural artifact "nation" has been so successful that it has become a universal; "in the modern world, everyone can, should, will 'have' a nationality" (1983:14).

Although the frames are formally comparable and universal, the content of each frame is unique. Collectivities, whether lineages, tribes, ethnic groups, or nations, are treated as "necessary and sufficient single units . . . organic autonomies, genetic identities" (Foucault 1979:170). This combination of the comparability of the frames and the essential uniqueness of the solid masses thought to fill them makes it difficult to conceive of a person belonging to more than one frame of any given framework. Although one may simultaneously be a member of groups at different levels within a framework, for example, a lineage and a tribe or groups in different frameworks, for example, an ethnic group and a nation, it is hard to think of a person belonging simultaneously to more than one nation or tribe.[7] The "essential" uniqueness of such collectivities also makes change difficult to account for.

There is no dispute that modern Western approaches to the material and social world have been powerfully effective. There are, however, indications that in a number of diverse contexts such approaches are no longer felt to be adequate—neither as a way of describing the material world (Capra 1982; Beyerchen 1989), nor as a model of the body (Martin 1992), nor as a template from which to organize production and control labor in U.S. corporations (Martin 1992), nor as a model of society (Wolf 1988) or culture (Dominguez 1992; Appaduri 1990; Clifford 1988, Moore 1989; and Fernandez 1986). My interest concerns the difficulties that arise when one attempts to understand collective identity via essentialist models.

THE DIALOGICS OF TRIBAL AND NATIONAL IDENTITIES

In the remainder of this chapter I sketch out some of the problems that essentialist models of identity pose for understanding both tribal and national identities in Jordan. I note a number of parallels in approaches to tribal and national identities, including the repeated attempts by scholars, patriots, and policymakers to define "true Bedouins" and "true Jordanians." These two instances of collective identity are not simply homologous, however, but are intricately related. The relationship between the two might be called "dialogic," to use a Bakhtinian term. As Bakhtin's editor Michael Holquist points out, "dialogism" refers to the "constant interaction between meanings, all of which have the potential of conditioning others. Which will affect the other, how it will do so and in what degree is what is actually settled at the moment of utterance" (Bakhtin 1981:426).

D. Eickelman (1989:127) delineated four forms or ideologies by which people "make" tribal identity in the Middle East:

> 1) the elaboration and use of explicit "native" ethnopolitical ideologies by the people themselves to explain their sociopolitical organization, 2) concepts used by state authorities for administrative purposes, 3) implicit practical notions held by people which are not elaborated into formal ideologies, and 4) anthropological concepts

noting that "in practice these notions are not mutually exclusive and frequently overlap each other" (1989:128). As this study will show, in the Jordanian case at least, these various meanings of "tribe" do not simply overlap but actively inform one another. Furthermore, given the extent to which tribes have come to represent Jordan, the dialogic process takes place not only between various constructions of "tribe" but also between these constructions and those of the Jordanian nation.

A number of scholars (Eickelman 1981; Abu-Lughod 1989; Street 1990) have commented on the fact that pastoral nomadic tribes have been disproportionately studied by anthropologists of the Middle East given their small demographic importance. As Eickelman observed, "As of 1970, pastoral nomads constituted only slightly more than 1 percent of the population of the Middle East, yet such nomadic societies have been more intensively studied by anthropologists than those in village or urban settings" (1981:63). These authors are no doubt right in attributing part of this scholarly emphasis to the "romantic attraction" the Bedouin hold for some Western ethnographers, as perhaps evidenced in William Lancaster's proclaimed desire to study "the most bedu" of Jordan's bedu (1981:3), echoing Donald Cole's (1975) *Nomads of the Nomads*.[8] There are, of course, other reasons than romance or demographic importance for studying tribes, as in our case, their centrality in Jordan's national imaginings.[9]

Tribes have been routinely linked to cultural constructions of the "Hashemite Kingdom of Jordan" in several different though related ways. One important source of this connection is the social composition of Jordan at the time of its establishment in the 1920s, which Mary Wilson describes thus:

> Virtually everyone in Transjordan was identified by family, clan, and tribal affiliation. This social organization reflected the territory's low level of urbanization and marginal relationship to centers of power. . . . In the absence of state security, tribal forms of protective social and economic affiliation expressed through kinship and usually associated with nomadic animal husbandry extended into the agricultural regions and villages. Hence, tribalism in Transjordan was not limited to nomads; rather, the tribes of Transjordan filled every economic niche from nomadic camel breeders to settled farmers, forming a complex web of integrative social alliances. (Wilson 1987:57)

Another source of this connection is found in the composition of the armed forces. A small Mobile Force, the precursor of the Arab Legion (Jaish al-ʿArabi), had been established in 1920 under the leadership of British officer Frederick Peake.[10] Initially the force was composed of ex-soldiers from the Ottoman army and local townspeople and had as one of its primary tasks the suppression of Bedouin raiding (Axelrod 1978).[11] In 1930 Peake was joined by Captain John Glubb who had extensive experience dealing with Bedouin tribes in Iraq. Glubb reversed Peake's approach to recruitment; the Desert Mobil Force he organized was composed largely of Bedouin (Gubser 1983:79–80; Jureidini and McLaurin 1984:18–22).[12] According to S. A. Brigadier El-Edroos (1980:213), "The eventual pacification and the successful recruitment of the Bedouin of Transjordan into the ranks of the Legion was due solely to the personal efforts, leadership and diplomatic skill of Major (later General) J. B. Glubb," and he suggests that the fact that the Bedouin played such a central role in Jordan's military may be an artifact of the British preference for the Bedouin as exemplars of a "martial race."[13]

Up until the present, Bedouin are still widely believed to account for the majority of the armed forces (Axelrod 1978; Day 1986; Jureidini and McLaurin 1984). According to Arthur R. Day, "The army is still drawn predominantly from those sectors of the population that have manned it in past years. The great majority of the senior officers are selected from the principal tribal groups in the country. . . . Junior officers and enlisted personnel have also come from these tribal groups and from other tribes and extended families that made up so much of traditional East Bank Society" (Day 1986:80). Sources for assertions like Day's that "the army is still a heavily bedouin army" (Day 1986:81) are rarely given and there is some dispute regarding the actual composition of the officer corps (cf. Axelrod 1978:29; Bocco, personal communication).[14] Nevertheless, it is almost axiomatic that in descriptions of Jordan tribes are credited with "providing the foundation on which the Jordanian government was built and the nucleus of the Jordanian Army which has ensured its stability" (Jureidini and McLaurin 1984:vii).[15]

A corollary of this view is the frequent assertion that "it is Jordan's tribes who uphold the monarchy." Irving Kaplan (1980:64) asserts that "Jordan was unique among primarily sedentary Middle Eastern countries in that the Hashemite government depended, at least until the late 1960s or early 1970s, for its most significant political support on the beduin tribes." Paul Jureidini and R. D. McLaurin also believe that "the importance of tribal consciousness is waning" and "given the centrality of tribal support in the security of the Hashemite monarchy in the past" this trend is perilous for the stability of the regime (1984:vii). This common view seems to confirm Iliya Harik's observation that most social science interpretations of politics in the Middle East assume that "if a regime is in power, then its power rests on a particular social class or ethnic group" (Harik 1981:69). In fact, the Hashemite rule of Jordan is more in keeping with what Harik (1981:71) suggests has been the typical pattern for Middle Eastern regimes throughout the twentieth century: reliance on a "strategic political minority" characterized by "multiple identifications," in this case one that includes both those who might be considered Palestinians as well as a whole range of Transjordanians.[16]

Bedouin are also sometimes linked to cultural constructions of the "Hashemite Kingdom of Jordan" directly through the person of the king. For nearly all of the over seventy years of its modern existence, Jordan has been ruled by two Hashemite kings, Abdullah bin Hussein (reign 1921–1951) and Hussein bin Talal (reign 1953–present). (Talal, Abdullah's son, and Hussein's father, ruled only for a short period, from 1951 to 1952, due to health reasons; a regency council relieved him and ruled until Hussein took the throne in 1953.) These two long-reigning kings have been so closely associated with their kingdom that people have periodically remarked that it is hard to imagine Jordan without them. For example, Day (1986:2) remarks that for most Americans, "to the extent that they are aware of it, [Jordan] is primarily King Hussein"; and he begins his book on Jordan with a description of the King's palaces, explaining that the King's personal life is a good place to begin because "the country the King rules from here is shaped in his image and that of his Hashemite grandfather Abdullah" (1986:8). Similarly, Jureidini and McLaurin (1984:68) assert that "the concept of 'Jordan' is so closely linked with King Hussein some find it difficult to conceive of Jordan without Hussein" and "Jordan is a Hashemite Kingdom in name, but Hussein's Kingdom in the public mind" (Jureidini and McLaurin 1984:68). Such observations are particularly prevalent whenever the issue of succession is raised, as it recently was by Hussein's surgery for cancer in September 1992. As one Jordanian analyst commented on that occasion, "For most of us, the man has been with us since the beginning of life itself. We don't know anybody else" (Fineman 1992:A-4).

Given such a close association of these monarchs with Jordan, the fact that they are so frequently mistakenly identified as Bedouin is especially important. The Hashemites are referred to as Bedouin in the movie *Lawrence of Arabia*, and both King Abdullah and King Hussein have individually been portrayed as Bedouin on numerous occasions.[17] According to Wilson (1987:6), Abdullah was often portrayed both in the Middle East and the West as a Bedouin despite the fact that he grew up in two of the most important nineteenth-century cities of the Middle East, Mecca and Istanbul.[18] King Hussein is also routinely identified as a Bedouin, at least by Western observers. For instance, Day (1986:2) describes the average Americans view of Hussein as "the courageous and very lucky bedouin king" and in an article in the *New York Times* Thomas L. Friedman (1988) asserts that "about two-thirds of Jordan's 2.8 million inhabitants are Palestinian, with the remainder Bedouins like King Hussein."

BEDOUIN, "TRUE" AND OTHERWISE

In Jordanian nationalist and tourist-directed rhetoric, much as in Western popular and social scientific discourse, "the Bedouin" represent the archetypical Arab "tribe" and frequently stand for Arab or Jordanian "tribes" in general. For example, in the many handbooks on Jordan one frequently finds the terms tribe, Bedouin, nomad, pastoralist, and desert Arab being used interchangeably.

The term *Bedouin* (*badū*) comes from the same root as *bādiya* (desert or steppe) and literally means desert dweller. Generally the term refers to pastoral nomads and encompasses a constellation of characteristics—residence location (the *bādiya*), residence type (goat-hair tent), residence pattern (nomadic), and a particular form of pastoralism (camel herding). Statistics on Bedouin are highly unreliable, and estimates of the number of "Bedouin" and/or their proportion of the total population at various moments in Jordanian history have varied significantly.[19] Part of the difficulty stems from the assumption, implicit in this four-part definition of Bedouin, that all these characteristics go hand and hand. In fact, figures vary depending what is counted. For example, if one counts tent dwellers one is likely to come up with a different number than if one counts nomads because, as I will discuss in chapter 3, many people, including agriculturalists, occupy tents for at least part of the year. Still a different number would be had if one counted those living in that part of the country administratively defined as the desert (*bādiya*).[20] For example, according to the 1961 population census of the East and West Banks of Jordan the total population living in tents was over 95,000. Of these only about half (43,000) lived in the *bādiya*; the remainder lived in the settled census districts of both banks. Counting "nomads" is even trickier business. The *bādiya* population was estimated to be 140,000 to 150,000 out of a population of more than two million by the mid-1970s; of these it was "estimated that far less than 50,000" were still nomadic (Gubser 1983:26), but no definition of nomadic is provided. Just how far and how often does one have to move to be "nomadic"? If one owns a house is one automatically disqualified?

There is more at issue here than a statistical problem. The cultural construction of "Bedouin" in this way is a clear example of the essentializing approach to collective identity discussed above. Bedouin are construed as a distinct, unique social type, or to borrow Foucault's phrase again, as an "organic autonomy." Camel herding, nomadism, and living in tents in the desert *naturally* seem to go together. If viewed from the point of view of an organic model of culture in which a culture is likened to a body, if any one of these elements were to be missing, say tent dwelling, the culture is maimed.

Such an organic model of tribal culture helps explain why the demise of the Bedouin has been so frequently predicted. For example, in the 1880s a British topographer wrote of one of the Jordan Valley tribes: "The 'Adwan are on a downhill path, and with the death of Goblan and his generation, their future seems to be that they will either become tillers of their own lands or else sink to the ignoble position of tourist guides . . ." (Conder 1892:355). He went on to predict that the "wilder" tribes of the ʿAnazeh and Beni Sakhr would, like the ʿAdwan "finally disappear" in the face of more "energetic and civilized races" (Conder 1892:356).

But it is not only an organic model of tribal culture that makes change among Bedouin so problematic, for in the case of Bedouin the mostly static model of cultural holism is normally joined with evolutionary models of social change.[21] Because most evolutionary models are premised upon the assumption that mankind advances through the move to sedentism and that all the glories of civilization hinge on this move, it sets up a double bind for Bedouin. On the one hand, Bedouin must settle to advance, but given the nostalgic construction of "Bedouin" as a repository of a pure primordial past, in the process of advancing they are simultaneously degraded and corrupted.

This is apparent in the concept of a "true" or "real" Bedouin and its tacit counterpart, the residual category of the "not-so-true" Bedouin. For example, according to Day (1986:81) there is a "relative scarcity of true bedouin in modern Jordan."[22] Gubser describes "the 'true' bedouin" as those "who depend mostly upon camels rather than sheep and goats for their livelihood, live in black (goat hair) tents, and do not settle in permanent houses" (Gubser 1983:24; see also Kaplan 1980:66). Similar definitions have been put forward by Jordanian anthropologists. For example, Mohammad Abu Hassan (1984) suggests that reliable measures for distinguishing Bedouin tribes from non-Bedouin tribes are 1) habitation in deserts; 2) source of livelihood, 3) tribal mobility, and 4) provisions of the law.[23] The construction of "true Bedouin" as the standard against which other tribes are measured recalls Foucault's discussion of "the power of the Norm" whereby certain characteristics deemed normal not only indicate membership in a homogeneous social body but also provide the means by which other individuals and groups are classified and ranked (1979:184).[24] Similar instances are found in North and South American constructions of "real Indian" (Clifford 1988; Jackson 1989; Jarvenpa 1992). For example, Robert Jarvenpa (1992) reports that the Euro-Canadians of Dawson City attribute "real Indian" status to those rare native individuals who still engage in winter subsistence hunting. "The presumptuous notion of 'real Indian,' of course, dismisses as false or less than worthy those who have changed or departed from a static ideal" (1992:15).

But in each case one must ask why it is that certain "native" practices seem to belong together and for whom this appears to be so. James Clifford has described the problems that an organic model of culture posed for Mashpee Indians in a land-claims suit in the 1970s. One of the reasons the Mashpee lost their case, Clifford suggests, is that their discourse was compromised and constrained "by powerful assumptions and categories underlying the common sense that supported the law" prominent among them being "the idea of cultural wholeness" (Clifford 1988:336–37). He writes:

> Indian culture in Mashpee might be made up of unexpected everyday ele-ments, but it had in the last analysis to cohere, its elements fitting together like parts of a body. The culture concept accommodates internal diversity and an "organic" division of roles but not sharp contractions, mutations, or emergences. It has difficulty with a medicine man who at one time feels a deep respect for Mother Earth and at another plans a radical real estate subdivision. (1988:338)

Clifford is only partially correct here, for it is not "the culture concept" that has difficulty with such a medicine man. One can in theory at least image a culture in which these two impulses are not viewed as contradic-tory. The observation that the Western concept of culture assumes that the various aspects of a culture will cohere still leaves unanswered the questions: By what criteria are "unexpected everyday elements" distin-guished from "sharp contradictions" and by whom?[25] For example, to return to our case, one might ask whether Jordanian tribespeople find living in a house a sharp contradiction or an everyday occurrence.

This question is one that I address at length in chapters 3 and 4. Here suffice it to say that the tribes of the Jordan Valley who changed in the last thirty years from being tent-dwelling, transhumant goat and sheep herders to house-dwelling agriculturalists evidenced no discomfiture with the changes, in their way of life or confusion about their identity. Even before these dramatic changes, they would not have qualified as "true Bedouin," and in the early eighties they would probably be de-fined according to the common four-stage model of sedentarization (nomadic, seminomadic, semisedentary, sedentary) as semisedentary. But these tribes do not think of themselves as "semi" anything; they refer to themselves collectively either by their proper name (that of their family, lineage, tribe, or tribal confederation, depending on the context) or generically as ʿarab.[26]

The perspective of people like the ʿAbbād provides an alternative ap-proach to collective identity. Tribespeople in Jordan do make distinc-tions between themselves on the basis of herding and residence prac-tices, but in so doing they utilize a elaborate vocabulary that contrasts with the simple, "Bedouin/not real Bedouin" distinction so often used by and to outsiders. For example, Alois Musil, writing in the first de-cades of this century, reports that

> the Rwala divide human beings into *hazar*, or those who dwell in perma-nent houses, and ʿ*arab*, or those who dwell in movable tents. Arab, there-

fore, is the name given throughout the desert to the inhabitants of a black tent only. . . . *ʿarab ad-dira* is the common name of the nomads who are found in the tilled areas and on their borders, irrespective of the tribe to which they belong. . . .

The dwellers in houses, *hazar*, are divided into *karawne* . . . , or those who never leave their permanent dwelling, and *raʿw* (or *raʿijje*), or those who change from their permanent dwellings during the rainy season to movable tents. After the sowing of crops in the autumn, the *raʿw* or *raʿijje* leave their villages and with their flocks of goats and sheep make their way into the steppe, where they dwell both in black goat's-hair tents and in gray tents of cotton fabric. At the end of April and in May, when the harvest is near, they return from the steppe to their houses.

The Arabs consist of *Bedouins* and *swaja* (or *jujan*). The *swaja* have two things black, . . . black tents of goat's hair and flocks of black goats and sheep. These flocks do not permit them to go into the interior of the desert, *ma jesarrezun*. They are limited to the territory where their is abundance of water and where annuals grow every year. They encamp on the edge of the desert and are therefore known as *ruhm ad-dire*, relatives of the (the people of) settled country; they do not undertake extensive raids, *razw*, and they acknowledge the supremacy of various Bedouins, to whom they pay a tax for protection, *hawa*. The Bedouins are arabs who breed camels exclusively, or at least in the main, and for ten months dwell in the interior of the desert, *jessarrezun*. At the end of June they move to the edge of the desert, *jerarrebun*, dwell among the settlers until the middle of August or the beginning of September, provide themselves with grain, clothing, and weapons, and then return to the desert again. (Musil 1928:44–45)[27]

Although Jordanian tribespeople do distinguish among themselves based on differences in herd composition and residence practices, in fact, of much greater importance to *ʿarabs* than mobility is the question of nobility. In this regard, indigenous classification is a much more either/or affair; tribes either are or are not *aṣīl* (noble) (although in practice, of course, there is a certain amount of negotiation and posturing regarding whether or not certain groups are in fact "noble"). (See Layne 1986.) But whether one speaks of differences in subsistence system or noble heritage, it is important to remember that such indigenous distinctions between tribes were utilized in the past to culturally construct the identity of particular tribes, not a tribal or Bedouin identity as such.

Anthropologists (including myself) who have studied tribes in Jordan and elsewhere in the Middle East have been aware of these distinctions yet when writing for Western audiences have almost inevitably opted for the term Bedouin.[28] For example, Abu-Lughod reports that the Awlad ʿAli of Egypt's Western Desert refer to themselves more frequently as ʿarab than as bedu (1986:44); and yet she refers to them in her writings as Bedouin. Similarly, J. C. Wilkinson (1977:189) explains that he uses the simple distinction "bedu" and "hadar" (settled and nomad) "for convenience" even though he realizes that "there are so many variables involved in the way of life of the people who inhabit the fringes of the desert that it is of limited value to classify their mode of life under such simple terms: the fact that people may not move around to gain a living does not, *ipso facto*, make them 'settled' any more than livestock-herding makes them 'nomads.'"[29] This use of the term Bedouin is comparable to the practice that Brian Street (1990:251) observed in Afghan ethnography where even indigenous anthropologists follow convention and use the colonial term Pathan for people who refer to themselves as "Paktuns" because the latter is more "accessible" to Western readers, especially British readers who are likely to be acquainted with the stereotypes of "wily Pathans" found in popular fiction and newspaper reports. That ethnographers, including myself, have made such choices in the recent past is testimony to the power of this discourse.

In certain administrative contexts the Jordanian government has adopted a different, but ultimately no less problematic, approach to defining "Bedouin." Up until 1976 people legally defined as "Bedouin" were subject to special laws, and to this day Jordanian electoral law prescribes a set number of seats for "Bedouin" representatives.[30] In both of these contexts those defined as "Bedouin" have been designated by proper names. For example, in The Bedouin Control Law of 1924 drawn up by the British Protectorate and Jordanian Emirate authorities, "Bedouins" referred to the members of nine named tribes (Oweidi 1982). Although all these tribes were camel herders of the eastern desert, not all such tribes were named (Bocco 1989b:278). As Bocco (1989a:147; translation mine) observed, the state apparently found the task of legally defining tribes and tribal spaces that had heretofore "been defined and represented in relation to kinship whether fictive or real" a problematic one, for the definition of Bedouin was revised in the Bedouin Control Law of 1929 and again in 1936 as well as in numerous electoral laws over the years.[31] The new laws dropped the names of some tribes and added those of others, but more importantly they added the clause "the tribes and sub-tribes under their protection and such other nomadic tribes as may enter Transjordan from time to time." In so doing the state effectively "safeguarded a space for negotiation," recognizing both the fluidity of tribal systems—the processes of "fission and fusion, division and alliances"—and the changing needs of the government vis-à-vis certain tribal groups (Bocco 1989a:148; 1989b:278).

JORDAN'S MUDDLED MOSAIC

Many of the definitional problems encountered by those seeking to define "true Bedouin" find parallels in efforts to define "true Jordanians." Open any of the handbooks on Jordan (Harris 1958; Naval Intelligence 1943; Sinai and Pollack 1977; Nyrop 1980; Gubser 1983), pass the section on climate and topography to the section on population and you will find the mosaic of Jordan sketched out.[32] Jordan's ethnic and religious minorities are each easily defined and neatly placed—the Circassians, about 25,000 "souls" originating in the Caucasus and like the vast majority of the Jordanian population Sunni Muslims; about 2,000 Sheeshans also originally from the Caucasus but, unlike the Circassians, Shia Muslims; the Christians (Greek Orthodox, Greek Catholic, Roman Catholic, and Protestant) totaling about 125,000 or about 8 percent of the total population; and small communities of Bahais and Druse, Armenians, Assyrians, Kurds and Turkomans.[33]

But when the authors of these handbooks address "the Jordanians" and "the Palestinians" their descriptions inevitably become muddled and confused. Their accounts are riddled with definitional problems; one finds that the terms of reference keep shifting. Individuals (and their descendants) who happened to be living in the area that became "Transjordan" in 1921 and the East Bank of the "Hashemite Kingdom of Jordan" in 1949 are variously referred to as "Jordanians," "Transjordanians," "true Jordanians," "indigenous Jordanians," "East Jordanians." "True Jordanians" are generally described as being "tribally organized and tribally oriented" (Kaplan 1980:53) but the meaning of "tribally organized and tribally oriented" is vague and unclear for many of the same reasons that Palestinians and Jordanians are so hard to define definitively.[34]

In addition to "true Jordanians," another conceptual category is something called "practical purpose Jordanians." For example, according to Kaplan (1980:76) the Majali family, the leading family in Kerak, although originally from Hebron in the West Bank are "for political and social purposes" considered "Jordanians." Other Hebronis who came as merchants before 1948 but unlike the Majalis remained "to a considerable degree outsiders, for the most part taking their spouses from the Hebron area and maintaining economic and other ties there," are also "for practical purposes" considered "Jordanians . . . having cast their economic and political lot with that country" (Kaplan 1980:76). Even some groups like the Ghazawis (from the Gaza Strip) who came to the Karak area after 1948 are included among those having cast their lot with Jordan and as a result are considered "Jordanians" in contrast with the Palestinian refugees living in or near Amman (Kaplan 1980:76–77).[35] The reader is left unsure as to whether the definition of "Jordanian" hinges on having moved to Jordan before an arbitrary cut-off date, residence (refugee camp or not), loyalty (the casting of one's economic and political lot with the country), or some combination of all three.[36]

These definitional problems are also apparent in more scholarly work. For example, Valerie Yorke defines Palestinian Jordanians as "those who came to the Kingdom from west of the Jordan river after 1948, and their descendants" (1988a:16), but later she cites evidence concerning their numbers based on birthplace or the birthplace of one's father. By "descendants" does she then mean only the children of male Palestinians? Is national identity, like tribal identity, presumed to be patrilineal?

Efforts to define Jordanians or Palestinians on the basis of social differences are no less problematic. "Palestinian Jordanians" were at one time thought to be distinguishable by virtue of being more sophisticated, better educated, more urbanized than East Bank Jordanians. For example, Daniel Lerner's 1950 survey of the levels of modernity in Jordan showed "consistently greater modernity" of refugee Palestinians over indigenous Jordanians" (Lerner 1958:307).[37] The refugees were "proportionately better educated, more urban, more active media consumers, and more widely empathic than the non-refugees" (Lerner 1958:307).[38] Although there were serious problems with Lerner's methodology, there is no doubt that there were differences between the East and West Bank populations at that period. However, those differences in health, education, and welfare have virtually disappeared in the intervening years. There are, of course, still important social differences in Jordan including differences in health, education, and welfare, but these differences are not easily summarized by the Palestinian/Jordanian distinction. For example, several authors have described economic and political differences (defined in terms of loyalty to the Hashemites) within the East Bank Palestinian population which they believe correlate with date of migration (pre-1948, 1948, 1967) and residence (refugee camps and or not) (Gubser 1983.16–17, Brand 1988:180–81). Neither is the Transjordanian population socially or politically homogeneous; religious (Christian/Muslim and divisions within the Muslim majority), rural-urban, north-south, and differences in political attitudes exist (Khouri 1981:105; Brand 1988:180).

Despite, or perhaps because of the ambiguities entailed in the cultural construction of "Jordanians" and "Palestinians" in the Jordanian context, the distinction is often considered the most significant in Jordanian society. For example, most Western analysts would agree with Gubser that Jordan's "national and cultural differentiations . . . are most vividly represented by the Palestinian Jordanians as distinguished from, for want of a better term, the East Jordanians . . ." and that "the distinction between the Palestinians and the East Jordanians constitutes the most serious and, at times, nation-threatening cleavage in Jordan" (Gubser 1983:14).[39]

It is not just Western observers who find this distinction important and problematic. Kamel Abu Jaber, a political scientist at the University of Jordan, addressed the issue in a book whose title signals this definitional ambiguity: *The Jordanians and the People of Jordan* (1980).

> In this century, we have mixed like we never mixed before. . . . the West has thrown us together. And here we are loving and hating it, constantly adjusting and readjusting to the new "realities," and the new "facts of life." Who are the Jordanians? The Palestinians? Where are they? Can't we find a new expression like the Pale-Jordanians? Jorpalians? Jorstinians? I wonder if we should, if we could, for the proud Palestinians though so ethnically, religiously, geographically and linguistically similar, enjoy or suffer distinct traditions and experiences. Why should they become anything but Palestinians, in the same sense that one wonders why should two brothers be alike? (1980:17–18).

In 1988, Fawaz Toqan, then Minister of Social Development, asserted, "There is nothing that is pure Palestinian nor pure Jordanian . . . I am a pure Palestinian born in Jerusalem and living here, and my wife is Jordanian. I have five children: So what are they?" (Ibrahim, *New York Times*, 18 Oct. 1988).

The concepts of "Jordanian" and "Palestinian" are not only ambiguous in terms of personal identity but in terms of national identity as well. Given the premise that a nation is by definition expected to be "self-contained, autonomous, and complete, asserting itself against a world of similar entities" (Handler 1988:194), the nationhood of Jordan like that of all the other Arab states is at odds with the notion of Arab nationalism.[40] The question as to whether or not an Arab nation currently exists or can ever exist is one that has been repeatedly debated, but if one accepts B. Anderson's (1983) definition of a nation as an "imagined political community," the Arab nation certainly qualifies.[41] And to the extent that nations are thought to be "necessary and sufficient single units . . . organic autonomies, genetic identities" it is difficult to reconcile the coexistence of an Arab nation with that of individual member-state nationalisms.[42] This tension which follows from a modern Western pigeon-hole-style definition of nation may account for the relative scholarly neglect of "nation-state nationalisms" in the Arab world on the one hand, and the isolation of the study of Arab nationalism from current trends in history and social sciences including the comparative study of nationalism on the other (Khalidi 1991:1363–64). As Rashid Khalidi noted, most of the important work done in recent years on comparative nationalism such as that by Eric Hobsbawm and B. Anderson make little or no use of Arab examples.

Although this apparent problem of simultaneous country-specific and pan-Arab nationalisms is one shared by all Arab states, the nationhood of Jordan is especially problematic (at least if defined according to the modern Western model) because of the circumstances of its creation and its special relationship with Palestine. The demands inherent in nationalist ideologies for clarity and closure with regard to boundaries have consistently been challenged by ambiguities in the relationship between Jordan and Palestine.[43] As Wilson (1987) has so well documented, the contours and status of the Jordanian and Palestinian nations and their relation to each other have been characterized by equivocacy since the breakup of the Ottoman Empire.

From 1516 onwards, the area that became modern Jordan had been part of the Ottoman Empire's province of Greater Syria (*bilād al-Shām*). In 1908–9 a group of Turkish army officers, who came to be known as the Young Turks, forced the Turkish sultan, Abdul Hamid II, to restore the constitution and to introduce parliamentary procedures and then ultimately deposed him. The new regime's efforts to centralize the Ottoman administration and to "Turkify" the empire sparked opposition among the Arabs. When the Ottoman Empire allied itself with Germany and Austria in 1914, Sharif Hussein of Mecca, King Hussein's great grandfather, broke away from the empire and asked for Britain's help in establishing an independent Arab nation. Sharif Hussein's sons, Faisal, Ali, and Abdullah (later the first King of Jordan), played central roles in what would come to be known as the Great Arab Revolt [against Ottoman rule] (*al-thawra al-ʿarabiyya*). Britain provided supplies, money, and military advisors (including T. E. Lawrence); but when the war was over, despite the British promises of postwar Arab independence, the British and French governments divided the Fertile Crescent among themselves. In March 1920 Faisal had been elected King of Syria but at the San Remo Conference in April of that year, Syria and Lebanon were put under French Mandatory rule, while Palestine and Iraq came under British mandate. The status of the East Bank of the Jordan (an area considered to be of limited importance to all parties) was left unclear. Under Faisal's rule, this area had been administered as a province of Syria. When France occupied Damascus and ousted Faisal, the British decided that Transjordan was not in fact a part of Syria and therefore the French had no jurisdiction over it. From that point on until 1948 the British administered TransJordan along with Palestine as part of the same mandate. Although Transjordan and Palestine had separate governments, a number of factors contributed to a particularly close relationship between the two countries throughout the mandate period. Wilson summarizes this relation thus:

> Their particular governments were different, but the two fell under the same mandate, causing administrative overlap and certain common cares. The high commissioner for Palestine was also the high commissioner for Transjordan. . . . The long border between Transjordan and Palestine was very permeable. Papers or passports were not generally needed to pass from one to the other. Trading ties had been encouraged ever since 1920 and the two territories shared the Palestine pound after its introduction in 1927. Transjordan served Palestine as a reserve of unskilled seasonal labor. Palestine provided Transjordan with trained men for its new bureaucracy. Economic problems in one reverberated in the other; political problems too resounded across the Jordan valley. (1987:103)

Britain had not intended for Jordan to exist as a separate political entity but gradually came to see the advantages of using Jordan as a buffer area between Palestine and the Arab nationalism of Syria, on the one hand, and the reformist, puritanical Islamic religious movement (Wahabism) gaining strength in central Arabia on the other.[44] Abdullah, who had entered Transjordan in the fall of 1920 on his way to Damascus to reclaim Syria for the Arabs, was gradually accepted by Britain as ruler of Transjordan and was made emir when the Transjordanian Emirate was established in 1923. Even after Britain's 1923 "assurance" to Abdullah that it would recognize the existence of an independent government in Transjordan under his rule, Britain's commitment to an independent Jordan remained provisional for some time and Britain periodically considered the possibility of merging the two entities (1921, 1937, 1948) (Wilson 1987:60,75,84).

Neither did Abdullah envisage Jordan as an independent nation unto itself. Abdullah, like his father, never gave up the dream for a united Arab nation under Hashemite rule, and devoted his life to attempting to merge Jordan with one or another of its neighbors. A merger with Palestine was effectively accomplished following the withdrawal of the British Mandatory forces in 1948 and the war with Israel that ensued. When the armistice was concluded between Israel and Jordan on April 3, 1949, Jordan remained in effective control of the West Bank including the old city of Jerusalem (only a portion of the United Nations–defined Arab areas of Palestine). Elections were held to select representatives of the West Bank as members of the Jordanian parliament on April 24, 1950, and the newly enlarged Jordanian parliament voted to unify the territory and populations of the two banks of the Jordan (Hassan 1981:41).

The Jordanian annexation of the West Bank resulted in the incorporation of roughly 460,000 residents of the West Bank into Jordan. At the same time, it is estimated that over half a million Palestinians fled from Israel to the East and West Banks; about 450,000 of these registered with the United Nations Relief and Works Agency as "refugees" (Gubser 1983:12). Jordan granted full civil rights (the only Arab host country to do so) and full rights of property ownership to all these new citizens (Haidar 1988:97–98).

In the June war of 1967 Jordan lost the West Bank to Israeli military occupation but continued to provide passports for West Bank residents, paid the salaries of thousands of government employees, and the West Bank continued to be represented in Jordan's lower house of parliament. Following the 1967 war, an estimated 310,000 individuals fled from the West Bank and Gaza Strip to the East Bank (Gubser 1983:12). The flow continued throughout the 1970s and 1980s, as many West Bankers moved to the East Bank and then, quite often, on from there to the Gulf.

Much as we saw regarding the statistics on "Bedouin," because of the definitional ambiguity and political importance of the categories "Palestinian" and "Jordanian," figures regarding the number and proportion of Palestinians and Jordanians in Jordan can vary widely.[45] Writing in April 1988 Yorke notes that

> it has come to be accepted that Palestinian Jordanians . . . comprise a majority of some 65 per cent of Jordan's East Bank population of just over 2.9 million. According to this estimate, Jordan provides a home for some 1.9 million Palestinians, the largest concentration of Palestinians living outside pre-1948 Palestine but in the Middle East, and nearly a third of the total Palestinian population worldwide (Yorke 1988a:16).

She goes on to observe that although "these figures are repeated so often they have become conventional wisdom," their source is obscure. Yorke questions these figures, citing two separate sources (a housing and population census and Family Books in the civil status department) which indicate that East Bank Palestinians (at least as defined by place of birth or father's place of birth) account for only 36 to 37 percent of the population (Yorke 1988a:16).[46] And just as the definition of Bedouin adopted by the government allowed a valuable degree of flexibility, the uncertainty regarding national population figures serves the same ends. For example, Yorke, writing in April of 1988, suggested a number of reasons that the Jordanian government might prefer the figures which suggested a Palestinian majority in Jordan. But in August of that same year, speaking at a press conference following Jordan's disengagement from the West Bank, King Hussein used the lower figures which downplayed the demographic importance of East Bank Palestinian Jordanians (*Jordan Times*, 8 Aug. 1988).

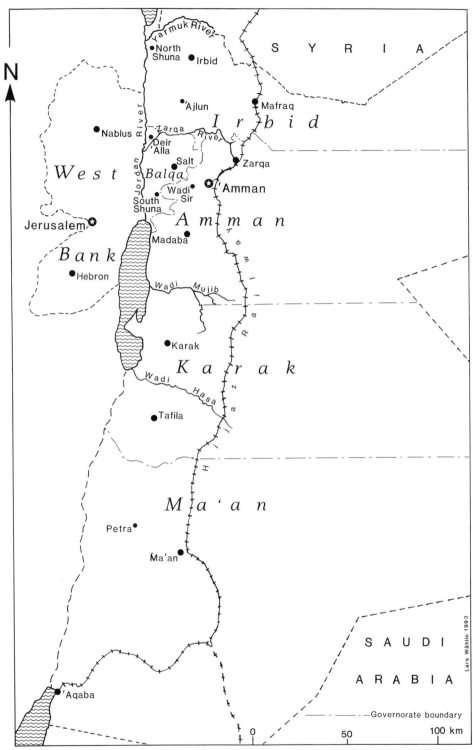

FIG. 3 Map of Jordan

THE VALUE OF AMBIGUITY: KEEPING
THE BORDERS FUZZY

Over the years, the ambiguities of the relationship between Jordan and Palestine have been in many ways beneficial to Jordan. In addition to a substantially enlarged territory (especially in terms of percentage of arable land), benefits have included a primary role in Mideast peace talks, considerable economic aid from Arab countries, a strong Jordanian dinar,[47] remittances of West Bankers, as well as Palestinian investments in Jordan.

At the same time, the ambiguity surrounding Jordan's relationship with Palestine and Palestinians has also entailed certain dangers. The most serious threat throughout the 1980s was the specter of Jordan being transformed into Palestine. In the early 1980s Israeli Minister of Defense Ariel Sharon proposed that Jordan, with its Palestinian majority, was de facto a Palestinian state, and the slogan "Jordan is Palestine" began to receive a good deal of attention in the Israeli and international press.[48] Implicit in the slogan is the assertion that Jordan was a country without a people or a history of its own, just as in an earlier era Palestine was portrayed as having been a land-of-dust in order to rationalize its occupation by Israel. Proponents of this position not only denied the legitimacy of the restoration of Jordanian authority in the West Bank but also called for the expulsion of an additional one million Palestinians into Jordan from the West Bank, a move that would greatly diminish the demographic importance of "indigenous Jordanians." Within weeks after Jordan's disengagement from the West Bank, the *Jordan Times* published an article from the *Jerusalem Post* reporting that "49% of Jewish Israeli adults believe that the "transfer" of Arabs from the occupied territories [to Jordan, presumably] would allow the democratic and Jewish nature of Israeli society to be maintained" (*Jordan Times*, 17 Aug. 1988:5).

Although the Israeli threat remained fairly constant, the shape and strength of Palestinian nationalism has changed radically in the last few years with the uprising on the West Bank beginning in December 1987 and the Palestinian Declaration of Independence in November 1988. (See Haidar 1988, Muslih 1988, and Brand 1988 for a historical survey of Palestinian nationalist development.) During the first seven months of the uprising the West Bank was still defined as part of the Kingdom, and thus the uprising and the anti-Hussein sentiment that accompanied it constituted a serious "internal" threat. A poll conducted on the West Bank and Gaza Strip in the summer of 1986 found that only 3.3 percent supported King Hussein as a leader in contrast with 72.2 percent in favor of the current leadership of the PLO (Shadid and Seltzer 1988:23). Furthermore, in the early years of the uprising there was concern among the Jordanian authorities that it might spill over onto the East Bank (Yorke 1988b:14).

Whatever the reasons that prompted the King to renounce legal and administrative links with the West Bank, both the act and the rhetoric of disengagement produced a Jordanian nation that conformed more closely to the modern, Western model of nation by clarifying and confirming the Jordanian "Self" and the Palestinian "Other." In his televised speech on July 31, 1988, to explain his decision, King Hussein proclaimed that "Jordan is not Palestine." Similarly, Marwan al-Kasim, chief of the royal court at the time, is quoted as saying "From now on Jordan is Jordan and Palestine is Palestine" (Ibrahim, *New York Times*, 10 Oct. 1988). The Jordanian Cabinet statement announcing the termination of the West Bank development plan in July 1988 explained that the purpose of this move was "to remove any doubt which might arise regarding Jordan's relationship with the Palestinian people under occupation, by virtue of Jordan's strong historical and geographical bonds with the Palestinian people . . ." (*Jordan Times*, 30 July 1988).[49]

The disengagement certainly clarified many of the ambiguities concerning the status and limits of Jordan versus Palestine, but no sooner had the King clarified the ambiguity concerning the extent of his sovereignty than he reintroduced a measure of ambiguity by reaffirmation of his commitment to the ideals of Arab nationalism. In the King's July 31 speech, he repeatedly invoked the ideals of the Arab Revolt. Arab nationalism was used to justify Jordan's unification with the West Bank in the 1950s: "We believe that such unity between two or more Arab peoples is a right of choice for every Arab People. Based on that, we have responded to the wish of the representatives of the Palestinian people for unity with Jordan in 1950" (*Jordan Times*, 1 Aug. 1988:2). Then, to justify Jordan's disengagement, the King explained that his decision was in compliance with the will of "our nation," that is, the Arab nation, and asserted that "these measures do not mean . . . relinquishing our faith in Arab unity" (*Jordan Times*, 1 Aug. 1988:2).

The Great Arab Revolt is one of the three key themes in Jordanian nationalist rhetoric along with the Hashemites' genealogical links to the Prophet Mohammad and their traditional role as protectors of Islam's holy places, and Jordan's "tribal" character. These three themes often overlap and reinforce one another.[50] For example, the War Museum in Amman celebrates the Hashemites' role in the Great Arab Revolt and their role in the establishment of Jordan. At the same time it celebrates the tribes' role in these enterprises and defines these events as blessed ones inspired by Allah. In certain contexts and periods, however, one or another of the themes tends to be emphasized. The Hashemites' role in the Great Arab Revolt and their role as protectors of the holy places strengthened the legitimacy of Jordan's administrative and legal ties with Palestine including the holy city of Jerusalem. In contrast, Bedouin tribes have come to symbolize Jordan's national identity in contradistinction to Palestine's traditionally more settled population and hence the tribal character of Jordan is often used to accentuate the autonomy of the two nations.[51] Given this, my initial prediction was that the tribal element would be pronounced in the context of Jordan's disengagment and the ensuing clarification of Jordanian and Palestinian national identities. I was wrong. In the weeks leading up to the July 31 announcement and during the months following the disengagement, the issue of Jordan's tribal nature was nearly completely absent from the local papers; so, too, was that of the Hashemites' holy lineage. In this context, the theme of the Great Arab Revolt seemed even more prevalent than usual.[52] The Revolt was invoked in circumstances as diverse as the occasion of the celebration of the thirty-sixth anniversary of King Hussein's accession to the throne in August 1988, during which Hussein's rule was described as "continuing the march of the Great Arab Revolt against backwardness, colonization and ignorance and as a manifestation of the people's cohesion with its leadership to confront all challenges facing the Arab Nation" (*Jordan Times*, 11 Aug. 1988:1) to the "Great Arab Revolt Scout Camp" organized by the Ministry of Youth to which boy scouts from a number of Arab countries were to be invited. On another occasion the minister of youth distributed awards to "prominent youths who presented creative work and offered a meaningful contribution to the Kingdom's celebrations of the Great Arab Revolt." A number of regional developments during this period were also described in these terms. The end to the Iraq-Iran war was portrayed as "a victory for all Arabs" and in response to an Iraqi gift to the Jordanian armed forces of weapons captured in the war Jordan asserted that they "will be exploited in the defense of the Arab Nation" (*Ṣawt al-Shāb*, 8 Aug. 1988). The establishment in February 1989 of a four-country Arab Cooperation Council (Iraq, Jordan, Egypt, and North Yemen) was praised "as conforming to the principles laid down by the leaders of the Great Arab Revolt" (*Jordan Times*, 21 Feb. 1989; 1 Mar. 1989).[53]

The King's decision to relinquish the West Bank was interpreted by many observers, as his actions almost inevitably are, purely in terms of cynical pragmatism. Most reporters tried to figure out "what he was up to" and characterized his decision as a "move," "ploy," or "tactic."[54] For example, in Thomas L. Friedman's (1988) article in the *New York Times*, "The King's Move," he suggested that the King's decision "be viewed with the same suspicion as a cat voluntarily offering a mouse a slice of cheese." In this vein, his invocation of the Great Arab Revolt in the context of the disengagement might be interpreted simply as window dressing designed to cover over and prettify his real, self-interested motivations.[55] It is a mistake, however, to dismiss mention of the Arab Revolt whether in the context of the King's speech or a scout camp as mere rhetoric, simply public relations copy, for the uses of the Revolt in public discourse reveal a good deal about Jordanian political culture. The King's framing of the disengagement in terms of the Arab Revolt not only contributes to the meaning of the disengagement, it also illuminates an alternate way of understanding both national and tribal collective identity making.

Richard Handler argues that in the realm of nationalist ideologies "there is no place for imprecision, for mixture, for hazily defined boundaries" (Handler 1988:48), and yet it would seem that it is precisely these qualities on which the Jordanian state thrives. Rather than welcoming the clarification of limits of the Jordanian nation-state, the King took immediate steps to compensate for this new level of clarity by accentuating the tentativeness of his borders (and those of his neighbors) when seen in the light of Arab nationalism. If seen from the perspective of modern, Western, organic models of collectivity, the ambiguity of Jordan's nationhood is a sign of weakness. And much like those tribespeople who do not conform to the Bedouin norm, a nation that does not meet the accepted standards for clarity and purity risks the charge of inauthenticity. But if viewed differently, either via the lens of postmodern theory or from an indigenous point of view, such an approach to collectivity may appear both natural and beneficial. In the chapters that follow I suggest that the way that Jordanian tribespeople and the King construct the spaces and boundaries of both their homes and homeland offers an alternative to the "highly localized, boundary-oriented, holistic, primordialist images of cultural form and substance . . ." (Appadurai 1990:20) which have characterized so much scholarship of the Arab world and I argue that this approach in some respects resembles postmodern cultural forms. For example, the glimpse of Jordan's body politic provided by the disengagement suggests a body not unlike the postmodern, "agile, anticipatory body," that Emily Martin (1992) has described. Like the new bodies being constructed in American immunological textbooks, the Jordanian nation-state could be described an "adroit, supple, nimble, innovative bod[y]," one capable of "agile response" and "flexible specificity," "poised to meet any conceivable challenge" (Martin 1992:11). And like the "lean, agile" companies now emerging in the United States through corporate restructuring, Jordan appears to be constructing itself in a way that enables it "to make links across all kinds of division," (Martin 1992:17) both within itself and between itself and other nation-states.

In other words, to comprehend Jordanian national and tribal identities, a more emergent model of collective identity is needed. Jordanian nationalism, like Mashpee identity and history described by Clifford (1988) is better seen as "a series of cultural and political transactions, not all-or-nothing conversions or resistances . . . a series of ad hoc . . . episodes, turns in an ongoing engagement" (1988:342). Although this sense of contingency has always been, I believe, a part of Jordanian notions of nationhood, events such as the King's decision to relinquish control over the West Bank certainly highlight this aspect.

In the remainder of this book I develop and explore an approach to collective identity that sees identity as meaning constructed on an ongoing basis through the everyday practices of making a place in the world, that is, adopting a posture in the context of changing circumstances and uncertain contingencies.[56] This posture-oriented approach to identity not only addresses the problem of abstractness and independence of identity from identity makers mentioned above, it also has built into it an expectation for change. In addition to stressing the ever-emergent aspect of identity making by placing social life in a temporal perspective, this approach also emphasizes the spatial dimension of identity making by focusing on how we place our embodied selves in relation to others and the material world.[57]

I begin by introducing the ʿAbbad tribes of the Jordan Valley and sketching the outlines of some of the important changes that have occurred in the Valley during the twentieth century. Topics of special importance to the aruguments developed in the book such as the ʿAbbadis' relationship to the land, the role of sheikhs, and the relationship of the Jordan Valley tribes to state structures under Ottoman, British Mandatory, and Hashemite rule are given particular attention.

In chapters 3 and 4 I focus on the ʿAbbadis' organization and use of space in their homes. I argue that their household practices are central processes by which the ʿAbbadis construct themselves. By exploring the postures that they adopt (both literally and figuratively) as they position themselves with and in their homes, I address much more than a private domestic world. Although the focus of most political anthropology in the Arab world has been on formal, all-male enterprises such as dispute settlement or raiding, I argue that the way that both men and women move with and within their homes illuminates the means by which the ʿarabs of the Jordan Valley practice politics and actively construct their social identities and their world. This study of ʿAbbadi homes also confronts the prevailing assumptions about the special conservatism of non-discursive knowledge. The ʿAbbadi case reveals a great deal of dynamism and provides ample evidence that the "private lives" of the ʿAbbadis are thoroughly enmeshed in wider social worlds. Finally, I show that although the ʿAbbadis' integration into capitalist systems of production is significantly changing the use of space in homes (through the separation of production from the home), ʿAbbadi homes are rarely charged with the symbolic function that homes so typically assume in Western class-based societies.

National discourses on tribalism are the focus of chapter 5. I show how in the early 1980s, "tribes" became key symbols in thinking about Jordanian selfhood and statehood. In chapter 6 I focus on the 1984 parliamentary by-elections in which tribespeople participated as both candidates and voters. These elections provide a rich case through which to examine the the ways that tribal identity is being dialogically constructed between sheikhs and ordinary tribespeople, tribesmen and women, tribespeople and a variety of outsiders including representatives of the state and to critically explore notions of citizenship and representation. I show that although the values of democracy and ʿarab autonomy reenforced each other, the meaning of autonomy as constructed in the course of the elections by Jordan Valley tribespeople differed significantly from that normally associated with exercising one's right of suffrage in Western democracies.

In the seventh chapter the dialogics of national representations and tribal self-representation are explored further. Using the examples of "traditional costumes" and a local exhibition of "tribal heritage," I show how tribespeople's views of what it means to be a tribesperson in Jordan today are articulated in dialogue with the views of Jordanian urbanites and official nationalist rhetoric. I argue that these dialogically produced self-representations should be understood as acts of resistance to the anonymous appropriation of their culture by the state.

In the final chapter I return to the problem posed by the participants in the study tour of Jordan that I led: namely, why is it that modern Western assumptions about collectivities and collective identity are so misleading when applied in a Middle Eastern context? In addressing this question I focus on the King as the ultimate symbol of Jordanian collective identity and suggest that the notion of posture (explored throughout the book) provides the key to understanding his role as symbol and leader. I argue that while utilizing modern Western notions of time and history, the King, like the tribespeople of the Jordan Valley, continues to employ a distinctively ʿarab sense of space. This sense of space, which has profound consequences for the experience and representation of collective identity, bears certain resemblances to approaches to space and identity now being articulated by postmodern theorists— and these two approaches have something to offer each other. On the one hand, new cultural theories provide an approach better able to make sense of processes involved in the making of Jordanian national and tribal identities; on the other hand, the Jordanian case highlights an approach to identity making that should help us to refine these theoretical tools.

NOTES

1. Apparently this metaphor is also sometimes applied to Israel. Dominguez (1989:104) reports that a bureaucrat from Israel's Ministry of Education referred to Israel as a "mosaic" while addressing a meeting of Oriental Jews from the East for Peace movement in 1985 on the topic "Israel in the Mediterranean Cultural Environment."

2. Whereas the mosaic image normally refers to the larger entity that various "pieces" of a society make up, in Kaplan's (1980:53) usage no such larger unit exists, at least in Jordan: "No consistent social system or set of attitudes binds even most of the people into one unit. Different stratification criteria, based on often contradictory values, operate among the different ethnic, cultural, and social groups."

3. This problem is not unique to segmentary theory, as Jeanne Favret observed: "Theoretically social groups have no substantial existence; in practice, researchers always forget that they exist only as relational systems." She goes on to note that if one tried to study local politics in rural Algeria with such an approach one would "miss the point" (1972:307).

4. In contrast interpretive anthropologists Dale Eickelman (1976), Lawrence Rosen (1979), and Hildred Geertz (1979), argued against the usefulness of thinking of tribes and other social units in the Middle East as corporate entities that govern behavior. For example, in their 1979 essays in *Meanings and Order in Morocco* and in Rosen's more recent work (1984), H. Geertz and Rosen focused on the cultural conventions by which interpersonal ties are built and rebuilt. They suggested that rather than being shaped by abstract norms, the relations among family members are shaped by the same sort of flexible and pragmatical cultural conceptions as those of friendship and patronage.

5. Alternative images of segmentary systems as imagined from the inside of such a system have been described by Oweidi (1982:108–9), Lancaster (1981), and Dresch (1986:315).

6. The fact that the National Science Foundation magazine is named *Mosaic* is telling. The meaning in this case is presumably that bits of scientific knowledge add up to a larger truth.

7. As I shall discuss in chapters 5 and 6, membership in a tribe is often thought to preclude full membership in a nation.

8. Eickelman (1981) also notes their centrality to core issues in anthropological theory such as segmentary lineage systems and human ecology. Abu-Lughod (1989) goes further, questioning how segmentary lineage came to be such an issue in the first place. Eickelman also mentions some of the "practical" reasons that Middle Eastern governments have encouraged anthropologists to

work with pastoral groups. He implies that the reason governments have supported these studies is their desire to document cultures which they are destroying, for many of these governments have been trying to settle nomads. The Jordanian case suggests that an alternative, or perhaps additional, explanation may be that the Bedouin are believed to provide a suitably honorable and glorious picture of Arab society.

9. I take this term from Benedict Anderson's *Imagined Communities* (1983).

10. Jordan's Arab Legion and later the Arab Army is one of the best studied elements of Jordanian society. See Axelrod (1978), Vatikiotis (1967), El-Edroos (1980).

11. It is interesting that El-Edroos's (1980) extensive study of the Hashemite Arab Army (1908–79) does not mention this role but concentrates instead on various rebellions within the country and the Wahabi raids from the south that this force countered.

12. See Oren (1990) for a description of Glubb's ouster in 1955.

13. He goes on to say that Glubb's attempts "to distinguish between Bedouin and non-Bedouin personnel were, however, less than successful [and] in the opinion of Arab Officers, . . . quite unjustifiable and suspect." He points out that although the outstanding officers of the Arab Revolt were all from the so-called *effendi* class, Glubb appeared "most uncomfortable when called upon to serve alongside educated, critical and not overly obsequious . . . Arab officers" (El-Edroos 1980:213–14).

14. The composition of the troops that accompanied Abdullah into Transjordan is also subject to interpretation, varying from Rinehart's (1980:21) description of "a motley force of about 2,000 tribesmen" to El-Edroos's (1980:206) account of "a sherifian *katiba* (battalion) of 400 regulars . . . and a tribal bodyguard of Hejazi retainers," and Dann's (1984:2) report of "a retinue of beduin body guards and Syrian nationalist refugees."

15. It is important to remember that only some of Jordan's tribes provided initial support for Abdullah's rule. (See Wilson 1987:57–58.)

16. According to Harik, these elites do not necessarily share ideological orientation; the important factor is their willingness to collaborate with the regime and use their local leadership to obtain compliance (Harik 1981:74).

17. Abdullah's brother, Faisal, is referred to as "a Hashemite Bedouin" in the film *Lawrence of Arabia* when Lawerence is ordered to go to Arabia to find him.

18. While researching her book on Abdullah in Jerusalem, Palestinians frequently asked Wilson why she was wasting her time on a Bedouin like that (Wilson, personal communication). Despite Abdullah's identification with the Bedouin, he apparently also at times used "*bedu*" in a similarly derogatory sense, privately denigrating Ibn Saud as "a mere Bedu" (Wilson 1987:44).

Although some British colonial officers were well aware of Abdullah's background and privately criticized him for pretending to be a Bedouin, others ended up believing in the myth that they had a part in creating (Wilson, personal communication).

19. For example, Lerner (1958:305) cites a 1944 estimate that "classified half the population as camel-breeding Bedouin or goat and sheep raising semi-nomads"; Gubser (1983:12) cites a 1946 estimate of 99,260 nonsettled Bed-

ouin of a total of 433,660 East Bank Jordanians; and Abu Jaber et al. (1978:11) mentions estimates of the East Bank nomadic population in the 1950s ranging between 150,000 and 220,000. These differences can be partially explained by the fact that it has not always been easy to locate nomadic groups for census taking. There are also, of course, always political implications to population statistics. The political import of statistics on Jordan's tribal population will be discussed below.

20. For administrative purposes the *bādiya* is defined as the area to the east and the north of Mafraq and the southern part of Jordan from Karak and Tafila down to the border with Saudi Arabia. Of course, the definition of the *bādiya* can be subject to debate. There is no reason to assume that the fixed cadastral definition established by the state coincides with that of various inhabitants.

21. For example, Glubb, the first leader of Jordan's Desert Mobil Force and author of numerous books on the tribal history of Jordan, suggests a model of sedentarization that takes place over a three-hundred-year period in which nomadic tribes come from Central Arabia to Jordan where they continue nomadic lives on the boundaries of the cultivated area but gradually reduce the distance of their annual migration and increase the numbers of sheep at the expense of camels. According to his model they eventually become complete agriculturalists, although retaining their tents for a considerable amount of time (Glubb 1938:449).

In addition to unilineal sedentarization models that address Bedouin tribes in particular, cultural ecologists and modernization theorists often posit all tribal societies as an evolutionary stage. For example, in Marshall Sahlins's book *Tribesmen* (1968), tribal culture is described as the form of social organization that displaced Paleolithic hunting and gathering societies and that was in turn displaced by "civilizations." See Godelier (1977) for a critique of the term *tribe* as used in the evolutionary literature and LaBianca (1983) for an example of "rebedouinization" in Jordan.

22. Day explains that by "a heavily Bedouin army," he is referring to the "traditional background" of the men, but what is meant by "traditional background" is itself unclear.

23. He bases his definition on those of classical Arab scholars such as Qalqashandi and Imam al-Razi who he says distinguished between the "Arabs, those people of the cities and the 'real' Arabs *al-arab* [who] are the desert dwellers" (in Abu Hassan 1984:2).

24. The special "authenticity" attributed to the Bedouin by at least some Jordanians will be discussed further in chapter 5. Another example of Middle Eastern ranking of tribes is reported by Wright who chose not to study "large, dominant tribal groupings" in Iran but to focus instead on "one of the myriad small tribal groupings, consistently weak in the face of neighbouring tribes and the state" (quoted in Street 1990:249). She found that the dominant discourse on tribes developed by European anthropologists had been passed on to local Iranian academics who had in turn influenced local administrators who, upon hearing Wright's description of her work, concluded that she was not working with "real tribes" (in Street 1990:250). See Greenwood (1985) on the notion of "true" and "false" ethnicity.

25. Though for the most part, Clifford's analysis focuses on the "form" of

the culture concept—a coherent whole—he does provide one important insight about the "content" of the particular culture he is examining although he attributes this characteristic to culture in general—"the idea of culture carries with it an expectation of roots, of a stable, territorialized existence." Clifford goes on to describe how the legal definition of "tribe" used in the Mashpee case had been designed to "distinguish settled, peaceful Indian groups from mobile, marauding 'bands'" and how during the trial whenever the question "How rooted or settled should one expect 'tribal' Native Americans to be?" was raised, "common notions of culture persistently bias[ed] the answer toward rooting rather than travel" (1988:338).

26. Bocco (1984:3) first drew my attention to this issue. Dickson (1948:108–109) refers to 'Arab-ad-Dar as the "Half Bedouin" in contrast with "pure-bred Bedouin," although he adds that many are of "good Sharif stock." See Lewis (1987:3) on the use of the term ʿarab in Greater Syria during the nineteenth century.

27. Compare this with Dickson's (1949:108–9) account of the "Badawin social system" in Kuwait and Saudi Arabia.

28. I must thank Lars Wahlin for questioning the appropriateness of my use of this term for the 'Abbad.

29. He goes on to say that "an Egyptian villager would probably tend to describe all Omanis as 'bedu,' even though they may have been living in villages for centuries, because their social organization remains 'tribal' and their attitude towards the land continues to exhibit somewhat ʿarab characteristics. To the Omanis themselves, on the other hand, there is a marked distinction between what they call bedu and hadhar" (1977:189). Wilkinson also observed that in "local legal works" in Oman Bedouin are designated as ʿarabs (1977:189).

30. See Bocco (1989b) for an analysis of the definition of "Bedouin" in Jordan's electoral laws.

31. See Bocco (1989b) for details.

32. Handbooks represent a particular literary genre; one characterized by the neat and essential categorization of population groups. Indeed, like the travelers' accounts that preceded them, a certain amount of "borrowing" tends to go on and these handbooks tend to recreate themselves in both structure and content. However, when they attempt to apply such a mold to "Jordanians" and "Palestinians" in Jordan, this approach leads irrevocably into a muddle.

33. These population figures come from Gubser (1983:19) for Circassians and Sheeshan, and from Kaplan (1980:94) for the Christians.

34. See Bocco (1989a and b), Wahlin (1992), and Wilson (1987) for thoughtful discussions of the meaning of these terms in the Jordanian context and Altorki and Cole (1989) for an interesting comparative case.

35. It is worthy of note that this entire discussion of "practical purpose Jordanians" is found under the subheading "Palestinians."

36. Following Jordan's disengagement from the West Bank a new cutoff date, that of July 31, 1988, the official date that ties were severed, became the determining one—in the eyes of Jordanian officials, at least. The statement issued by Prime Minister Zaid Rifai on August 20 regarding new civil status rules

"defined 'Palestinians' as all those permanent residents of the West Bank as of July 31, 1988. All such residents are 'Palestinian, not Jordanian'" (*Jordan Times*, 21 Aug. 1988:1).

37. Lerner's sample included 131 "refugees" and 157 "nonrefugees" (1958:308).

38. Renee Hirschon's (1989) study of Asia Minor Greek refugees in Greece provides an interesting parallel case of what she calls "superior subordinates" (1989:12). The Greek refugees she studied (like the Palestinian refugees in Jordan) shared religion, language, and close similarity in most aspects of culture and tradition with that of the host society and yet maintained a separate identity and a sense of cultural and moral superiority. In both cases the refugees are "distinguishable in conceptual terms but not by readily observable criteria" (1989:5) and thus tend to construct a separate identity "by emphasizing minutiae of detail, of difference of degree rather than kind" (Hirschon 1989:246).

39. Similarly, Day (1986:56) describes as "the most suspect seam in Jordanian society . . . that which binds Palestinian-Jordanians to East Bank Jordanians."

40. Cf. Lisa Anderson (1991b:72).

41. As Laroui (1977) pointed out, foreign observers generally consider "the Arab nation" a myth in the pejorative sense of the term. He argues that the frequency of inter-Arab crisis paradoxically "proves the existence of a real inter-Arab system [which] objectively limits the sovereignty of each state . . . No Arab chief of state . . . is totally free in his movements. He must assure for himself the good will of his counterparts, and he must not offend pan-Arab opinion" (1977:4–5).

42. See Boyarin (1990a) for a critique of organic models of nation with regard to Israel.

43. Jordan has the longest border with Israel of any Arab state. In the King's July 31 speech, he pointed out that Jordan's border with Israel is "longer even than the combined borders of the West Bank and Gaza" (*Jordan Times*, 1 Aug. 1988:2).

In addition to the many boundary changes between Palestine and Jordan over the years, the Jordan-Saudi border remained in dispute until 1948. Kirkbride (1956) provides a firsthand account of the laying of boundaries on the Syrian/Jordanian frontier.

44. I draw here on Wilson's (1987) excellent account of the period.

45. The estimated total population also varies. The offical estimate of the population of East Bank Jordan in 1989 was 3,111,000 (*Statistical Yearbook 1989*, quoted in Wahlin [1991a:26 n. 101]).

46. She suggested that these larger figures suited the regime because the idea of a Palestinian majority supported the Hashemites' responsibility for the Palestinians and because Transjordanians might be more likely to cling to the King if they believed they were outnumbered and needed him to protect their interests.

47. The value of the dinar declined sharply when the King started signaling his intentions to relinquish the West Bank in May 1988.

48. A poll in 1985 showed that another supporter of this solution to Israel's

Palestinian problem, American Rabbi Meir Kahane, had the support of 42 percent of Israel's high-school students (Day 1986:1).

This threat is still felt in Jordan. With the recent concern about King Hussein's health following his surgery for cancer and speculation about what Jordan would be like without Hussein, one journalist reports, "The unspoken fear is that the prince [Crown Prince Hassan] will be unable to manage a post-Hussein crisis that could result in Jordan's becoming a de facto Palestine" (Fineman 1992). See also the *Washington Report*, 6 Sept. 1982; Ryan and Hallaj (1983); and L. Dean Brown (1982) on "Jordan as Palestine."

49. Disengagement entailed the dissolution of the lower house of parliament, the abandoning of a 1.3-billion-dollar plan for West Bank development, and the cutting off of the salaries of some 21,000 government employees on the West Bank (teachers, health workers, municipal employees, and others). In addition, Jordanian citizenship was revoked and two-year passports to serve strictly as travel documents were issued to West Bank Palestinians. In line with this decision the Ministry of Occupied Territories was disbanded and matters concerning the West Bank were transferred to the Foreign Ministry (*New York Times*, 6 Aug. 1988). Restrictions were also placed on the amount of time West Bankers might reside and work in Jordan. Whereas in the past, West Bank residents were able routinely to cross the Allenby Bridge for indefinite stays on the East Bank, following the disengagement they had to apply for permission to extend a stay longer than a proscribed period and might have to return to the West Bank for such permission. Many of these restrictions were challenged by Jordan's parliament (Andoni, *Middle East International*, 19 Jan. 1990:9).

50. It is not coincidental that two of the three symbols of Jordanian nationhood are neither Jordanian nor Palestinian but refer exclusively to the Hashemites.

51. In both cases, formulations of Jordanian national identity are informed by Jordan's special relationship with Palestine and Palestinians. In other words, the Palestinians are at once Self and Other. In some contexts, Palestine is the Other that the Jordanian Self is constructed against. In other contexts, Palestinian is included within the boundaries of the collective Jordanian Self.

52. The *Jerusalem Star* and the *Jordan Times* were examined from June 1988 through April 1989. The *Jordan Times* includes an English translation of an editorial from each of the Arabic-language dailies, and the Arab Revolt was referred to frequently in these editorials as well.

53. This emphasis on Arab nationalism had other practical consequences. Jordan's concentrated efforts to establish cooperative agreements with other Arab countries, (e.g., a tourism agreement with Tunisia in March 1989 and progress on the al-Wahdah Dam to be constructed with Syria along the Jordanian/Syrian border) as well as the establishment of the Arab Cooperative Council helped to compensate for the loss of the West Bank in terms of Jordan's importance in the Arab world and served as a much-needed, if limited, boon to Jordan's crippled economy.

The theme of the Great Arab Revolt has continued to be especially useful in responding to the many challenges that faced Jordan in the late 1980s and early 1990s. In April 1989, riots broke out in southern Jordan in response to austerity measures adopted as part of an IMF agreement. In his address to the country on April 26, the King asserted that "the difficulties we are facing came as a result of regional and pan-Arab circumstances . . ." The King remarked that the national infrastructure and the armed forces (two of the major sources of state expenditure during the previous decade) both served to "bolster our defense and enable us to protect the Arab Homeland" and mentioned "defense of the longest confrontation lines with Israel" as one of the reasons Jordan had borrowed. In this text, pan-Arab issues are not only implicated in the problems Jordan confronted, the heritage of pan-Arab struggle is given credit for his faith in the country's ability to survive the pain of "economic adjustment": "Those nations which refuse adjustment and adaptation to new situations and prefer to remain frozen are bound to disintegrate and perish. But we can never be counted among them because we have inherited those who raised the standards of the Great Arab Revolt and who devoted their life to the defense of its principles" (*Jordan Times*, 27 Apr. 1989).

Similarly, in August of 1990, following the Iraqi invasion of Kuwait, the King addressed the members of parliament and, in the context of describing U.S. plans to break up Iraq into multiple spheres of influence and voicing his resolve to support Iraq, told the members that if they wanted to honor him they should call him Sharif Hussein, thereby identifying himself with his great-grandfather's commitment to Arab unity.

54. According to Harkabi (1988), Israeli government spokesmen took the line that Hussein's move was only "tactical." An article by Herzberg (1988) in the *New York Times* (perhaps written in response to that of Friedman) is entitled "This Time, Hussein Isn't Being Coy." For additional references to cynical motivations for his decision see *Newsweek*, 15 Aug. 1988:31.

55. These motivations were typically believed to be either that the King hoped to force the Palestinians to beg him to come back or that he was punishing the Palestinians. See, for example, the column from *al-Hadar* reprinted in *Middle East International* 26 Aug. 1988. Cf. Andoni (1988).

56. I am indebted to Schumacher's *Human Posture: The Nature of Inquiry* (1989) for drawing my attention to the importance of posture.

57. This approach, while in marked contrast with the essential, static notions of identity presumed by the mosaic metaphor and implied in the questions of the American tourists, resonates with the Greek concept of meaning as something "recognize[d] in *action*, a term that includes speech but does not necessarily give linguistic meaning any special priority. It is an essentially *poetic* notion, in . . . that it concerns the means in which significance is conveyed through actual performance" (Herzfeld 1985:xiv). It is also complementary to Caton's (1990) depiction of the social construction of tribesmen in Yemen, although his study focuses on discursive forms (poetry) whereas mine has greater emphasis on non-discursive practices.

CHAPTER 2

A Generation of Change

MUḤAMMAD ḤUSSAIN AL-ṬĀLIB (head of the household featured in chapter 3) was born to Mahra Bahadla and Ḥussain al-Ṭālib[1] in 1928, the same year Jordan's first constitution was promulgated. Although the area known today as the Hashemite Kingdom of Jordan has experienced many periods of prosperity and decline throughout its long history, there has probably never been such rapid change as that which has taken place in Muḥammad al-Ṭālib's lifetime.

The ʿarabs of Jordan have a patrilineal system of descent and so Muḥammad, like his father, Hussain ʿAli Fālah Sālim Ṭālib Sālah Ghanān, belongs to the Ghānānim tribe. The Ghānānim are one of the eighteen tribes that make up the ʿAbbād confederation.[2] Although the Ghānānim trace their descent back nine generations to their common ancestor, Ghanān, from whom they derive their name, the ʿAbbādis, as a whole do not consider themselves to share an ancestor. Legend has it that their name comes from the root ʿabd, which means love and refers to the fact that they loved each other enough to join forces against the ʿAdwan tribe in 1812.

During the waning years of the Ottoman Empire (the late nineteenth and early twentieth centuries), the ʿAbbād tribes practiced transhumant goat and sheep herding in the Jordan Valley and its piedmont in the region known as Balqaʾ.[3] The Valley had been at earlier periods of history (during the Umayyad era [661–750] and under the Ayyūbid-Mamlūk rule [1187–1516]) a prosperous, settled agricultural region, but from the seventeenth century onward herding tribes dominated the Valley.

The Jordan Valley, known in Arabic as ʿal-Ghōrʾ, literally "the Lowlands," is that part of the Great Rift Valley which stretches from Lake Tiberias (200 meters below sea level) to the Dead Sea (the lowest spot on earth at 400 meters below sea level). (fig. 4). Because of its low elevation, temperatures in the Jordan Valley are on average five to seven degrees centigrade higher than on the plateau and humidity averages about 10 percent higher (Jordan 1971). The Jordan River flows the length of the Valley and is flanked by fertile floodplains. An eroded zone of uncultivable land separates the floodplains from the rest of the Valley floor which stretches eastward between four to sixteen kilometers until it reaches the foothills which rise at a rate of fifteen to twenty-five meters per kilometer up to the Jordanian plateau, a thousand meters above sea level.

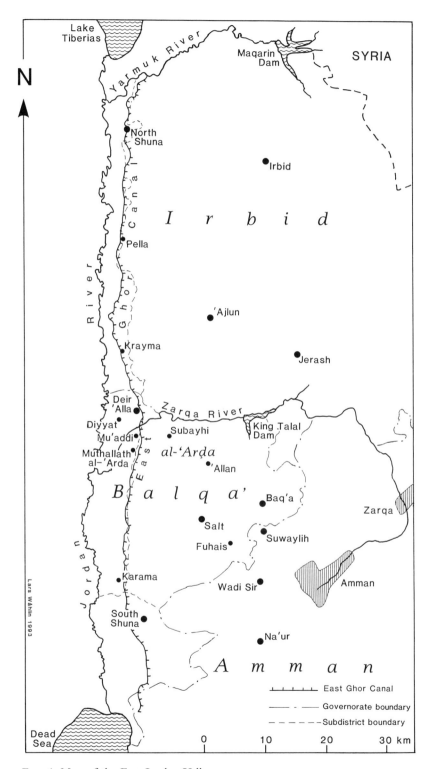

FIG. 4 Map of the East Jordan Valley

This distinctive landscape provided the ʿAbbādis with mild winter temperatures, abundant sources of water, rich soil for crops (mostly wheat and barley), and early spring pasturage for their flocks. In the summer, the tribes moved with their flocks into the hills of the East and West Banks of the Jordan where temperatures were cooler and pastures greener. They sold or traded wool and dairy products in Jerusalem, Nablus, and Salt in exchange for coffee, tea, sugar, and other supplies. A visitor to the Valley in the 1940s reports ʿAbāddi herds totaling approximately twenty thousand sheep (Oppenheim 1943:227).

Up through the 1940s goat-hair tents and caves were the primary forms of shelter, while structures made of mud brick or stone were used for storage.[4] Grazing rights and the constitution of "tribal territory" were probably similar to that of the Rwala of eastern Jordan where, according to Lancaster, the notion of "ownership" or "rule" of a territory (and of the wells, grazing, and wild animals in it) refers to "a prior claim of usufruct (a claim not a right)" (1981:121).[5] A person "only rules [territory] when he is there and he only owns it under the same circumstances . . . [The Rwala] only 'own' [their tribal territory] by right of dominance and have no exclusive right to it at all. As they cannot possibly cover the whole area the whole year round other tribes use parts when the Rwala are not there or, by custom, when they are" (1981:121).[6]

Claude Reignier Conder, one of the members of the Palestine Exploration Fund's topographical survey team who visited the Valley in 1881–82 reported that even though the tribal territory and cultivation rights of the ʿAdwān tribe in the Jordan Valley and its piedmont were well defined, the Beni Sakhr, an eastern nomadic camel-herding tribe, freely entered this territory to water their flocks in the course of their wider-ranging migrations (Conder 1892:316, 129).

Agriculture played a greater role for the ʿarab tribes who utilized the valley than for Bedouin tribes such as the Beni Sakhr or the Rwala, and it appears that rights concerning agricultural land were more precisely defined. According to Conder, property rights for cultivable areas were a matter of importance and subject to dispute in the Valley. "The fields in the Jordan valley have distinct owners . . . the ʿAdwān are acknowledged by the Turks to be proprietors of the lands in which they dwell, and the colonist must buy them out if he wishes for their country" (Conder 1892:355). Although this report by Conder is in accordance with the Ottoman Land Code of 1858 which was in effect at the time, other sources (Walpole 1948:55; Abu Shaikha [1971]; and Wahlin [1988a]) suggest that the mushaʿ system of tenure continued in some places in the Fertile Crescent even after it was forbidden by the Turks. Wahlin's (1988a) map showing the type of tenure of agricultural land in

439 Jordanian villages in the 1930s through 1950s indicates that *musha'* was used for agricultural holdings in the northern section of the Jordan Valley. Under the *musha'* system an

> estate is held, as a unit, by a corporate body, usually a village or a tribe, and apportioned among the different members . . . The tenant, therefore, does not get a definite piece of land which he keeps year after year and then passes on to his heirs; he gets a right over a share in the estate. . . . In most instances, the *sheikhs* (or headmen) divided the estate into as many rigorously equal parcels (*sahm*) as there were males in the tribe; one *sahm* being assigned to each by agreement or by lot (Klat 1955:54–55).[7]

The 'Abbādis' subsistence system afforded a high degree of autonomy among households for everyday tasks. However, larger groups were sometimes needed for dealing with disputes or defending or making claims on territory.[8] Like other *'arab* tribes, the 'Abbādis marshaled ties of descent and alliance to mobilize larger units when needed (for example, for the various confrontations that took place between the 'Abbādis and the 'Adwān war between 1812 and 1841).

One feature of this type of system is that political authority is dispersed. Leaders are found at all levels, from the household on up to major tribal alliances.[9] The title of *shaykh* was given to the leader of a tribe, *'ashīra*, and the leader of a confederation of tribes was known as the sheikh of sheikhs.[10] In Jordan, as in many other parts of the Middle East, sheikhs are said to be the first among equals. Sheikhdom is not rigidly defined or automatically inherited, but sheikhs normally belong to families from which previous sheikhs have come. Noble birth is only one of the many traditional criteria for tribal leadership. Personal characteristics such as bravery, generosity, charisma, and leadership abilities are important attributes of a sheikh; and these attributes played a role in determining which of a sheikh's sons would succeed him. In the past, a tribal sheikh acted as a spokesperson for the tribe when dealing with sheikhs from other tribes (within and outside the confederation) or with Ottoman authorities. These sheikhs also mediated disputes within and between tribes, and their homes served as meeting places for community decision making.[11]

During Muhammad al-Ṭālib's lifetime a number of factors led to a profound alteration in the meaning of "tribe" as a political unit. From the time of Ottoman conquest of the area in 1516, the Ottoman government never had more than limited success in controlling the *'arab* and Bedouin tribes of the Syrian provinces (Ma'oz 1968; Karpat 1974; and Zenner 1972). Efforts at subduing the Transjordanian tribes were intensified during the construction of the Hijaz railway from Damascus to Medina, 1900–1908. Tribal discontent with Ottoman rule during the period just before World War I coincided with broader Arab opposition to Ottoman rule (Wilson 1987:20).

Some Jordanian tribes participated in the Hashemite-led revolt against the Ottomans and, as discussed in chapter 1, tribespeople have been important sources of support for the Hashemite rulers of Jordan. But since the establishment of the modern state, tribespeople have come under increasing control of the ever-growing state apparatuses. As early as 1932 the Desert Mobil Force of Bedouin led by John Bagot Glubb had practically eliminated intertribal raiding (Gubser 1983:79–80; Jureidini and McLaurin 1984:18–21). Although the sons of sheikhly families took on leadership roles in the army, there was no longer any need to mobilize tribes as such. When war broke out or rebellions had to be put down, the units of mobilization were now brigades and regiments made up of men hailing from different tribes. The settlement of tribal disputes also became the responsibility of the central government. Even though tribal leaders continued to play an important role in dispute settlement, theirs was no longer the final authority in these matters.[12]

A number of events during this period also contributed to a decline in the pastoral economy. One of the earliest administrative offices instituted by the British Mandate authorities was the Department of Land and Surveys. The first task undertaken by this department upon its establishment in 1928 was a village cadastral survey which was completed in 1933. A land settlement law was enacted which gave judges a free hand in determining ownership (regardless of whether a formal Ottoman title could be produced), and the department began to settle individual plots of land working from the northern territories south.[13] In addition to facilitating tax collection and increasing agricultural production, G. F. Walpole, the first director of the department, listed among the benefits of the new land system a loosening of "the hold of the tribal sheikhs on their tribesmen" (Walpole 1948:58). Another, perhaps unforeseen, consequence of the new land policy which did away with communal land tenure was that "communal responsibility for land preservation ended and problems of overgrazing began to appear. Herd sizes were not reduced, though individual pastures could not support the numbers. Overgrazing of confined pastures resulted in stunted animal growth and increased disease and parasites" (Shoup 1981:2).

Jordan gained its independence from Britain in 1946, and in 1948 Israel was created and the first Arab-Israeli war ensued. In 1950, the year Muhammad al-Ṭālib married, the West Bank of Palestine was annexed by Jordan.[14] Many Palestinians settled in the Valley, most of whom were skilled farmers, and they soon introduced more sophisticated agricultural techniques.

The opening of schools also played a major role in transforming life in the Valley. When Muhammad al-Ṭālib was a boy he studied, as was the custom at the time, with an itinerate teacher who taught him the Koran and the three Rs.[15] The first government school in the Valley was opened in 1950 for boys. In the years following King Hussein's ascension to the throne (1953), schools proliferated throughout rural Jordan. By 1981 there were twenty-two schools in the Deir ʿAlla Subdistrict of the Valley alone (nine for boys, nine for girls, and four mixed elementary schools). According to one ʿAbbādi sheikh who could not read or write, schools were the main factor in the ʿAbbādis' decision to settle: "Schools were built and we all settled around them." Another ʿAbbādi, born in the foothill territory of al-ʿArda, now a lawyer based in Amman, explained how schooling worked toward diminishing the viability of pastoralism: "Schooling reduced the availability of shepherds. The first educated men married outside of the clan, then girls started to go to school and they in turn wanted educated husbands. They tried to look citified and to show that they were cultured so as to be attractive brides and they considered it below their level to milk or bring fodder (personal communication)."

By the eve of the 1967 war with Israel, pastoralism in the Jordan Valley had declined to the extent of being considered of "negligible importance" economically (Mazur 1979:178). Grazing land was diminished, the remaining areas were overgrazed, and the livestock had a low average weight (Mazur 1979:146).

These changes in the economy and demography of the Valley were accompanied by a burst of construction, primarily in mudbrick, between 1951 and 1967 (table 1). The Deir ʿAlla Subdistrict in the middle region of the Valley, for example, grew from a total of 118 dwellings before 1950 to 921 in 1965. Among these was the two-room house that Muhammad al-Ṭālib built in Muʿaddi (see chapter 3).

The 1967 Arab-Israeli war totally disrupted life in the Valley. The West Bank was occupied by Israel, and at least 300,000 Palestinians crossed the bridges over the Jordan River (Khouri 1981:109). About half of these stayed in emergency camps in the Jordan Valley, and the eastern bank of the Valley became a base for the Palestinian fedayein fighters. The Israeli bombing of the Valley resulted in a mass exodus causing most of the civilian population to flee, and it is estimated that more than 60 percent of the houses in the Valley were destroyed (Dajani et al. 1980:20). The Valley remained a battlefield during the internal civil strife in Jordan which lasted through 1971.

Since 1971 the Jordan Valley has been the target of Jordan's most extensive and expensive development programs.[16] The Valley represented Jordan's greatest potential for agricultural growth,[17] and plans

Table 1
New Dwellings—Deir ʿAlla Subdistrict, 1950–1978

Year	Total	Mud	Concrete	Cement
1978	54	10	14	30
1977	99	20	30	49
1976	77	21	22	34
1975	129	54	18	57
1974	118	41	26	51
1973	89	31	18	40
1972	91	56	5	30
1971	34	22	4	8
1966–70	381	309	38	34
1961–65	360	318	15	27
1956–60	275	267	3	5
1951–55	188	180	2	6
Pre–1950	118	116	2	–
Total	2,013	1,445	197	371

Source: Jordan: The Population and Housing Census Pretest, 1978

had been discussed for the development of the Valley for some time (Khouri 1981). The first seventy kilometers of the East Ghor Canal had been completed in 1966 but had been bombed by the Israelis in the 1967 war (fig. 4). In the 1970s, the canal was repaired and an eighteen-kilometer extension added. The postwar plan for rehabilitation and development of the Valley (1972) aimed not only at increasing food production but also at providing social services in order to improve the life of the area's inhabitants. During the period from 1973 through 1980 the government of Jordan established central marketing centers, a vegetable-processing plant and crate factory, farming cooperatives, and agricultural research stations and carried out a program of land redistribution in the Valley. During the same period the government provided a whole set of social services including paved roads, electricity, piped domestic water and sewers, municipal streetlights, housing, health clinics, vocational training centers, and more public schools. The government had limited success in attracting new residents to the Valley, so the primary "beneficiaries" of the projects were the local tribespeople in whose name the land had been registered in 1952.

The project succeeded in transforming the eastern bank of the Jordan Valley into Jordan's most productive agricultural area. An article on the green revolution in the Arab East states that "of all the examples of progress, none is more dramatic than the 100-kilometer (sixty-mile)-long Jordan Valley where, in 1981, Valley farmers grew $141 million worth of fruits and vegetables," accounting for over 63 percent of Jordan's agricultural output that year (Aramco 1983:31).

The land brought under cultivation reduced the area available for grazing, but more importantly, the sheer profit potential of farming accelerated the transition from a primarily pastoral economy to a highly intensive system of agriculture. By 1978 greenhouses, drip irrigation, pesticides, and chemical fertilizers were used extensively; and double and triple cropping were the norm. The 1978 agricultural census reports that nearly all privately owned land was cultivated, irrigated with water from the canal (Jordan 1981:103).[18] About 80 percent of the irrigated land was cultivated with vegetables (tomatoes, cucumbers, green peppers, eggplant, and cauliflower); the remainder was used to cultivate grains, especially wheat and barley. These figures represent not only a marked decrease in the amount of land devoted to pastoralism but also a significant change from subsistence crops to cash crops. The percentage of dunums used for field crops dropped dramatically during the period from 1975 to 1979 with, for example, a 60 percent fall in areas devoted to wheat (Seccombe 1981:51–53).[19] Valley residents now consume only a small portion of their agricultural produce, selling the bulk of their crops to the government at a central market where they are graded and packed for sale in Jordanian and international markets.

Grazing lands lost to cultivation were not made up for by the cultivation of fodder despite government projections. By 1979 fodder crops (clover, vetches, and maize) accounted for less than 0.5 percent of the harvested area.[20] The livestock, an average of just over one animal per capita in 1978,[21] was sent with shepherds to graze in the foothills on state lands and in the desiccated zone that separates the riverbed from the floodplains.[22]

Despite their insignificance in terms of agricultural production, during the period of my research goats and sheep continued to play an important social role. Sheikhs still maintained relatively large flocks as a status marker and to fulfill the continuing requirements of traditional hospitality; most families tried to keep enough goats for home dairy consumption and one or two lambs on hand for feast days and other ritual needs.

Contrary to the common belief that Arab pastoralists despise farming, the tribespeople of the Jordan Valley have become avid agriculturalists.[23] State subsidies have guaranteed a level of financial success, and the prevalent pattern of family farms grants tribespeople a degree of personal/familial autonomy that is highly valued.

The 1978 census found both tribesmen and tribeswomen actively involved in farming.[24] On the majority of agricultural holdings in the Deir ʿAlla subdistrict (709 of the 1,070 agricultural holdings in the subdistrict), the bulk of the work was done by members of the owner's household with some supplemental help by hired workers, mostly Egyptian and Pakistani men and local women (Jordan 1981:201).[25]

However, farming is not the only enterprise the ʿAbbādis engage in. Lars Wahlin's survey of ʿAbbādis in al-ʿArda showed that 26 percent worked in transport, 21 percent in agriculture, 16 percent in crafts, 16 percent in the armed forces, 11 percent in administration and clerical work, 5 percent in sales, and 5 percent in other fields in 1978 (1982:55). Given the higher profit potential of farming in the Jordan Valley, a much greater proportion of Valley ʿAbbādis were engaged in agriculture—a 1980 report estimates that agriculture accounted for about two-thirds of total employment in the Jordan Valley (Dajani et al. 1980:10). Nevertheless, in 1980 nonfarm employment was growing at a faster rate than farm employment in the Valley (Dajani et al. 1980:10).

The concentration of ʿAbbādis in transport—truck and taxi driving and vehicle repair—is suggestive of Dawn Chatty's (1980, 1986) findings among Syrian Bedouin where truck driving was seen as an acceptable occupational replacement for pastoral nomads because of the symbolic associations between motor vehicles and camels. Although Wahlin does not give details of employment in the transport sector, the ʿAbbādis I knew working in this area owned their own vehicles and/or garages and thus enjoyed the autonomy that self-employment afforded.[26]

Education has provided young people with the skills required to work in the growing service sector of the economy. The new generation has been able to fill some of the jobs that were created in the Valley as a result of the East Ghor Canal Project, while others commute to government jobs in the regional and national capitals. In 1980 there were still not enough skilled Valley residents to fill the government posts in the school system, the Jordan Valley Authority, the clinics, marketing center, and so forth. Many of these positions were filled by Jordanians from other parts of the country (many of whom commuted) and by Palestinians and other Arabs. For example, in 1980 the teaching staff at the Deir ʿAlla Secondary School for Girls was made up of twelve teachers from the regional capital, Salt (all of whom commuted); five originally from Palestine; three from the Valley, and one from another location in Jordan. The all-male faculty at the Muʾaddi Secondary School for Boys was made up of ten teachers from the Valley; eight Palestinians; three from Egypt; four from northern Jordan; and one other Jordanian.

As in the past, many individuals and most families are engaged in more than one type of economic enterprise.[27] The al-Ṭālib household was typical in that they practiced farming, raised a few sheep and goats, operated a small shop, and one of their members was employed by the government. This mixed economy which combines pastoralism, agriculture, trade, and wage labor has tribal precedents. As Riccardo Bocco (1984) has noted, even archetypical camel-herding Bedouin were probably never exclusively pastoralists but relied on a multiresource economy that included raiding, the collection of tribute (*khūwa*), and trading for their subsistence.

One of the goals of the East Ghor Canal Project had been to encourage population settlement in the Valley. The Valley had been depopulated during the war, and although most of this population returned after hostilities ended, the Plan for Rehabilitation calculated that a population increase of approximately 8,000 a year (i.e., a projected 96,000 by 1975 and 150,000 by the completion of the Maqarin Dam) was necessary to meet the manpower needs of the expanding agricultural sector. The hope was, as I understand it, to stem the tide of rural-to-urban migration by rerouting villagers from other parts of Jordan to the more profitable agricultural lands of the Valley. The plan had limited success in this regard. Instead, the needed labor was provided for by expatriates. The deficit in farm labor was made up in large part with Egyptian migrant farm laborers, while large construction projects in the Valley—as elsewhere in Jordan in the 1980s—were frequently contracted to Asian firms which brought in their own expatriate construction crews.[28]

Despite the development projects' failure to attract large numbers of new residents, they did serve as an enticement to the tribal residents of the Valley to remain in the area. Following the rise of oil prices in 1973, Jordan became a major source for labor for the oil-producing nations of the Arabian Gulf (Keely and Saket 1984). The tribespeople of the Jordan Valley were a noticeable exception to the trend of out-migration. My household survey of the Ghānānim tribe in 1981 found that out of about five hundred members, only four men and two women had moved for work to the Arabian Gulf. Two brothers had gone to Saudi Arabia for a few years, where they earned enough money to return and open a garage in Mu'addi and to buy one of the government-built housing units in the village. One unmarried man was working in public relations in Abu Dhabi and another as an army nurse in Kuwait. Two Ghānānim women had married schoolteachers (from other tribes) and had accompanied their husbands to Saudi Arabia and Oman.

Nor had there been significant rural-to-urban migration from the Valley. In 1981 two Ghānānim men who were officers in the army were stationed with their families in the town of Zarqa. Other than that only three Ghānānim families had moved to Jordanian cities, and two of these families continued to maintain a home in the Valley or al-'Arda.[29]

Despite the many changes that have taken place in the lives of the 'Abbād tribespeople, most 'Abbādis continue to live together and to maintain a keen sense of their tribal identity—although, as I will discuss, the meaning of this tribal identity is changing. In the following two chapters I focus on the way the 'Abbādis organize and use the space in their homes, arguing that household practices were and continue to be key to the way they make themselves as ʿarabs.

NOTES

1. He was the first of four sons and a daughter. His father later took two additional wives. The second wife had nine children; the third wife died leaving no children.

2. The confederation is divided into two main sections: the al-Jrumiya section made up of the Yasgin, Ghānānim, Nuimat, Manasir, Ramadhna, Khatalin, Asalma, Hajahya, Hwarat, Maadat, and Sanabra tribes and the al-Jburaya section made up of the Bqur, Fqaha, Jbara, Rahamna, Salahin, Zyadat, and Zyud (Peake 1958:166–68). Most of the Jubarah section tribes live on the Jordan Plateau in the towns of Wadi Seer, Mahas, and Arak al-Emir, which were practically suburbs of the capital by 1981, whereas most of the Jrumiya tribes live in the Valley and its foothills. See Layne (1986, chap. 2) for more on the history of the ʿAbbād confederation.

3. Archaeological evidence indicates that a system of transhumance has been used by people exploiting the Jordan Valley and its piedmont for at least 60,000 years—first by foraging societies such as the populations that inhabited the southern edge of the Jordanian plateau during the Late Quaternary and later by pastoralists (Henry 1984).

4. See Glueck (1951:240–46) for a description of the housing he observed in the Valley in the early 1970s.

5. This system of land use in the Valley may have been that of hima which according to Shoup (1990:195) was developed by "nomadic pastoralists but . . . enjoyed widespread use by nonpastoralists as well." "The hima system is based on the principle of communal (tribal) land tenure in which all members of the tribal unit have equal rights to pasture land regardless of size of household herds. Hima takes its name from the fact that certain range lands are held in reserve (hima) for specific use, such as bee-keeping or grazing during the various seasons of the year. Other areas are left untouched, to be used only during periods of crisis such as drought" (Shoup 1981:1).

6. He goes on to say that "in most cases it didn't matter much if they did meet, for most of these other tribes were small ones who paid khuwa in return for grazing" (1981:121). The arrangement of khuwa payments is very difficult to reconstruct, as tribes are reluctant to admit having been in a subordinate position to other tribes at some time in the past.

7. According to Klat, "These allotments were valid for a short time only, usually a full crop rotation period, after which the different parcels were brought again together and a new distribution made (1955:55)." Whereas Walpole writing of the mushaʿ system in Palestine reports that the reallotment occurred at fixed periods varying between two and nine years (Walpole 1948:55).

8. See Layne (1986:77–78) for accounts of some of the intertribal battles the ʿAbbād engaged in during the nineteenth and early twentieth centuries.

9. For comparative accounts of tribal leadership, see Musil (1928:50–60) and Lancaster (1981) among the Rwala, Caton (1990) and Dresch (1989) on Yemen, and Wilkinson (1977:180–82) on Oman.

10. Among the ʿAbbād and Mashālkhah tribes the terminology for different tribal groups is used ambiguously, probably because usage is changing. Although all agree that a *qabīla* is bigger and usually more prestigious than an *ʿashīra*, which in turn is bigger than a *ʿāila*, (family), there is no consensus as to which of these terms should be used for a particular group. I never heard the term *ḥamūla* (lineage) used among the ʿAbbād of the Jordan Valley (cf. Wahlin 1992:49).

11. See Gubser (1973), Antoun (1979), and Lancaster (1981) for excellent accounts of tribal leadership in Jordan.

12. See Oweidi (1982) for a history of tribal law in Jordan.

13. In the Jordan Valley individual titles were settled in 1952, although contested cases appeared before the court until June 6, 1957. See Bocco (1989a) for an analysis of the impact of the new system of land tenure on the Huwaytat of southern Jordan.

14. In addition, the influx of Palestinian refugees from the area that had become Israel created an unemployment problem which affected all of Jordan including the Valley until the rise in oil prices in 1973. Franken mentions a surplus of unemployed and widespread emigration to West Germany from Deir ʿAlla, one of the largest Palestinian population centers in the Valley, during the period from 1959 to 1964 (Franken 1969:xvi). My sense is that the migrants to Germany were predominantly Palestinian. One of the students at the Deir ʿAlla Secondary School for Girls was the daughter of a Palestinian man and a German woman who lived in Germany but sent their daughter back to the Valley for her high-school education.

15. See al-Tall (1979), Wahlin (1982), and Diab and Wahlin (1983) for a description of this type of education in rural Jordan.

16. According to Dajani, the development of the Jordan Valley was one of the most expensive per capita development projects in the world (Dajani, personal communication). The cost of the development projects undertaken on the east bank of the Jordan Valley between 1973 and 1980 (known as Stage I Development Projects) amounted to 245 million dollars (Dajani et al. 1980:25). Even at "full development" entailing the completion of the Maqarin Dam and extension of the East Ghor Canal to the Dead Sea at an additional cost estimated in 1980 at over one billion dollars, the population of the Valley was not expected to exceed 150,000 inhabitants (Dajani et al. 1980:24, 31).

17. In 1975, agriculture, including livestock production, accounted for 9.6 percent of the Gross Domestic Product in Jordan, and in 1980 it was the main source of livelihood for about 14 percent of the country's labor force (Jordan 1980:4,293). Although agricultural products form an important part of Jordan's exports, local agricultural products do not meet the country's food needs (Khouri 1981:16; Jordan 1986:532). In spite of steady growth in agricultural output during the period from 1973 to 1985 (from JD 23.6 million to an estimated JD 112 million), the agricultural sector was not able to meet the increasing demand [for food]—especially for meat and dairy products." Food imports

increased from an annual average of JD 41 million in 1973 to JD 179.9 million for the period 1981–1985, "representing 16.5 percent of total imports" throughout the first half of the 1980s (Jordan 1986:532).

18. The Jordan Valley is divided into three administrative subdistricts (*qaḍāʾ*) of about equal size: North Shuna in the north, Deir ʿAlla in the middle, and South Shuna in the south. (See fig. 5) The following figures on agricultural production in the Deir ʿAlla Subdistrict, the area in which I conducted my research, give a fairly accurate picture of the Valley as a whole. One dunum equals 0.1 hectares or about one fourth of an acre. Out of a total of 44,971 privately owned dunums in the Deir ʿAlla Subdistrict 33,670 dunums were cultivated; of these 33,500 dunums were irrigated. Fruit crops are more important in the South Shuna Subdistrict. There were one hundred twenty holdings planted with a total of over thirty thousand citrus trees (Jordan 1981:126).

19. This change was not anticipated; the projected figure for field crops during that period was 49.6 percent (Seccombe 1981:53).

20. Although the government planned for an increase in fodder cultivation, by 1979 only "1,117 dunums of fodder crops (clover, vetches, and maize) were cultivated, accounting for less than 0.5 percent of the harvested area compared to 2,242.6 dunums in 1975," and that year no alfalfa was grown in the Valley, even though the Jordan Valley Commission had planned for alfalfa to make up 13.2 percent of the total cultivated area (Seccombe 1981:53).

21. The 1978 census reported a total of 7,757 sheep, 4,591 goats, and about 951 dairy cows in the Deir ʿAlla Subdistrict (Jordan 1981:156, 168,173,178).

22. See Tapper (1979) for a detailed discussion of the implications of herd size and composition for subsistence versus market production.

23. According to Wilkinson (1977:142–43) in ninth-century Oman, Arab tribespeople became cultivators and "introduced their ʿarab (bedu) system of social organization into village life." As they did so, "the old prejudices against working the land disappeared."

An interesting comparison can also be made with the Basque case documented by Greenwood (1976). Greenwood argues that the abandonment of agriculture by Basque farm families following the commercialization of agriculture can only be understood in terms of Basque ideas about work and dignity. Although commercialization made farming more profitable, it cost them in "additional managerial effort, speculation in future markets, and in their subjection to the movements of prices over which they have no control" (Greenwood 1976:147).

24. The census reported 1,441 male and 694 female permanent unpaid farm workers (presumably family members). Most of those females were between fifteen and thirty-four years of age, whereas most of the men were between thirty-five and fifty-four years of age (Jordan 1981:208).

25. The census reported 343 males and 21 females employed year-round and 4,161 males and 2,330 females hired on a seasonal basis (Jordan 1981:209).

26. See Wahlin (1991a) for a historical account of the growth of various means of transportation in Jordan. Wahlin calculates that in 1989 there was "one private car to every 23 inhabitants, or a vehicle of some kind to every 12" (1991a:26).

27. Similarly, Bocco (1984:6) found that "in analyzing the economic activities of the members of different 'bayt' (extended family) of the al-Khraisha. . . .
I could hardly find one, whose members all practiced the same economic occupation."

28. According to *The Population and Housing Pretest* (Jordan 1978), there
were 151 non-Jordanian Arabs, 35 Pakistanis, 46 Indians, and 306 South Ko-
reans out of a total population of 15,309 in the Deir ʿAlla Subdistrict in 1978.
These figures, especially with regard to the non-Jordanian Arabs, seem to me to
be low.

29. The family that did not maintain a second home within the tribal territory was an ex-slave of the Ghānānim who married a Palestinian woman and
moved to Amman. Most, but not all, of the ʿAbbād tribes had slaves until slavery
was abolished in Jordan in the 1929 constitution. (See Gubser 1973, Lancaster
1981, and Layne 1986 for more on slavery in Jordan.)

CHAPTER 3

‘*Arab* Architectonics

THE INCLUSION OF THE ‘ABBĀDIS’ TRIBAL TERRITORY within the confines of a modern state has profoundly influenced the meaning and constitution of social space. Bocco provides valuable comparative material in his explorations of the changing meaning of tribal territory in the context of state intervention among the Khrayshah living southeast of Amman (1985) and the Huwetat of Southern Jordan (1989a:145). He notes, "At the beginning of the century, mobility, group cohesion, strategies of alliance and military force constituted the critical elements of control of a territory and of survivial for a tribe of pastoral nomads" (Bocco 1989a: translation mine). The emergence of a state made tangible by its military, politico-administrative, and economic systems meant the loss of military autonomy and a progressive limitation of mobility for such tribes and threw into question the very notion of "tribal territory" (Bocco 1989a:145). Of special import was the new system of land tenure which defined both state lands and those available for private ownership. The new code made cultivated lands the only lands that could be privately owned. Henceforth, at least theoretically, pastures that had been the mainstay of tribal territories were open to all parties. This policy was reinforced in the late 1930s when the government constructed wells and cisterns in the arid areas which remained state property, accessible to all (Bocco 1989a:147). Changes like these regarding access to resources in the arid zones required a renegotiation among Bedouin groups, and the new land-tenure laws regarding the private ownership of lands in cultivated regions changed relationships between nomadic and sedentary groups (Bocco 1989a:147). According to Bocco, however, although some state policies undermined the traditional meaning of tribal territory, other policies—such as the laws regarding the division and allocation of land within tribes, special provisions in the electoral laws and Bedouin control laws, and the sedentarization of Bedouin in arid lands—in fact encouraged the social reproduction of tribal territories, if in a significantly altered form.

Because the tribes of the Jordan Valley have never legally been considered to be "Bedouin" not all these policies have affected them.[1] In their case, more important than policies directed especially at them as tribespeople have been the more generalized repercussions of integration into a modernizing state system perhaps most clearly manifest in the state intervention in the development of the Valley in the 1970s and 1980s described in the previous chapter. And like the cases described by Bocco, although state-run economic and politico-administrative systems have undermined some tribal identity-making practices, they have also provided new resources and opportunities for the social construction of tribal identities.

In this and the following chapter I focus on domestic space in examining the meaning and constitution of space by Jordan Valley tribespeople in the context of their increased integration into an ever more elaborate state system. According to the social scientific definition of "Bedouin" described in chapter 1, three of the four defining characteristics of "Bedouin" deal with where and how tribespeople make their homes—in tents, in changing locations, in the desert. Despite the limitations of this type of definition (discussed above), it is true that residence practices were and continue to be central to the processes by which the 'Abbādis construct social identities.[2]

In the past the tent was the primary locus of all social activity. In addition to the household matters of eating, sleeping, and raising children, the household was the fundamental unit of production and the tent the principal locus for political and economic decision making. The indigenous and interrelated concepts of *aṣiil* (noble origin) and *awāʿid* (code of conduct) provided guidelines for the "proper" way to go about all these activities. Although *aṣl* (origin) is an important basis of ascribed status, it is complexly modified with the actions of individuals and groups (their achieved status), because *aṣl* also refers to the accumulated reputation of one's patrilineal group.[3] As Ahmad Oweidi, an indigenous anthropologist of the 'Abbād tribes, notes, *uṣul* (the plural of *aṣl*) refers to "rooted customs; decent characteristics; principles; and . . . right behavior" (1982:xiii).[4] Oweidi defines *awāʿid* as the code of honorable conduct appropriate to a person of noble lineage (Oweidi 1982:96–100).[5] This code, systematized in customary tribal law, is designed "to protect and maintain among [the community's] members certain moral values which they consider a deep-rooted part (*uṣul*) of their identity, handed down to them through and from their ancestors" (Oweidi 1982:2).

The activities regulated by *awāʿid* typically reported by tribespeople and cultural anthropologists alike have been those areas codified in customary law.[6] There are two important consequences of this: 1) activities that fall under this purview are those governed by discursive practice, and 2) they are activities typically undertaken by men.[7] But *awāʿid* also entail guidelines for behavior governed by nondiscursive knowledge. And hospitality, as important a component of *'arab* honor as practices

like raiding or protecting women's honor, is as much women's responsibility as it is men's. (The primary locus of hospitality is, of course, the
home.)

Pierre Bourdieu has illustrated the special importance of the house in
the reproduction of "habitus," that is, a system of transposable schemes
of perception, thought, and action within a given culture (1977:82–83).
Based on his study of the Kabyle house he concludes:

> Inhabited space—and above all the house—is the principal locus for the
> objectification of the generative schemes; and, through the intermediary of
> the divisions and hierarchies it sets up between things, persons, and prac
> tices, this tangible classifying system continuously inculcates and reinforces
> the taxonomic principles underlying all the arbitrary provisions of this
> culture. (1977:89)

Some behaviors within the house are explicitly dealt with in customary law under the rubric of *ḥurmat al-bayt*, literally, the inviolability of
the house.[8] But most everyday practices and household tasks are informed by tacit norms about how one might best go about such activities. These are not rules that "govern" behavior but cultural meanings
that "orient practice without producing it" (Bourdieu 1977:21). The
way one conducts oneself in these matters, whether in choosing what
clothing to wear, what seat to offer a guest, or the way one holds one's
body while performing household tasks or walking in the street, is the
minutia out of which judgments concerning the honor (*muḥaram*) of
individuals and, by extension, their families are made (see chapter 7).

As Bourdieu has noted, to a large extent these values and meanings
are inculcated in the body. By paying attention to gestures and postures
of adults, children learn with/in their bodies "a way of walking, a tilt of
the head, facial expressions, ways of sitting and of using implements, . . .
a tone of voice, a style of speech" (1977:87).

In the following description of the way that ʿAbbādi tribespeople design and live in their houses I examine the contours of *ʿarab* posture. I
use "posture" here in all three senses of the term explored by Schumacher in his book *Human Posture*: "i. . . . the position and carriage of
the limbs and the body as a whole; . . . ii. position of one thing (or person) relative to another; . . . and iii. a state of being; a condition or situation in relation to circumstances" (from the *OED* in Schumacher
1989:17). Posture, in each of these senses, reveals a critical aspect of
identity making among the ʿAbbādis. For example, the way that
ʿAbbādis move and position their bodies when sitting or reclining on a
mattress or when entering a tent or house exemplifies some of the ways
that tribesmen and women construct themselves as tribespeople, honorable tribespeople. There is more to this than simply politeness. It is not

just a question of knowing, for example, that it is rude to sit in a way that directs the soles of one's feet toward another. A person's bearing as he or she moves when walking in the street or moves to accept a seat that has been offered expresses self-control and self-respect, or the lack thereof.[9]

In the second sense of posture, I describe the way that 'Abbādis position themselves vis-à-vis others both by moving their residences and rearranging themselves and their furniture within their houses. I show how, despite some significant changes in the last thirty years in both 'Abbādi vernacular floor plans and residence patterns, 'Abbādi housing practices still exhibit a high degree of dynamism and fluidity. These movements continue to be critical to the negotiation by the 'Abbādis of the dual tribal values of autonomy and sociability. Finally, I argue that the way that the 'Abbādis move in and with their homes, constantly repositioning themselves in relation to one another and the material world, is the basis of an '*arab* architectonics. Indeed, the postures that the 'Abbādis adopt in their homes are much more than household practices; they exemplify the means by which the '*arabs* of the Jordan Valley practice politics and actively construct their social identities and their world.

'ABBĀDI HOMES: TRADITIONAL FLOOR PLANS IN NON-TRADITIONAL STRUCTURES

Among the 'Abbādis the word *bayt* represents not only their homes but also the people who inhabit them. For example, the Muḥammad Hussain al-Ṭālib family is sometimes referred to as *bayt Muḥammad Hussain*. The term *bayt*, when used alone, implies a goat-hair tent (*bayt al-shaʿr*). Other kinds of houses must be specified, for example: *bayt lubn* (a mud-brick house), *bayt ḥajar* (a stone house), or *bayt cement* (a cement house). The 'Abbādis consider goat-hair tents (*bayt al-shaʿr*, plural *byut al-shaʿr*), as homes in contrast with the tents (*khayma*) used by the army and refugees. (I follow English usage in referring to the 'Abbādis' goat-hair houses as "tents" and their mud-brick or concrete dwellings as "houses".)

Up through the 1940s goat-hair tents and caves were the primary forms of shelter of the tribes of the Jordan Valley. Nelson Glueck reported in 1943–44 that "the Arabs living in this district (near Pella) and indeed in almost all of the valley, are still tent-dwellers" (1951:244–45). He recorded a number of settlements, particularly north of Wādi Zarqa, where there were "several crude mud-brick and stone houses . . . used as storage houses rather than dwelling places" (1951:244,240,246). In 1952 there were only 118 houses in the area now designated as the Deir

ʿAlla Subdistrict as compared with over 2,000 houses there in 1981 (Jordan 1978).

Since the 1950s the ʿAbbādis have been building houses in the Valley and in al-ʿArda—first in mud brick and, since the 1970s, out of poured concrete or cement block.[10] In designing and building permanent dwellings, regardless of the building material, the ʿAbbādis have replicated, to a large extent, the layouts of the various types of goat-hair tents they use.[11] They have used new materials and technologies to build according to traditional principles. The dimensions of rooms and house plans as a whole are similar in many ways to the spatial organization of tents.[12]

Goat-hair tents are woven by women in the open air on ground looms.[13] They are woven in strips 60 to 80 centimeters wide of varying lengths and sewn together. Goat-hair tents usually consist of six to eight strips totaling 3.5 to 4.5 meters in width. Tents vary in length rather than width and are differentiated by the number of center poles (*wasat*) which serve as dividing points between each room. The space between poles can vary only to a certain extent, between 3 to 4 meters, without the roof sagging. Whatever the distance, it is equal between each of the poles. In other words, in order to make a larger tent, rooms of equal size are added laterally. Lancaster reports that the Rwala of eastern Jordan prefer tents with an uneven number of central poles (or in a Western manner of thinking, with an even number of rooms) so that the two sides are equal in size to show that family and visitors are of equal importance (1981:161).

This principle of starting with a basic unit, typically a rectangle, and adding space by annexing additional units is transferred to the construction of other kinds of dwellings. In vernacular structures, as in goat-hair tents, the size of the rooms vary within the 4 to 5 meter range. Hence rooms, although typically oblong, may be square (4 by 4 m or 4.5 by 4.5 m). The salient cultural convention affecting the dimensions of rooms in a multiroom dwelling is that the rooms should be of equal size (fig. 5). Houses are frequently built in stages; rooms are added on gradually as needs change and/or finances permit.

People do not live in tents larger than they require. Today, as in the past, most nuclear families' tents consist of two rooms. The ideal size for tents is one room for each conjugal couple and a room for receiving guests. Hence, three-room tents are usually used by extended families, the third room being occupied by a son's family. Only sheikhs had four or five-room dwellings. To live in a tent larger than one's needs would be considered to be making pretensions of being a sheikh, and demands of hospitality might be made accordingly. Furthermore, larger tents are more cumbersome to move. However, the cultural conventions and practical considerations that kept the size of tents to the minimum

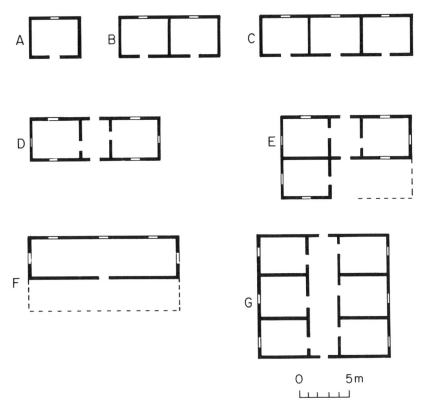

FIG. 5 Vernacular house plans

needed do not pertain to houses. Not only are considerations of moving a dwelling no longer a problem, people are now also accumulating capital goods and require more space to store their belongings.

Alterations in the social limits of house size for ordinary tribesmen also affect and reflect changes in the social relationships between tribesmen and tribal sheikhs. Building a house as large or larger than those of sheikhs is a challenge to the special status and authority of tribal sheikhs. This type of challenge is typical of the "low-key" politics described by Richard T. Antoun (1979). In the Jordan Valley, as in the northern Jordanian village described by Antoun, claims of relative status, honor, and purity ("prizes" that are themselves ambiguous) are often made by "generalized confrontations" rather than confrontations directed at a specific individual (Antoun 1979:151–52).[14]

The most simple 'Abbādi house, a one-room structure made of sun-dried mud bricks or of concrete (fig. 5), is comparable to the *kharbūsh* tent.[15] The nomenclature for different types of tents varies among the tribes of Jordan but among the 'Abbād *kharbūsh* refers to a tent made of sacking. The *kharbūsh*, because of its light weight, was easier than a goat-hair tent to move and was typically used by shepherds for temporary shelter, not as a home. A one-room house is typically four by five meters large. Very few families live in single-room dwellings because they do not accommodate the cultural convention that requires separate spaces for men and women—or, to put it another way, separate spaces for public and private activities. However, many families use noncontiguous single-room structures as part of their housing complex.

More common are two-room houses made of mud-brick or concrete (fig. 5). In Muʿaddi many of the larger concrete houses still use adjacent two-room mud-brick houses for supplementary shelter and storage. Of the two-room structures being used as a complete dwelling in Muʿaddi, about half are made of concrete and half of mud brick. Two rooms of equal size, usually four by five meters, are built next to each other. These two-room houses are comparable to the common *gatbeh*, the one-poled goat-hair tent. A one-poled tent is divided into two equal parts, the *shigg* (literally "half" or "side," considered to be the men's section) and the *rabʿa* (literally "living quarters," considered to be the women's section). The *shigg* and the *rabʿa* are not structurally different from each other but equal sides of the domestic space. In order to move from one side of the tent to the other—from the *shigg* to the *rabʿa* or vice versa—one must go outside the roofed area and then reenter the tent. This circulation pattern is replicated in two-room houses, which typically have an entrance to each room located in the front wall and no internal passage between rooms.

In both two-room tents and houses mattresses are stacked in the middle of the structure. In houses they are usually stored on a low cupboard (*khizāna*) similar in shape to the table or platform (*maṭwa*) on which mattresses are stacked in a tent.[16]

The three-room house is most frequently made of mud brick. It resembles the two-poled tent, the *faza* or *wasaṭayn*. Three rooms of equal size are built in a row. As in the one- and two-room houses, the doors are located in the center front wall of each room, and there is no way to pass from room to room without going outside (fig. 5).

By the early 1970s new floor plans for concrete and cement-block houses had become popular. The ʿAbbādis' use of the Western terms *corridor*, *sala* (also used for "corridor"), and *veranda* mark the innovativeness of these new designs. The simplest of the new designs consists of two four-by-five-meter rooms divided by a corridor three by five meters in size (fig. 5). The ʿAbbādi corridor, unlike a Western one, is not simply a passageway but is often one of the most used domestic spaces.[17] A door leads in and out of the house at either end of the corridor. This permits more circulation of air than there is in the previously mentioned house designs. Doors to the two rooms are located catercorner to each other in the walls of the corridor so that people may enter a room without seeing or being seen by people in the other room. Household members can also move from one room of the house to the other without stepping outdoors.

The corridor contributes to a more segmented and privatized use of space in homes. Henry Glassie suggests that a similar development, the evolution of the central hall in eighteenth-century Middle Virginian vernacular architecture, was the result of the emergence of the familial isolation of industrial capitalism and the demise of the face-to-face community (1975:189–90). A similar process may be occurring here. The 'Abbādi corridor acts as a divider between the men's and women's sections and between the values and activities associated with new and traditional furniture (see below). However, the intensive use of the corridor by members of both sexes in some families may represent resistance to this separation.[18]

Larger houses are usually an extension of the two-room and corridor plan (fig. 5). The introduction of the corridor changes the axis of lateral extension. An additional room is added on in front of, rather than next to, one of the original rooms and a covered veranda is built in front of the corridor entrance and the other original room. The veranda may also be enclosed to make a fourth room. In this way, tribespeople can build homes larger than their tents without replicating the shape of sheikhs' tents.

SHEIKHS' TENTS AND HOUSES

Size is a sign of status in both tents and houses and sheikhs had, and continue to have, larger tents than ordinary tribesmen. These tents serve as a sign of the sheikh's status (and by extension that of the tribe). In a similar fashion the royal palace of King Hussein is regarded by many tribespeople as *al-bayt al-ʿāmm* or *bayt al-jamiʿ/al-ʿumam* (the house of all Jordanians) following the principle that *bayt al-Shaykh, bayt al-ʿumam* (the house of the sheikh is the house for all the tribe) (Oweidi 1982:74).

In the past, these large tents were needed to accommodate sheikhs' large families and to meet the special demands of hospitality incumbent upon them. Sheikhs tend to have more wives than other tribesmen. Wives were a sign of status in and of themselves, but they also served to strengthen alliances with other groups, and to produce numerous descendants for the sheikh, thus strengthening his family. Although the status of having multiple wives seems to be waning, the labor of many women is still needed in order to extend the hospitality required of a sheikh.

Each of the ʿAbbādi sheikhs still has a four- or five-room tent, and although they are privately owned, the tribe has the right to use them. Such tents are used for weddings, funerals, litigation, and the receiving of important guests. Tribes loan these tents to other tribes of the same confederation for such occasions when more than one tent is needed.[19]

Because of the permanency of walls between rooms in houses, a four-room house cannot be used for the large meetings and celebrations normally held in tents of a comparable size. Accordingly, sheikhs did not built four- and five-room houses to replicate their four- and five-room tents. Instead, they built long, open halls the length of four- or five-room tents for these purposes (fig. 6). These halls tend to be separate from the living quarters of the rest of the household and are sometimes built as a second story above the family's living area.

For example, Sheikh Sālah al-Naim of the Mashālkha tribe uses a large meeting hall which his father built in the village of Diyyat.[20] This hall is known as an ʿallīa (from the root ʿalā [high]) because it is located on the second story of a building. The meeting hall and veranda occupy the entire second floor. The ground floor consists of open and enclosed storage areas in which his Mercedes is garaged and his tent is stored when not in use (both visible to anyone approaching the building). The ʿalliāh is furnished with chairs and couches arranged around the circumference of the room and with thick, wool mattresses and pillows which are stacked at one end of the room when not in use. Sheikh Salah sleeps in the ʿalliāh near the door on a regal stack of three mattresses. Visitors may safely approach the building at any time of the day or night without fear of disturbing the privacy of the women of the household. Tea and meals are brought to the sheikh in the ʿalliāh by one of his many grandchildren and consumed in the company of his ever-present guests either indoors or in the open air on the veranda.

The rest of his large family lives in an adjacent building in which rooms of equal size line both sides of a corridor. The rooms are occupied by one of the sheikh's sisters and her unmarried children, and three of his four wives and their children. (The fourth wife lives in his house in Amman.) Each room is referred to by its occupants as their "house" (hathā bayti).[21] The corridor is used communally as a large living room, and one of the rooms near the door is a communal kitchen.

In other words, while sheikhs continue to distinguish themselves by distinctive family structure and household architecture, the new house designs of ordinary tribespeople reflect and effect their integration into a capitalist mode of production and challenges to the status and authority of sheikhs.[22]

TRANSHUMANCE IN A NEW KEY

During the period of my research, 1981–83, most 'Abbādi families owned permanent dwellings. Despite the preponderance of permanent domestic structures, many 'Abbādis maintained a modified pattern of seasonal transhumance. Present-day transhumance has been adapted to the existence of these new forms of shelter and to the transformation of the local economic system. For example, the 'Abbādis who settled in the Valley still move to al-'Arda in the summer to escape the heat. This migratory pattern, which was based in the past on the requirements of the livestock, persists even though the importance of pastoralism has significantly declined. The traditional summer grazing areas in al-'Arda have been planted with olive trees or are used to cultivate cash crops such as tobacco or summer vegetables. Consequently, those who own livestock now leave most of their flock in the Valley while they are at their summer residences. Only lactating goats and those intended for immediate slaughter are brought along in the summer. Economic considerations still influence settlement patterns, but migrations now follow agricultural seasons and the school year rather than green pastures.

Nor did the presence of concrete houses indicate the demise of tent dwelling. In fact, historical records indicate that tents and houses have been used simultaneously in Jordan for over one hundred and fifty years. In the 1820s, John Lewis Burckhardt reported that "in the village of Ketherabba there were about eighty houses with tents pitched in between the houses" (1822:396), and he found that the "Christians and Turks" of Karak and villagers of Khazyre in the southern Ghor (whom he judged as "little better than Bedouins") lived in tents at harvest time (1822:397,388).[23]

I soon learned that just because people owned houses did not necessarily imply that they would choose to live in them. Many families (like the al-Ṭālib family with whom I lived) live in concrete houses during the school year in the Valley and in a tent in al-'Arda during the summer. And many of the year-round al-'Arda residents leave their permanent dwellings in the summer and move into goat-hair tents. Some say they do this so as to be closer to their fields while cultivating summer crops, but most say they just enjoy the life-style, at least when the weather is fine. Sometimes they rent or loan their vacant houses to Valley 'Abbādis who do not own their own tents. Tents are also still used for rites of passage (funerals, weddings) and other special occasions such as ṣulḥas (legal conciliation ceremonies), or for visiting dignitaries. I was told that entertaining a guest in a goat-hair tent shows more respect to the guest, bestows more honor, than having him in a house. I was not surprised, then, to see that when King Hussein visited the Valley in 1983, tents were set up by the tribes to receive him as he processed from north to south through the Valley.

Some of the al-ʿArda-based ʿAbbādis move to the Valley in the winter to farm and to enjoy the warmer climate. For example, one family that owns two houses, a three-room concrete house adjacent to their 280 dunums of farmland in al-ʿArda and a government-built housing unit in Muʿaddi, move to the Valley every winter because of the economic opportunities of farming in the Valley. In the winter of 1981 they lived in their concrete house in the housing project, but in the winter of 1982 they rented this house to another family and lived instead in a two-room tent which they jerry-rigged out of green-house plastic and plywood on the land in the Valley that they were sharecropping that year.

As in the past, people continue to exercise a large degree of discretion on a daily basis about where and near whom they will live. Like the Basseri of South Persia described by Fredrik Barth, ʿAbbādi households made up of elementary families were the basic units of production and consumption. Households combined to form herding groups, but the relationship among members of a herding group were always open to change—"at any time, a member of a herding unit may withdraw from that group and work alone, or join another unit; and through time the constellations of households in herding units change completely" (Barth 1961:22). Barth observed that

> unlike a sedentary community, which persists unless the members abandon their house and land and depart, a camp community of nomads can only persist through continuous reaffirmation by all its members. Every day the members of the camp must agree in their decision on the vital question of whether to move on, or to stay camped, and if they move, by which route and how far they should move. These decisions are the very stuff of a pastoral nomad existence. (Barth 1961:25–26)

This element of contingency and sense of possibilities continues to color the ʿAbbādis' way of life. Now as in the past, the ʿAbbadis' way of being in the world has a particularly aleatory quality.[24] Through movement between and within residences they keep clearly before themselves the possibility of reordering and reconstituting their social world (cf. Schumacher 1989).

There are many factors that influence the choice of residence—such as the quality of current relations with relatives or neighbors, household finances, proximity to schools, farmland, and office jobs. Because of Islamic inheritance laws and the large average size of families, shares to a single house are often inherited by many different people. In order to enjoy more autonomy, some of the heirs may choose not to occupy the same house with their co-owners and rent a house or live in a tent instead. Although autonomy has always been highly valued by 'arab tribespeople (Oweidi 1982; Lancaster 1981; Abu-Lughod 1986), the parameters of autonomy are being renegotiated as the following example illustrates. A schoolteaching couple from Mu'addi decided to rent a unit in the employee housing project in Mouthalth al-'Arda and to rent out their own home in Mu'addi even though it was a longer drive for them to work. They told me they preferred Mouthalth al-'Arda because they didn't know many people there. (Indeed, they were probably the only local family in the employee project.) This meant more privacy. The husband complained that relatives who do not work do not understand that when he comes home from school he wants some time to himself, to sleep, be quiet, or to study. "They don't understand this. And sometimes they come and look in our refrigerator just to see what there is, and I can't complain because they are my relatives. Furthermore, people don't make an appointment to visit. This way [because the relatives have to come about three kilometers from Mu'addi] they come less often and they're more likely to let us know that they are coming."

Although mobile residence patterns facilitate autonomy, they also enhance opportunities for sociability, as the following story illustrates. One day Sulaymān al-Ṭālib, my research assistant, came to see me. I was not in, and he left word that I could reach him at Um Waṣfi's house next door. I was puzzled. I had been living at Nada's for several months and thought I knew all our neighbors. I learned that Um Waṣfi had moved next door that week. She and her husband Abū Waṣfi (one of Sulaymān's paternal uncles) had been living on the other side of the wādi, but when Abū Waṣfi went to Iraq with his younger brother Ḥamad, Um Waṣfi "was alone" (Um Waṣfi explained that she didn't have any neighbors there) and so moved with her three children into Ḥamad's vacant house next door to us. As she had hoped, Um Waṣfi had lots of company while her husband was away. When I went to find Sulaymān, two neighbor women (another member of the Ghānānim tribe and a Palestinian) were there visiting, and one of Abū Waṣfi's unmarried sisters and Sulaymān (one of his nephews) had temporarily moved in with her.[25] My field notes for the day record my first glimmer of understanding of the extent to which domestic mobility persisted in the context of what appeared to me to be "permanent dwellings"—"No wonder I'm having trouble keeping things straight; everyone keeps moving!"[26]

The construction of low-cost government housing projects (iskān) in the Valley has facilitated the tribal preference for domestic mobility.[27] A total of 1,880 housing units was built in twenty villages in the Valley by the Jordan Valley Authority in 1978. The government feared that the success of the East Ghor Canal Project would be hampered by a lack of labor and so built these housing projects in the hope that low-cost housing would encourage the tribes to settle there and would attract new labor for the agricultural projects. One hundred of these sixty-two-square-meter cinder-block houses were built in the predominantly ʿAbbādi village of Muʿaddi.[28] About half of these houses were purchased by local tribespeople.[29] Most of the ʿAbbādis who bought houses in the government projects already owned houses. They either rented or loaned their second homes to others or used them on a seasonal basis. For example, in 1982 ten of the local owners (one-fifth of the units owned by locals) were living in other houses in Muʿaddi, and five al-ʿArda-based families owned units in the Muʿaddi housing project.

Two units in the project were being loaned to others free of charge. In one case the house was owned by an ʿAbbādi who lived in the town of Salt. He loaned his house to three of his nephews from al-ʿArda so that they could attend the Muʿaddi Secondary School for Boys as there was no secondary school in al-ʿArda. In the second case, a local landowner who lived in a house on his farm loaned his house in the project to employees in his agricultural supply company.

Fourteen (nearly half) of the thirty-one units that were inhabited when I conducted my survey in the spring of 1982[30] were occupied by tenants. The renting of houses, although contributing toward the maintenance of the indigenous system of domestic mobility, signals a profound change in the meaning of a home, for in the past and still today, tents were sometimes loaned or shared but never rented.

In 1982 the rent was either JD 20 or JD 25 a month, a sum that covered the owner's mortgage payment and in the latter case provided a surplus of JD 60 per annum. Thus in a radically different way the house remained a locus of production. In addition to the transformation of houses into an income-producing commodity, the emergence of renting as a socially acceptable practice has widened the range of types of relationships that ʿAbbādis can have with themselves and others. ʿAbbādis were renting their houses to other ʿAbbādis as well as outsiders. Six of the Muʿaddi units were being rented to other ʿAbbādis, three of which were rented to newlywed couples. Non-ʿAbbādi tenants included two families from neighboring towns, four West Bank families, two Egyptian men, two Jordanian agricultural engineers,[31] and me. Two of the houses had been rented previously to other tenants (to a West Bank schoolteacher and to two male laborers).

PEOPLE MAKING PLACES

The fluidity and dynamism with which ʿAbbādis choose where to live is replicated in how they live within their homes. Several elements of the ʿAbbādis' distinctive definition and use of space in their homes may be highlighted in comparison with the definition of middle-class American domestic spaces. The nomenclature of domestic spaces in American English indicates a highly specialized division of space according to function. Rooms are often named with reference to a permanent fixture that defines the primary activity of that room—for example, the terms *bedroom, bathroom*. Other terms refer to the activity directly such as the *study, dining room*, and *washroom* or *laundry room*.

In contrast, spaces in 'Abbādi goat-hair tents and houses are multifunctional. Because of the portability of *'arab* furnishings such as mattresses and water pitchers, almost all the nonproductive household activities can and are done in a variety of places throughout the tent or house. One can sit, eat, visit, sleep, and wash one's face after a nap, perform ablutions, and carry out a variety of light tasks on a mattress. Mattresses are moved from one location to another depending on the time of day, the people involved—their sex, age, status, and degree of kinship or familiarity—and the duration and purpose of the occasion. Ablutions and prayers, performed five times a day, are carried out more or less wherever one happens to be. The only requirement is that prayers be performed in a clean place, and this is assured through the use of prayer rugs.

In goat-hair tents spaces are defined more by reference to the kinds of people who are likely to use the space than by the purpose for which the space is used. In addition to the two main divisions of a goat-hair tent, the *shigg* (men's section) and the *rab'a* (women's section), some particular places are named according to this principle. The *nasab* is the lover's place, where a young man courting is likely to sit; the *ṣadr* is the place for an honored guest; and the *makān manī'* is the prisoner's place.

Because spaces are defined by people and not by places, they are not permanent or fixed. It is the social action of individuals that makes a house. This premise is apparent in the verb to sleep some place (*bayat*), which comes from the same root as house (*bayt*). Within this cultural system, space must be continually created and re-created. The essence of *'arab* architectonics is the creation of space through the routine establishment and reestablishment of domestic space in the desert expanse.

In America, an individual's "living room," "bedroom," "backyard," and so forth, exist whether or not the individual is present. But after the camp is dismantled, the spaces that were once, for example, the *shigg*, the *rab'a*, or the space behind the *rab'a* no longer exist and will not exist until they are reestablished through the force of social interaction. For example, although among the 'Abbād the *shigg* tends to be located on the left of the *rab'a* when facing the tent, this is not a hard-and-fast rule but varies from one household to the next. Therefore, there is nothing a priori that makes one side of the tent the *shigg* and the other the *rabʿa*. The mere construction of the tent does not create the space. It is the placement of social actors (as male and female, young and old, known and unknown, kin and nonkin, as individuals having honor, status, authority to a greater or lesser degree) in relation to one another that creates a space. As Gilsenan (1982:171) put it, although in a rather different ethnographic context, "Space means relationship."

Another manifestation of the way that spaces are defined, not by walls, but by a configuration of social actors in spatial and social relationships to one another, can be found on ʿAbbādi birth certificates. They define their "place of birth" in terms of social location rather than geographic location: that is, an infant's place in relationship to others. As of 1982 some tribespeople of the Jordan Valley were still recording their tribal name as the place of birth on the birth certificates of their children.

A similar phenomenon was reported by Musil at the beginning of this century among the Rwala. "If herdsmen or hunters meet an unknown nomad in their territory, they inquire: ent mine en ja walad, where art thou from, man?" If he says:" Min hal-ʿarab, from these arabs," they ask: "Fahmin annak min al-ʿarab mar min ajj al-ʾorban, we know that thou art from the Arabs, but from which of the various Arabs?" (Musil 1928:44).

This cultural salience of people over places results in an important conflict between Bedouin law and civil law in Jordan. In civil law there is a concept of delimited territorial jurisdiction, *al-iktisas al-makani*, according to which a court holds jurisdiction for crimes committed within a specific area. Whereas, for the Jordanian Bedouin tribes, the choice of a judge is based on the particular competence of a judge and on finding a judge "acceptable to each of the parties, normally without taking account of the residence of the judge and/or the litigants" (Oweidi 1982:28).[32]

The precedence of practice over physical structure in constructing social space is also evident in the ways that the ʿAbbādis handle privacy. Unlike the typical urban homes in Jordan, the tribes of the Jordan Valley do not rely on high walls to protect the privacy or property of their homes. What is seen or is not seen in a home has little to do with walls. A Bedouin saying "the back tent curtain never knows what happens inside the tent (*irwaq al-bayt mayirif waysh iysir juwwah*)" expresses this notion (Oweidi 1982:112). Two examples from my field experience illustrate the processes by which privacy is created and maintained in an open physical venue.[33]

In a tent young women change clothes in the *rabʿa* section while squatting facing the back of the tent. One night I was changing clothes in this position when a vehicle drove up to the front of the tent with its headlights shining directly into the area where I was changing. Immediately the three unmarried daughters rushed to stand in front of me holding their skirts out to shield me from view. I was mortified. I asked them whether or not they thought I had been exposed. They answered with certainty that I had not been seen because no man would look into the *rab'a*, at least not the type of person who would visit their tent.

On another occasion a nephew of the male head-of-household was taking a nap in the *shigg*. An important visitor from Amman arrived, and a mattress was laid out for him in the *shigg*. The sleeping nephew awoke but remained lying down with his eyes closed until he ascertained the identity of the visitor. He sat up with his back to the visitor, facing the back of the tent. Without a word being spoken, one of the young sons of the household brought him a pitcher of water and a towel with which he washed his face. He put on his shoes, then stood up and turned around and, as it were, entered the room to greet the guest.

WOMEN'S WEALTH AND THE MAKING OF SOCIAL IDENTITY

The creation of social space in an *'arab* home is accomplished with the aid of props such as mattresses and pillows, and these furnishing are one of the major forms of *'arab* women's wealth.[34] The average *ma'jal* (initial bride-wealth payment) was JD 1,000 during the period of study, equivalent to approximately $3,000. About one-third of this was spent on gold, one-third on traditional furnishings, mainly mattresses, and one-third on "modern" furniture.[35]

In 1981–83 bride-wealth payments normally included a modern living-room set consisting of a plush couch with four to six matching overstuffed armchairs and coffee tables, and a bedroom set consisting of a queen- or king-sized bed with a headboard (sometimes equipped with radio, ashtrays, and reading lights) and matching side tables, a vanity with stool, and a closet. This Western furniture was not replacing traditional furnishings but rather was being incorporated as an additional resource. Those households that owned both styles of furniture, usually furnished one room with Western living-room furniture, and another room was used for receiving guests on mattresses.[36] These rooms did not take on an enduring definition because the furniture was frequently moved from room to room.

Even though the new living-room sets share some of the elements of comfort and abundance with mattresses (they are always overstuffed), they are less readily portable and are more individuated. Western couches share with *'arab* mattresses the capacity to seat more than one person, but Western chairs (even the overstuffed models most favored by ʿarabs) only seat one person at a time. And whereas the elements of a modern living-room set are separated by tables (end and coffee-tables), there is no intervening furniture between mattresses. The ʿAbbād associate Western chairs with modernity and high status and consider them to be more appropriate for Western clothing. However, they strongly feel that mattresses are more comfortable than chairs and because it is a host's duty to make a guest comfortable, mattresses are still preferred, especially for long visits. In a similar vein, many newlyweds who owned Western bedroom sets found sleeping on traditional mattresses more comfortable than their new beds and so used the bed for tasks such as folding laundry but laid out a mattress to sleep on every evening.

Although gold and Western and indigenous furniture each serve as indicators of personal and familial wealth, mattresses play by far the greatest role in creating the social universe. The importance of a thing within a culture is often indicated by the richness of the vocabulary associated with it (e.g., snow in Eskimo languages, the Nuer names for cows, and the ninety-nine names for God in Arabic). There are at least ten terms in the Arabic dialect spoken by ʿAbbādi tribesmen to indicate different kinds of mattresses, covers, and pillows, each of which is a component of a traditional sitting or sleeping space. The difficulty an English speaker has in finding an accurate term to describe these varied items generically emphasizes the important cultural difference between our mono-functional furnishings and these multifunctional ones. Pillows, mattresses, and covers are all included in the English term *bedding*. But *bedding* is essentially mono-functional—for sleep; essentially private; and except for the conjugal bed, ideally individual. In contrast, ʿarab mattresses are multifunctional, both public and private, and valued for their ability to be used both individually and communally.

The different terms in Arabic distinguish size and use rather than material. Almost all the mattresses and pillows may be made out of wool, cotton, or *swenge* (foam rubber), or *nafish* (shredded old clothing or shredded foam.) Cotton is cooler and so is preferred by some for summer use, but it is more expensive because it is not locally produced. Wool is used for the most prestigious mattresses.

The selection of the cloth to cover one's mattresses and pillows is, like the selection of a china or crystal pattern by brides in the West, a topic of teenage contemplation and a sign of one's style and taste. The cloth coverings also distinguish one person's mattresses from another. In 1983 a mattress that had been stored in al-ʿArda over the winter was stolen and was later identified and reported to the owner on the basis of the fabric.

A woman's bridal mattresses, although paid for by the groom's family, are usually prepared by her own mother (with the help of her neighbors and friends). One bride explained that it is better to have the mattresses made by one's mother than by one's mother-in-law because "no one cares for a girl like her mother." In addition to the mattresses given by the groom, the bride's family often makes a gift to their daughter of one or two additional mattresses. A woman's first quilt is also usually made for her by her mother on the occasion of her marriage.

In a goat-hair tent, bedding is usually stacked in the middle of the tent on the *rab'a*-side of the center pole, thus serving as a dividing wall during the day between the *shigg* and *rab'a* sections of the tent. Paradoxically, the time a division is most needed, when there are guests present, is the time when it is least effective, as mattresses are taken down for the guests. A dividing curtain (*saḥaḥ*) is therefore sometimes hung in addition to the stack of mattresses.

The items are stacked on a platform (*maṭwa*) according to size and use, with the least-used and bulkiest items on the bottom. The hand-woven rugs (*basuṭ*) are kept on the bottom as they are laid out only on very special occasions such as a marriage or the visit of a highly honored guest. I was told that in the past rugs were hung out like flags or banners when the King visited.

Next the large mattresses (*farāsh*) of either cotton or wool are stacked. Mattresses are a standard one by two meters large but vary in thickness. A large mattress contains from six to ten *raṭal* of wool, or twenty to thirty kilos, and costs about JD 30 ($90).[37] Thinner mattresses (*janbiyya*) are stored on top of the *farāsh*. These vary in size from about three to seven centimeters in thickness, are commonly made out of foam rubber, and cost between JD 1.500 ($3) and JD 5 ($15), depending on thickness.

Pillows are stored on top of the *janbiyya*. *Mukhadda* or *wasāda* are oblong pillows, a standard one meter in length, that is, the width of a mattress.[38] They contain about one *raṭal* of wool or cotton and cost about JD 8.200 ($25) complete with decorative covers. The plain white cotton cover is sheathed in brightly colored *satan* for about ten centimeters on each end, and the middle section is encased in a slip-on cover called a *wajah*. Although *wajah* were typically white cotton with pastel-colored machine embroidery, *wajah* of synthetic fabric printed with colored portraits of famous singers or romantic scenes were also available in the markets. *Mukhadda* are used, usually in twos or threes, as props for formal reclining on mattresses. In houses, they are also placed behind one's back when sitting on a mattress and leaning against a wall. *Mukhadda* are also used as pillows for sleeping, either placed on top of the mattress, or underneath the mattress to elevate the head. Smaller pillows (*girna*) are about forty centimeters square. They are used for sitting and can be placed directly upon the ground.

Next on the stack come the quilts, blankets, and ground covers. Heavy cotton quilts (*laḥāf*, pl. *luḥuf*) contain an average of five to six *raṭal* of cotton at JD 1.750 per *raṭal*. These are covered on one side with brightly colored *satan* and then usually covered again with a removable, washable cotton cover. *Luḥuf* are made to order in a specialized shop and sold without covers for about JD 8 ($24). Covers are made at home or can be bought ready-made. Both cotton and synthetic blankets (*ḥaram*, pl. *ḥaramāt*) were available in the markets in 1981. The older cotton blankets were being superseded in popularity by synthetic ones imported from Spain. *Mafrash*, two-ply quilts made from squares of old fabric, could be used either as ground cloths or as lightweight covers for naps. Finally, on the top of the stack, the ground cloths (*ṣafīḥ*) made from sacking are kept when not in use. *Ṣafīḥ* are laid out under most other kinds of mattresses in a *bayt*.

The process of laying out mattresses is a domestic ritual and, as such, is a source of moral vitality. Mattresses are not left out in expectation of a guest but are put away after sleeping and after the departure of guests, only to be brought out again upon the arrival of new guests. Every time a new person arrives, all present rise to greet and be greeted by the new arrival. The seating arrangement is then renegotiated. If needed, more mattresses are brought and arranged. In any event, all present rearrange themselves taking into account the new individual/s. When a person leaves, this process is recommenced. All rise to bid farewell, and all those remaining once again position themselves vis-à-vis one another before taking seats again. In the course of a typical evening visit, this process may occur five or six times.

Mattresses belong to women, and carrying them is women's work. Full mattresses weigh twenty to thirty kilos and are very bulky. Although unmarried women do not generally own mattresses, they are usually the ones to whom the task of carrying and placing mattresses falls. Thus young women are allowed a degree of choice in defining the situation by their choice of a mattress and its placement.

The offering (and accepting) of a seat is part of an ongoing negotiation of social status and an indicator of the nature of specific social relationships. The process of offering a seat can be divided analytically into three steps: the choice of the seat to be offered, the placement of the seat, and the placement of people on the seating arrangement provided.

There are a number of considerations that influence the choice of a seat (degree of intimacy, purpose of visit, projected length of visit, etc.). (Some of the considerations that influence the choice of Western versus ʿ*arab* furnishings have been discussed above.) Family members, neighbors, or close friends who stop for a short informal visit may simply squat or sit on a stool or nearby crate. Women working at home often lay out a *janbiyya* for themselves, or simply sit on a *girna* or *mafrash*. *Farāsh* are used for prolonged or formal visits. Status is indicated by the thickness of the mattress (the farther from the ground, the higher the status), the quality of the cloth cover, and the number of pillows. The symbolic value of thick mattresses is also manifest by the practice of sheikhs sleeping on two or three of the largest-size mattresses piled on top of one another. Similarly, when dignitaries visited from Amman, two thick mattresses were placed on top of one another all around the sides of the receiving room (whether in a tent or house). This conspicuous display showed both the means of the host and the esteem in which the host held the guest. In addition, at this height the honored guests, who usually wore Western-style clothing, could sit on a mattress as in a chair, that is, with their legs in front and without having to remove their shoes.[39] The converse of the height/high-status principle is seen at times of death. On these occasions one of the ways that the immediate family expresses their wretchedness and sense of loss is by sitting directly on the ground.

The space that will be used for seating depends on the time of day, the people involved—their sex, age, degree of kinship or familiarity—the length and purpose of the visit, and status. For example, the space behind the *rabʿa* is a favorite place for women, especially young women, to visit because it is usually cooler than the *rabʿa* where the stove is in nearly continuous use for cooking or heating water for washing or bathing. Formal visits, on the other hand, always take place in the *shigg* or the equivalent part of a house. Within a *shigg* (or equivalent) different locations have different statuses. The status hierarchy of locations in 'Abbādi meeting rooms is quite similar to that described by Susan Wright for men's meetings in the homes of the Mamasani, an Iranian tribal group (1981:142), C. Eickelman (1984) for women's visiting in sheikhly homes in inner Oman,[40] and by Whitney G. Azoy for a khan's guest house in Afghanistan (1982:38–42):

> In the subtle, but universally acknowledged, language of proxemics, the relative status of each individual is reflected in where he sits. . . . Highest status individuals sit . . . "high" along the narrow end of the rectangle farther from the door. The highest status individual of them all occupies the center spot. The long sides of the rectangular room are lined with men of progressively lower status with the very lowest at the end nearer the door. . . . Thus the newcomer can tell with one look who is who in relative status. . . . Like all those who have arrived before him, he too must now find—and be found—his proper place. (Azoy 1982:39)

But unlike the Iranian, Omani, and Afghan cases in which these practices pertain to single-sex gatherings, the 'Abbādis frequently meet together in mixed company. Most evenings, married couples either go to the home of a relative for a visit or receive visitors in their home. Unless there is such a large crowd that everyone will not fit in a single room[41] and if all present are known to one another (usually related through blood or marriage), men and women will sit in the same room and visit together.

New arrivals begin at the doorway and work their way around the room shaking hands and greeting each person.[42] Respect is shown by rising to greet the newcomer/s. Thus the greeting ritual provides a moment in which the relative status of all present is asserted and/or challenged. Although everyone usually at least makes the move to rise, sometimes the seated person may delay his/her movement slightly. At this point the newcomer can either wait, but in so doing risk public embarrassment, or go ahead and shake the person's hand. Similarly, a newcomer might quicken his/her movement and greet someone before that person had come to a full stand, thus displaying respect for the seated person. However, because families tend to arrive in a group consisting of individuals of differing statuses (i.e., men and women, adults and children), and because most ʿAbbādi families consider themselves to be more or less social equals, in the ʿAbbādi homes I visited the whole roomful would usually rise and stay standing until the greetings had been completed.

When the newcomers had greeted everyone, someone would invite them as individuals or as a group to sit near him/her. Others might call out "No, sit here near me" or protest that the first offered seat was not well enough positioned. The newcomer/s had to select a seat from those offered—ideally one that was neither presumptuously above his/her status nor demeaningly lower. Throughout this process—entering the house, making the round of greetings, and then finally moving to accept a seat—people generally move slowly and deliberately, but with ease.

The final dimension of seating is the position of actors on the mattresses. The ideal is to have a full mattress to oneself on which to recline (*kawi*) on one's side with one's shoulders elevated by a *mukhada* or two. Women are accorded this honor much less frequently than men and participate in their definition of themselves as unmattress worthy.[43] Women often loan their mattresses to relatives or neighbors for weddings and help set up the separate tents in which male and female guests will be entertained. In the men's tent/s they lay mattresses out around the perimeter of the tent and place several *mukhada* at the end of each mattress so that during the celebration men will be able to recline comfortably. Even if there are plenty of mattresses available, women do not lay out mattresses in the women's tent because, they say, "We do not know how to sit on mattresses." When I questioned this, they explained that they have children who are dirty and would spill on the mattresses. Yet although women do not usually take the trouble to lay out a mattress for themselves at home, they do offer this courtesy to a female guest even if (as is almost always the case) she is accompanied by children.

As we have seen, the process of laying out mattresses remains a domestic ritual in the many and varied structures the 'Abbādis now make their homes. With the aid of these portable, multifunctional furnishings, the 'Abbādis create, at one and the same time, space and social identity.

POSTURE AND THE COMAKING OF COLLECTIVE IDENTITIES

I have argued elsewhere (1985) that the household practices described above by which 'Abbādis continue to position and reposition themselves in relation to one another and the material world are one of the reasons that the 'Abbādis have not gotten "lost" in the midst of the rapid change going on about them.[44] These household practices are also important because they are illustrative of collective identity-making in Jordan more broadly. As we have seen, homes, like tribal territory, are constituted through movement, and in chapter 8 I will argue that this approach to space is also evident in the cultural construction of the nation as well. Homes (and I will argue the Jordanian nation) are not only culturally constructed on an ongoing basis by the active, embodied movement of those who occupy them—to sleep someplace is to make a home of that place—they are also in some sense indistinguishable from that movement. Homes (and the homeland) are both the space/structure and the people who inhabit the home, and neither the home nor the individuals who make up a home are essentially constituted a priori. The identity/meaning of a *bayt* (in both senses of the term: the physical structure and the family who inhabits it) is constructed on an ongoing basis through the everyday practices of making a "place" in the world— that is, adopting a posture in the context of changing circumstances and uncertain contingencies. In the following chapter we shall explore the consequence of some of these changing circumstances.

NOTES

1. They have not been given special consideration in the civil or electoral laws. Another point of difference stems from differences in the physical attrib-

utes of the territories in question. As discussed above, the Valley is one of Jordan's lushest regions.

2. The descriptions of the organization and use of space among the ʿAbbādis that appear in this and the following chapter originally appeared in "Village-Bedouin: Patterns of Change from Mobility to Sedentism in Jordan," in *Method and Theory for Activity Area Research—An Ethnoarchaeological Approach*, ed. Susan Kent (New York: Columbia University Press, 1987), 345–73.

3. Marriage restrictions are one of the most important ways that the *aṣl* of a tribal group is expressed and maintained. For example, the ʿAbbād and the Mashālkhah tribes of the Jordan Valley do not intermarry. Both groups assert this principle by saying "We neither give nor take women from them." In this, according to Patai, they differ from Arab villagers who usually only restrict the marriages of their women to lower-status men (Patai 1971:258–59).

4. Similarly, Rosen (1984:23–25) has observed, *aṣl* can also mean "strength of character," "authentic," "proper," "indigenous." According to Rosen (1984:23–27), *aṣl* is not simply a genealogical pedigree, but also an attribute of personal identity based on the idea that individuals draw much of their character from their physical and social environment. Rosen argues that to possess *aṣl* implies a kind of predictability about the sort of behavior one can reasonably expect from such a person: "To say of another *ʿandu asel* (he has *asel*) means that he is so well rooted in the sources that have nurtured him that he will probably act in recognizably acceptable ways" (Rosen 1984:27).

5. These values include piety, hospitality, generosity, courage, the protection of honor, and self-control. Oweidi mentions treachery (*ghadr*), not protecting one's honor (*ʿird*), and weakness (*duʿafaʿ*) as evidenced by not raiding other groups as examples of despicable behavior condemned by tribal customary law (1982:128).

6. See Stewart (1987) for a review of the literature on tribal law in the Arab world.

7. When women are discussed in customary law it is usually in terms of what appropriate action men should take in response to women's improper behavior rather than guidelines for women's proper behavior.

8. *Ḥurmat al-bayt* applied to any crime that was committed in someone else's home. In addition to the punishment for the crime itself, the fact that such an act breached the code for acceptable behavior in a person's home would also be subject to punishment (Oweidi 1982:89). The area covered by *ḥurmat al-bayt* varies among different tribes, although all include the area inside of the tent and that around it extending to the end of the guy ropes (Oweidi 1982:92). Lancaster (1981:62) explains that Rwala smugglers knew they were safe when they reached camp because "the camp was 'home' and therefore sacrosanct. If there was any suspicion that an overzealous customs officer was going to ignore this convention, the loaded trucks were driven straight into the *muharram* where they became, literally, untouchable." He reports that once when a customs officer disregarded this principle he was immediately posted elsewhere. (See also Lancaster 1981:60, 61.)

9. Given my southern Californian upbringing, learning to walk with an acceptable level of restraint was one of the hardest things for me.

See Caton (1990) and Abu-Lughod (1986) on the tribal values of self-control or self-mastery and the channeling of emotions into the conventions of poetry.

10. See Wahlin (1992; 1991b; 1988b:6–7) for a discussion of village settlement in the Jordan Valley and al-ʿArda and for material on ʿAbbādi land ownership and use in al-ʿArda.

11. For a comparison of these vernacular designs with the government housing project units see Layne (1984b).

12. See Khammash (1986) for a description of Jordanian village vernacular styles and plans.

13. Musil (1928:61–64) describes similar techniques of tent construction among the Rwala early in the century. See Weir (1976) on weaving and tent construction by contempoary Jordanian Bedouin.

14. In chapter 6 I describe other more directly confrontational manifestations of the changing social position of sheikhs. See Lancaster (1981:130–31) on the changing role of the sheikhs among the Rwala Bedouin of Jordan.

15. See Musil (1928:72) on tent nomenclature among the Rwala.

16. Khammash (1986) illustrates a built-in mud brick *maṭwa* in a village home.

17. Although in many ways the presence of a corridor between rooms is a radical innovation on goat-hair tent design, in its long and narrow shape, the flexibility of circulation through four doors, and the creation of a breezy indoor climate, the corridor resembles a tent.

18. C. Eickelman (1984:58–67) provides the floor plans for one sheikhly and nonsheikhly house in Oman. In the nonsheikhly house the women of the house spend most of their time in "a long, well-ventilated room" which much resembles the ʿAbbādis' corridor. One must pass through this room to enter the small rooms that are used for sleeping and the storing of personal possessions. In the sheikhly house women receive guests in part of the wide corridor that circles the open courtyard on the second floor. This room provides a pleasant climate (cool, shaded with a sense of openness) and permits women to see the ground floor, courtyard, and the main street in front of the house.

19. Oweidi, writing in 1982, reported that the tent of the spiritual leader of the Bani Sakhr tribe, Ibn Izhayr, is so "revered" (*muḥābāh*) that sometimes in complicated or serious Bedouin judicial cases his tent is borrowed for the conciliation meeting: "It is believed that in the case of parties to a dispute who refuse the intervention of the tent for concilation [sic], or give it no 'reverence,' they would be cursed by God, and the spirits of their 'holy ancestors' would be evoked against them by their living descendants" (Oweidi 1982:138). Usually it is the offender's kin who must bring such a tent, thus bringing honor to the victim's kin and giving them an excuse to accept the *diya* and allow conciliation to take place. Likewise, the tents of spiritual leaders give good fortune when borrowed for weddings (Oweidi 1982:138).

20. I did not get to know the ʿAbbādi sheikhs well, and so in this section I must rely on my knowledge of a Mashālkhah sheikh.

21. A similar usage is reported by Centlivres-Demont (1982) in the house of a local notable in a village in northern Afghanistan.

22. C. Eickelman (1984:222) describes a similar example of new housing designs and locations being used to loosen "patron-client ties between shaykhly households and persons from client tribal groups" in Oman.

23. In a similar vein, after completing an archaeological survey of the Jordan Valley in the 1940s, Glueck concluded that "in ancient times a large part of the sedentary population of the Jordan Valley must also have resided in tents, but they were attached to permanent sedentary settlements in built-up villages and towns" (1951:312).

24. "The word 'aleatory' is derived from the Latin word for a die; . . . what is aleatory depends upon the 'throw of a die,' upon 'uncertain contingencies'" (*Oxford English Dictionary*, quoted in Schumacher 1989:5).

25. There are several reasons that they might have joined her—to keep her company, to chaperon her in her husband's absence, to get a break from their own families, or some combination of all three.

26. Lancaster observed a similar phenomenon with the Rwala. He describes an encampment of the Rwala in eastern Jordan saying, "Ar-Risha in 1972–3 . . . is a fairly permanent encampment in that it has buildings as well as tents but this should not be taken to mean that it has a permanent population. Of the 500 or so family units at Ar-Risha in 1972 only about 8 remained in 1979; the other 200 were newcomers" (1981:10).

27. Data on the sedentarization projects in southern Jordan studied by Bocco indicate a high level of domestic mobility there as well. According to Bocco (1984), in the first fifteen years since the housing projects were built in al-Jafr, twenty-six of the forty-two units had changed owners and only about one-third of the inhabitants were original owners (1984:7). The Jordan Valley housing projects were still too new in 1981–83 to judge whether there would be a comparably high rate of resale.

28. Statistics show that there were only 13 houses in Muʿaddi before 1951. In 1978, there were 202 houses and 1 villa in Muʿaddi, of which only 198 were inhabited (Jordan 1978).

For a detailed description and evaluation of the housing project in the village of Muʿaddi see Layne (1984b).

29. The ratio of locals to nonlocals varies a great deal in different areas of the Valley. In the projects south of Muʿaddi, that is, closer to the capital, Amman, some of the projects are owned almost exclusively by Amman residents, whereas in projects to the north, some projects are almost completely locally owned.

30. Several units were owned by unmarried tribesmen who, in accordance with social conventions, continued to live with their families. (There had been several other cases, however, where despite the disapproval of others, unmarried *iskān*-owning males have lived in their units.) Three other units were owned by young men who had gone to fight for Iraq in the Iraq/Iran war with the voluntary Jordanian Yarmouk Force; one was owned by a man who was working as a mechanic in Saudi Arabia; and two were owned by tribesmen who were performing their compulsory military service. Eight of the units were used regularly on the weekends by nonlocals.

31. These engineers were working for the Jordan Valley Farmers' Associa-

tion. The association had twenty engineers in its employ, but only five units were reserved for the association in the Muthallath al-'Arda employees' project; so the remainder were responsible for finding housing on their own.

32. An interesting twist on this occurred during the 1989 parliamentary elections when three candidates from tribes considered Bedouin under the electoral law tried to run for seats in the governates where they resided rather than for the specially designated "Bedouin" seats (Bocco 1989b:280). The minister of the interior refused their candidacy.

33. Gilsenan has noted, in the quite different social setting of a village in northern Lebanon, that "'seeing' is a socially determined act and not a question merely of images on the retina and physiological process. Just as an insult can be negated or avoided if one can affect not to 'see' it and if anyone else present at the time is also willing to go along, so potentially problematic situations can be neutralized by not 'seeing'" (1982:171).

34. An interesting comparison might be made with Strathern's (1972) and Weiner's (1976) accounts of the relationship between women's wealth and men's prestige in Papua New Guinea.

35. Girls own and wear gold jewelry before marriage but do not normally own furniture.

36. These two rooms resemble the contrast described by Gilsenan beween the "majlis" and "salon" in homes in a northern Lebanese village. The salon is "a 'cold' space: neutral, empty . . . a consumption object that is no more than the sum of its parts, an agglomeration of expensive, shining surfaces. You do not sleep, play, joke, sprawl, meet, eat, or pray there" (1982:185). Whereas the majlis is "characterized by the wide range of transformations that can occur within it. It is usually a space of extreme simplicty of appearance: cushions, mats, or low divans are placed all around the walls facing inward. There may be a place for making coffee in one corner . . . The setting is austere. Everything within this uncluttered space is functional and draws no attention to itself. It can be made to serve many purposes" (1982:182). But rather than these two types of spaces coexisting in the same home as they did in so many Jordan Valley homes, in the case Gilsenan describes, the "salon" had nearly completely replaced the "majlis" in village homes in northern Lebanon.

37. The following prices are for 1981. Each *raṭal* is equivalent to a little over three kilos. In 1981 a *raṭal* of wool cost about JD 2 in the Jordan Valley. The price varied depending upon whether the wool had been cleaned before weighing or not. Taking into account the additional cost of fabric, large wool mat tresses cost an average of JD 30 apiece for raw materials, and labor was usually done by family members free of charge.

38. These dimensions appear to be standard, for Musil reports the use of pillows one meter long and thirty centimeters broad by the Rwala in the early part of this century (Musil 1928:64).

39. In houses, shoes were normally removed and left at the front door. In tents, shoes were typically removed immediately prior to sitting on a mattress and placed behind one.

40. C. Eickelman attributes the preference for seating persons of high status

(be they family members or visitors) along the wall opposite the entrance to the visiting area to the fact that it is near the windows that overlook the street and therefore gives these individuals more control over the social situation in that they have advance notice of who is about to visit (1984:65–66). In Jordan this same location would be reserved for the highest-status individuals simply because it is the farthest removed from the entrance.

41. At large gatherings such as weddings or funerals, men and women gather in separate spaces.

42. See Caton (1986) on the importance of ritual greetings.

43. The issue of "how many to a mattress?" may be another context (like the choice of residence location) in which the dual values of autonomy and sociality are negotiated. The fact that women tend to share mattresses much more frequently is certainly suggestive in this context.

44. Of course, there is no a priori connection between flexibility with regard to domestic structures and flexibility and adaptability in the face of social change. One can imagine people who are flexible in one of these domains and not in the other. But the crux of my argument is that in Jordan there is such a connection. Nevertheless, other factors such as the economic opportunities that accompanied the development of the Jordan Valley and the relatively secure and privileged political position of ʿarab tribespeople in the Kingdom have certainly also been critical in this regard.

CHAPTER 4

Capitalism and the Politics of
Domestic Space

THE PRECEDING DESCRIPTION of the way that ʿAbbādis move with and within their homes introduced an important area in which nondiscursive knowledge orients ʿAbbādi identity-making practices. Although agreeing with Bourdieu on the importance of the experience of living in a home (and of observing adults' behavior therein) for inculcating in the body "transposable schemes of perception, thought and action," the case of the ʿAbbādi ʿarabs challenges Bourdieu's assumptions about the special conservatism of such nondiscursive knowledge. Bourdieu asserts that

> principles em-bodied in this way are placed beyond the grasp of consciousness, and hence cannot be touched by voluntary deliberate transformation, cannot even be made explicit. (1977:94)

Sherry B. Ortner concurs that "it is precisely in those areas of life—especially in the so-called domestic domain—where action proceeds with little reflection, that much of the conservatism of a system tends to be located" (1984:150).

Both Bourdieu and Ortner arrive at these conclusions because they presume insularity—of simple societies[1] in the case of Bourdieu and of the home in Ortner's case. According to Bourdieu, in simple social formations there is "a quasi-perfect fit between the objective structures and the internalized structures which results from the logic of simple reproduction" (1977:166). "The play of mythico-ritual homologies constitutes a perfectly closed world, each aspect of which is, as it were, a reflection of all the others, a world which has no place for *opinion*" (1977:167) [or, I might add, of dialogics]. Only in cases of culture contact or by the political and economic crises associated with class division does Bourdieu posit structural transformations or the questioning of "the universe of possible discourse" (1977:169).

In a similar fashion, Ortner presumes that domestic life is insulated from the rest of the social system. Because so "much of systemic reproduction takes place via the routinized activities and intimate interactions of domestic life. . . . To the degree that domestic life is insulated from the wider social sphere, . . . important practices—of gender relations and child socialization—remain relatively untouched" (Ortner 1984:156–57). For this reason, she concludes that "the capacity of practice to revise structure must thus in all probability encompass a long-term, two- or three-generation developmental framework" (1984:156).

Neither of these presumptions stands up to scrutiny, at least for the societies on which they base their analysis.[2] Nor do they apply to contemporary Jordan. Jordanian tribespeople in the 1980s were neither insulated from other societies nor was their "private" life untouched by wider social forces.[3] In this chapter, through a detailed case study of the domestic practices of a single ʿAbbādi household in both their concrete house and goat-hair tent, we will explore further the contemporary context in which the ʿAbbādis make themselves in the process of making their homes.

A CASE STUDY: THE AL-ṬĀLIB HOUSEHOLD

In 1981 while doing research at the Deir ʿAlla Secondary School for Girls I was introduced to Fātima al-Ṭālib, the best student in the senior class that year. She invited me to visit her at her home, and I soon developed a friendship with her family. I became a regular visitor in the al-Ṭālib home in Muʿaddi and was their guest in al-ʿArda for the three-month summer holiday in 1982. The household consisted of Mr. and Mrs. Muḥammad al-Ṭālib,[4] three unmarried sons, and four unmarried daughters—Āmina, Sulaymān, Fātima, Kulthūm, Ghīdāʿ, Khālid, and Ṣalāḥ. The al-Ṭālibs' three oldest children were married and no longer lived at home.[5]

Mr. al-Ṭālib farmed, operated a small business, and raised a number of goats. He owned about twenty-eight dunums of land in an adjacent village which he was renting to another farmer. Instead of farming his own land, he preferred to farm a smaller parcel closer to his home. In 1981–82 he sharecropped eight dunums in Muʿaddi, which belonged to one of his brothers. His unmarried sons and daughters helped with the farming in their free time after school.[6] He also owned twelve dunums in al-ʿArda, which he had planted with olive trees in the late 1970s. The trees, still too young to bear fruit, required only a couple of days' care in the summer. The family also kept a small number of goats, which they sent to graze every day with a village shepherd for a monthly fee, and owned a half share in a small grocery in Muʿaddi which Mr. al-Ṭālib and his son Khālid took turns running.

Sulaymān, the eldest unmarried son, commuted to Amman where he worked as an accountant for the government. Āmina, the eldest unmarried daughter, had never finished her schooling but had dropped out of elementary school to help her mother with the housework. She did most of the daily household chores (baking bread, cooking, cleaning, and laundering). Mrs. al-Ṭālib was in charge of the care of the goats and all dairy processing, as well as more seasonal tasks such as making and maintaining mattresses, spinning, tent repair, and cleaning wheat. The three youngest daughters and two youngest sons were students at the local junior and senior high schools.

THE AL-ṬĀLIB GOAT-HAIR TENT IN AL-ʿARDA

In 1982 as soon as school was out the al-Ṭālib family prepared to move some thirty kilometers east to the hills of al-ʿArda where they set up a tent on their land for the summer holidays. Mr. al-Ṭālib and Khālid would commute to the Valley to look after the shop, and Khālid had enrolled in a summer course at the Vocational Training Center in the Valley. Because of my presence, Sulaymān, the oldest unmarried son, lived that summer at his cousin's house up the road from the al-Ṭālib tent and commuted from there to his civil service job in Amman. For the unmarried al-Ṭālib girls and myself, it was summer vacation. We spent the mornings doing household tasks and the afternoons napping, listening to soap operas on the radio, and visiting friends and relatives in the area. This routine was punctuated with occasional shopping trips to Salt or the Baqʿa refugee camp.

On the day of the move to al-ʿArda I arrived at their house at 6 a.m. Ghīdāʿ, Kulthūm, Sulaymān, Khālid, and Ṣalāḥ had gone up the day before and spent the night at their grandmother's (actually the youngest and only living wife of their father's father). I found Āmina, Fāṭima, and Mr. and Mrs. al-Ṭālib preparing the household belongings for the move. Fāṭima and I went on ahead with a load in my car while Āmina and her parents waited for the truck they had hired to arrive. We unloaded the car at the tent site and then went to her grandmother's house for breakfast. When we saw the truck go by, we returned to the site to help unload. The tent that Mrs. al-Ṭālib had woven in the early years of their marriage had been left in storage at a relative's house in al-ʿArda. Sulaymān had retrieved it and brought it to the site the night before. Because Mr. and Mrs. al-Ṭālib were fasting, it being the month of Ramaḍān, the sons and daughters put up the tent with their father shouting out instructions and encouragement.[7] I was surprised that the children didn't seem to know what to do, but they explained that they had stayed in the Valley the previous three summers and were too young to remember how the tent had been erected before that. They positioned the tent, like others in the neighborhood, on a north-south axis with the front facing the road. They placed the tent behind two olive trees, which effectively blocked the view into the tent from the road.[8] After getting the tent erected, they attached the rear wall (*sawak*) to the roof with wooden spikes. Although the basic structure was now in place, it did not remain static. Throughout the summer, at various times of the day, depending on the temperature, position of the sun, and direction of the breeze, the *sawak* would be rolled up and/or the poles of the tent rearranged to adjust the tent to the changing conditions.

The al-Ṭālibs' tent was a *gatbeh*, a one-center-pole tent, and as soon as the tent was up mattresses were laid in the section to the left of the center pole, thereby creating a *shigg*. Tea was made, and soon a second truck arrived with those mattresses that they kept in al-ʿArda. The driver had a cup of tea while the truck was unloaded. Ghīdā and Fāṭima were sent to a neighbor's house to get well water while Āmina organized the *rabʿa*. She set up the two-burner gas stove on a crate in the back exterior corner of the *rabʿa* and arranged the foodstuffs and dishes on a low table along the northern edge of the structure. Khālid and Fāṭima set up the *maṭwa* for the mattresses in the center of the tent. It was not as wide as the tent, so they extended it with vegetable crates and reenforced it with rocks until it was three meters—long enough to stack three mattresses folded in half, side by side. They put a twin bed alongside the *maṭwa* and another at right angles to it along the rear wall. Āmina arranged Mr. and Mrs. al-Ṭālib's clothing and that of the boys in cloth bundles and cardboard boxes under the table in the kitchen area, and Fāṭima, Ghīdā, and Kulthūm organized their personal belongings under the *maṭwa*. This work was frequently interrupted throughout the afternoon as families from the neighboring tents came over to say hello and have a cup of tea.

Once the family's belongings had been arranged, we all helped move the heavy water tank to a location near the *rabʿa*, and a short while later a water truck arrived to fill the tank. Most houses in al-ʿArda have rain-water wells, and tentdwellers such as the al-Ṭālibs borrow water from their neighbors' wells for drinking but use water from tanks for washing and cooking. Every day or so, the al-Ṭālib girls carried well water in plastic buckets or tin cans on their heads and stored it in a traditional ceramic jug and/or in Styrofoam thermoses in the tent.

After a few days the al-Ṭālibs built a semicircular stone fireplace (*nafīla*) in the far front corner of the *shigg* (fig. 6).[9] These fireplaces, symbolically associated with manhood, are the distinguishing feature of a *shigg* and are customarily used to prepare the delicious cardamom-flavored coffee the *ʿarabs* are known for. In the al-Ṭālib household, coffee was prepared in the *nafīla* in the morning after the goats had been

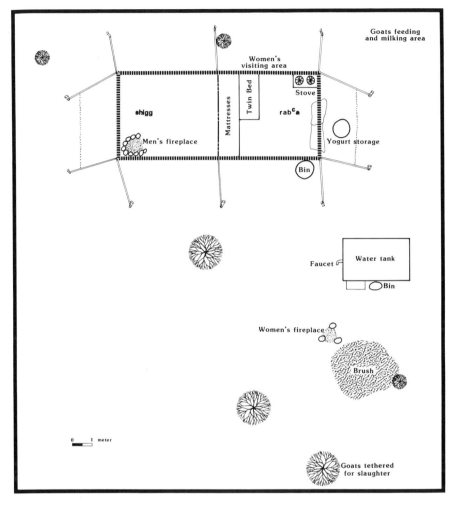

FIG. 6 The al-Ṭālib tent

tended, the bread baked, and breakfast eaten. In the past coffee was kept warm by the fire and served throughout the day to guests but the al-Ṭālib's, like many of their neighbors, now used an insulated thermos to keep the coffee warm.

Although the *shigg* and *rabᶜa* sections are thought of by the ᶜAbbādis as the men's and women's sections, in the al-Ṭālibs' tent as in other ᶜAbbādi tents, these divisions were not rigid, particularly with regard to women's use of the tent. The al-Ṭālib women used all parts of the tent.[10] Although the women had full run of the house, Mr. al-Ṭālib rarely entered the *rab'a*. The boys and their male cousins, though, sometimes came to the *rab'a* to grab a bite to eat or for a quick chat with their sisters working there.

The *rab'a* was not as comfortable as the *shigg*. Although the square footage of the *shigg* and *rab'a* were equal, there was much less open space in the *rab'a* because of the household furnishings (kitchen equipment, etc.) and personal belongings (both male and female) stored there, and it tended to be uncomfortably hot because of the stove.[11] Traditionally families bathed in the *rab'a*, but in this household people no longer felt that the tent provided enough privacy, so they either went to their grandmother's house to bathe or heated water in the *rab'a* and carried it in tanks to their new, still-uncompleted house next door (see below). The unmarried daughters did all the cooking and laundry in the *rab'a* but preferred the *shigg* or the area behind the *rab'a* for resting or activities that did not require the use of the stove. The outdoor area behind the *rab'a* was a favorite place for women, especially young women, to visit because it was protected from the view of passers-by and was usually pleasantly cool in the shade of a large oak.

In the al-Ṭālib tent the *shigg* was used by both men and women for resting, napping, and visiting during the day. Women also performed tasks such as cleaning lentils, knitting, or sewing covers for the bed quilts in the *shigg*. Household members of both sexes often ate meals in the *shigg*. People tended to eat at different times—Mr. al-Ṭālib and Sulaymān would eat when they came home from work, Mrs. al-Ṭālib usually ate by herself whenever she felt hungry, while the girls, being on summer vacation and having a live-in guest, prepared more elaborate meals for themselves which they served in the *shigg*. Despite these informal functions, the explicit function of the *shigg* was of course to receive guests. The girls would lay out mattresses for the guests in the *shigg* for any formal visit; and if there were unknown men, the women of the house either retired to the *rab'a* or if they weren't needed to prepare food and beverages for the guest/s, they might go visit their own friends elsewhere.

In addition to household chores, the al-Ṭālib women performed their prayers in the *rab'a*. The al-Ṭālibs did not have a television, but several of their neighbors did and used car batteries to power them. Although portable and moved from place to place, televisions were often watched by young people in the *rab'a*. We unmarried women slept in the *rab'a* at night. Mrs. al-Ṭālib and her young children slept in the *shigg* at night and Mr. al-Ṭālib slept in front of the *nafīla* fireplace, just outside of the *shigg*, thereby blocking the entrance to the *shigg* in which his wife and young children slept.

During the month of Ramaḍān households in the area took turns hosting the breaking of the fast. This meal was often served in front of the *shigg* and the adults would linger, visiting under the open sky with their friends and neighbors until the early hours of the morning, long after the host's young children had been put to bed in the *shigg*.

Mrs. al-Ṭālib also chose the outdoor area in front of the *shigg* to perform a number of tasks. This is where she tended her mattresses, opening them one by one over a series of days; removing and cleaning the wool (by beating, fluffing, and sunning it), and then reassembling them. She also cleaned wheat and spun goat hair into thread for tent repair in this area.

Dishes were washed at the tank and set out to dry on top of the tank and on a pile of brush nearby. The *ladaya*, a three-stone fireplace used for baking bread on a cast-iron disk, was built near the tank next to the pile of kindling. Āmina would rise earlier than the rest of the household to make the bread. Mrs. al-Ṭālib and I would rise soon thereafter to milk and feed the goats, which were tethered for the night behind the tent a short distance from the *rabʿa*. The goats that were destined for immediate slaughter were tethered under an oak in front of the tent, apart from the nursing she-goats and their kids. The rest of the children would get up at about the time when Āmina would start cooking the bread and drink tea next to her while sitting on stools. We often ate breakfast of fresh bread and yogurt or goat-milk butter there. This outdoor area next to the *rabʿa* is also the location where Mr. al-Ṭālib slaughtered lambs or kids and the girls slaughtered the much more frequently consumed chickens. On feast days men (Mr. al-Ṭālib and some of his brothers) and women (Mrs. al-Ṭālib and some of her sisters-in-law) worked together in this location to prepare *mansaf* (pl. *manāsif*), an *ʿarab* speciality consisting of lamb or goat meat served over a bed of rice with a sauce prepared from dried yogurt and clarified goat butter. While the men prepared the meat, the women set about the arduous task of making a yogurt sauce from dried yogurt.

During the summer I lived with the al-Ṭālibs, they began construction of a poured-concrete house adjacent to the tent site. Mr. al-Ṭālib and his son Sulaymān decided on the dimensions of the two rooms and corridor, and the whole family participated in clearing the site. Hired construction workers built the house, and the al-Ṭālib women prepared meals for them while the house was under construction. The following summer, the al-Ṭālibs lived in their new house and did not set up their tent. When I returned to visit in the spring of 1986 the house had been expanded and Sulaymān, who had recently married, was living there with his wife year-round.

THE AL-ṬĀLIBS' CONCRETE HOUSE IN MUʿADDI

When the summer was over, the al-Ṭālibs returned to the Valley to their three-room-and-corridor concrete house in the village of Muʿaddi. They built the first two rooms in 1965 and then added the third room, corridor, and veranda in 1977.

Since the completion of the canal, building in the Valley has been restricted to zoned areas in villages and towns so as not to infringe on the irrigable land. As a result, houses are clustered together at some distance from the fields. Because of the new distance between house and work, most people now construct a shelter on their farmland.[12]

Unlike most residential areas in the U.S. where houses back onto one another, the houses in Muʿaddi were not built back to back but only side by side, forming residential blocks one house deep. In this way the village resembled the siting of ʿAbbādi tents in al-ʿArda where tents were positioned side by side facing the roads, with the area behind the tent sheltered from view and often used for elimination. Nevertheless, houses in Muʿaddi were much more densely spaced than tents in al-ʿArda both in terms of next-door neighbors and in terms of proximity of other homes to the rear. In the village setting, property lines were also more clearly demarcated than at tent sites.

The al-Ṭālibs' concrete house in Muʿaddi is located on the eastern edge of the village on the border between the village and the government housing project. Like other houses in Muʿaddi, it is bordered at the front and back by dirt streets. On one side, they are separated from their oldest son, Omar's, house by a driveway and on the other side a vacant lot separates them from the road. Their house is situated on the lot differently than those of their neighbors. Most other houses on the block have the entrance to the corridor facing the street. Perhaps because of their location on the corner, the al-Ṭālibs oriented their house in the opposite direction.

One of the three rooms in their house was used as a *shigg* to receive male visitors. However, this was an abridged version of the *shigg*, maintaining only the male, formal functions. Here Mr. al-Ṭālib prayed, rested, visited, ate, and slept. It was bare of furnishings other than a carpet on the floor and a table in the corner on which a television and the Koran were kept, and mattresses were brought in whenever they were needed. If the weather was fine, mattresses would be laid out for guests outside on the concrete veranda or on the larger dirt veranda beyond.

A second room was used by the four unmarried daughters.[13] There they studied, entertained their guests, prayed, slept, and often ate. The

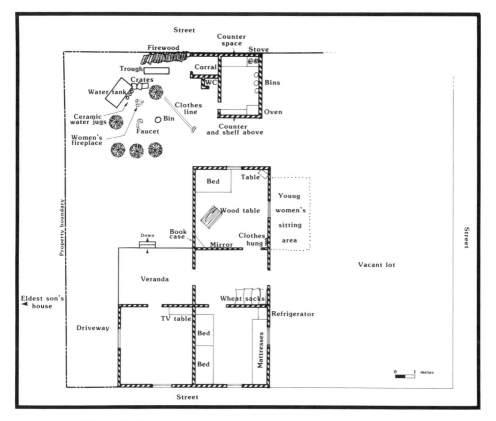

FIG. 7 The al-Ṭālib house

room was furnished with a double bed, a desk and straight-backed chair, a corner shelf used for schoolbooks, a small table, and a mirror on the wall. The room was decorated with a pictorial carpet hung over the head of the bed, a picture of King Hussein, and a Korean picture calendar. Clothes were hung on hooks behind the door. The girls brought mattresses from the room across the corridor and laid them on the floor when they had guests and to sleep on at night.

This room differed from the *rabʿa* in several important respects. For example, household tasks were not performed here, and the room contained only the personal belongings of the girls rather than those of the entire family. In addition, because of the greater distance and concrete walls separating their room from their father's meeting room, they were unable to overhear conversations taking place there.

In this house the girls frequently sat on stools outdoors behind their room to visit in the afternoon, much as they sat behind the *rabʿa* of their

tent in the summer. Although shielded from the entrance to their father's room and therefore the arrival of male guests, they were well
placed, facing the main street, to keep an eye on the goings on about
town.

The corridor in the al-Ṭālib house was little used in comparison with
other households in Muʿaddi. In this household its primary use was for
storage. Several large sacks of wheat were stacked to one side.

The room across the corridor from the girls' room combined some of
the storage functions of the *rabʿa* and the sleeping/eating functions of
the *shigg*. This is where the two younger boys slept, on twin beds that
lined one wall, and where they usually studied and ate their meals. The
family's mattresses, pillows, and blankets were stored here, too, as was
the clothing of all household members other than the girls, as well as
many other household items including sets of drinking glasses and dishes.
Here, too, was the family's refrigerator. The al-Ṭālibs, like other tribespeople in the Valley, used their refrigerator primarily for cold drinks. In
the past, the exigencies of life in this climate required that prepared foods
be consumed rapidly to avoid spoilage. There is still no concept of "lefto-
vers," and refrigerators are rarely used to preserve foodstuffs.

In the yard behind the girls' room a kitchen-bath-laundry-and-toilet
complex had been built out of cinder blocks. It contained a gas oven,
stove, and several large bags of staples such as sugar and wheat which
stood on vegetable crates in a row along one wall. Stools were brought
in and breakfast and other informal meals eaten off a tray placed on a
crate. The kitchen-bath-laundry was referred to simply as *maṭbakh*
(kitchen), even though the family also bathed and did the laundry in this
room. And although the "kitchen" was the only location in which food
was cooked (other than bread baking), it was not the only room from
which food was served: cold drinks and snacking food like pumpkin
seeds, dried garbanzo beans, and candies were served from the main
house. Because the "kitchen" was detached from the main building and
did not have electricity, it was little used after dark.

The family had constructed a windbreak in the yard using the water
tank, vegetable crates, and two large ceramic water jugs. The three-
stoned *ladaya* fireplace was located in the middle of this protected area.
They had not build a *nafila* fireplace at their concrete house, so bitter
coffee was made on the same fireplace used for bread baking. Here
Mrs. al-Ṭālib performed most of her daily tasks and received her friends
during the day. This is very similar to the use of the space in front of the
shigg in their tent. A clothesline was strung between a tree in the center
of the yard and a wooden pole. Behind this area was a trough for the
animals. The sheep and goats were kept at night in a lean-to stable made
out of corrugated iron that was attached to the rear of the *maṭbakh*. A

barrier constructed out of scraps of wood marked the border of their property.

'Abbādis do not refer to rooms in houses by tent terms, nor do they use the terms that are used by urban Jordanians such as *ghurfā al-nōm* (literally, the room of sleep) because of the continuing multifunctional use of these rooms.[14] An exception, at least in the al-Ṭālib house, is the use of the term *al-maṭbakh* (kitchen) for the detached structure used for both cooking and bathing. Otherwise they refer not to rooms but to where people are, for example, '*and al-bināt* (with the girls). They do not reify the connection between people and places in the house by making a construct phrase "the girls' room."

CAPITALISM AND THE USE OF SPACE

We have seen, using the case of the al-Ṭālib household, that the 'Abbādi use of space in both their new houses and traditional goat-hair tents is relatively multifunctional.[15] Some activities that take place in separate locations in tents are being combined in new ways in houses. For example, as we noted, at the al-Ṭālibs' house in the Valley the *ladaya* (female) fireplace is used for both bread baking and coffee preparation, activities that in their tent are performed in separate locations, on fireplaces of markedly different construction and symbolism. Some of the storage functions and food-preparation activities that took place in the *rab'a* of the tent are combined in the house with the sleeping, eating, and studying space of the small boys—activities that had most frequently taken place in the *shigg* of their tent.

Nevertheless, overall the use of space in 'Abbādi houses is more privatized, more mono-functional, and more sexually segregated than that in their tents. The informal and productive activities that they perform in the *shigg* of their tents have been removed from the equivalent space in their houses, leaving only the formal functions of the *shigg* space. The kitchen/bathroom functions have been detached and removed from the central unit of the house. Much like the process of "parlorization" that took place in nineteenth-century America, the connection between work and private life has been broken as the 'Abbādis create a special area where the family receives guests, separate from areas where other household activities take place (de Bretteville 1979).

These changes in tribal residential practices cannot be understood apart from their inclusion in the Jordanian nation-state and the subsequent transition from a subsistence-based economy to integration into the world system of capitalism.[16] Although Jordan had participated in capitalist exchanges since at least the nineteenth century, capitalism was not the dominant mode of production. Until the twentieth century, the capitalist system in which the people of Jordan participated was one of merchant capital, that is, one in which the products circulated were the surplus of individual producers' immediate needs or products specifically produced for exchange under certain conditions such as slavery, petty commodity production, and so forth. In such systems surplus labor is not appropriated through the buying and selling of labor. The emergence of circulation capital in Jordan destroyed pastoral production in the Jordan Valley and in so doing set the tribespeople's labor-time free for investment in other activities such as farming cash crops and a service economy.[17] The conversion of the productive base from one dominated by the production of goods for consumption to one dominated by the production of commodities for exchange has many far-reaching implications, including alterations in the division of labor and in the use of domestic space.[18]

As a result of these changes in the lives of the Valley tribespeople, productive tasks are no longer associated with the family unit or with the home. With the major productive activities taking place away from the home, most activities now performed at home are reproductive and consumptive. As Veronica Beechey has noted, in a capitalist mode of production domestic labor fulfills "the function of reproducing the commodity labour power, on both a generational and a day-to-day basis. Generational reproduction involves biological reproduction, the regulation of sexuality, and the socialisation of children, while day-to-day reproduction involves numerous tasks of domestic labour such as shopping, cooking meals, washing, cleaning and caring" (Beechey 1978:194).[19]

In the Jordan Valley, as throughout the Kingdom as a whole, children contribute less and less to production due to ever-increasing tenures at school. Elementary and preparatory education is compulsory and with the expansion of secondary schools in the rural areas, more and more children are continuing to high schools and beyond. Many of the new generation of ʿAbbādi men and women are wage earners who work outside the home. Educated sons and daughters are now employed as teachers in local schools and as salaried employees in the service industries that have accompanied the economic development of the Valley. Less-educated young people find work in the fields or in the armed services. Because family members now work outside the home, the number and types of activities performed in the house is much more limited.

The only members of the al-Ṭālib household whose work is still located at home are Mrs. al-Ṭālib and her daughter Āmina. Both continue to perform many of the same tasks that they would be if they were still pastoral transhumant tent dwellers. Yet even they are participating in capitalist production by raising children who will sell their labor as adults.

Many of women's traditional domestic tasks are being eliminated. More and more local girls are being trained to work as teachers, secretaries, and clerks. Mothers are not teaching their daughters to spin and weave. And although most girls know how to make Bedouin coffee and some know how to make Bedouin bread and yogurt, these and many other household products are now being produced commercially, substantially affecting the use of household storage and activity loci. Because of the smaller size of flocks today, there is less milk to be processed and fewer dairy items are being made. For example, although many middle-aged and older women continue to make yogurt and butter from their milk, few still make cheese or drained yogurt. These dairy-processing tasks have not been replaced by vegetable processing, now that the dominant means of subsistence is farming. Although most families now produce a variety of vegetables on their farms, they do not preserve any vegetables except for drying Jewish Marrow and mint.[20] The same holds true for many extractive tasks. Now people buy meat from one of several butchers in town instead of slaughtering an animal of their own for regular home consumption. Thus the time-consuming tasks of preparing the skins and cleaning and treating the stomachs to make them into liquid storage containers is done much less frequently at home.

The family also operates as a primary locus of consumption, which is essential to the circulation of commodities in the capitalist mode of production. The consumption of nonperishable mass-produced goods has resulted in a geometrical increase in material culture of the ʿAbbād. Despite diminishing household storage needs for foodstuffs, more storage space is required now than in the past because of the durable consumer items such as electrical appliances and tableware that the ʿAbbādis now own.

HOUSES AND IDENTITY: A BRIEF
U.S.-JORDANIAN COMPARISON

I have been arguing throughout this and the previous chapter that the house is a critical domain for the construction of social identity among the ʿAbbādis. This assertion probably would not strike a member of America's middle class as a novel or surprising claim, for in the United States the home also plays an important role in identity making. However, even given the recent integration of ʿAbbādis into capitalist systems of production and exchange and the concomitant changes in the ways they use their homes, the role of the home in each of these cultural settings is quite distinct.

As a number of scholars have noted, in the United States, houses are important symbols of social class and status. Paul Fussel has described houses in the United States, along with nearly ever other aspect of American material culture, as a "visible sign" of social class. He describes various aspects of the structure and design of houses including things like the length and material of the driveway, the way the street number is displayed, and the types of flowers and shrubs used to landscape the front yard, as well as home furnishings and other details of interior design as clear indicators of class (1983:76–96).[21]

Constance Perin has also analyzed the symbolic meaning of houses in the United States in terms of social status. She believes that "in American society the form of tenure—whether a household owns or rents its place of residence—is read as a primary social sign, used in categorizing and evaluating people, in much the same way that race, income, occupation, and education are" (1977:32). Perin describes how these two forms of tenure and different types of dwellings (apartments, multifamily dwellings, town houses, condominiums, and the American dream—a single-family detached house) feature in widely shared beliefs about the correct chronology of life, each stage of which should be "matched by appropriate marital status, amount of income, ages of children, school years completed, leisure tastes, tenure form, and housing type" (1977:32).

The ʿAbbādis also have widely shared ideas about the correct phases of life and how one should live at each stage, but these ideas have more to do with whom one should live than where and in what type of dwelling one should live. For example, although a number of unmarried men bought units in the government housing project in Muʿaddi, they were prevented from living in them by the shared social norm that young men should live with their natal families at least until they are married.

Neither do houses symbolize differences in social class among the ʿAbbādis. There are relatively small differences in wealth; and although houses and tents do vary somewhat in size, as described in the preceding chapter, there is an extremely high degree of regularity of floor plans, minimal differences in terms of home furnishings, and a nearly complete absence of distinguishing decorative features on the exteriors of homes. Nor do houses express the recognized social difference between ʿAbbādi tribespeople and their ex-slaves. The size, design, location, and furnishings of the houses of freed slaves are virtually indistinguishable from those of ordinary tribespeople. Although ʿAbbādis live in dwellings that they own, rent, or borrow, they do not appear to distinguish social status on the basis of tenure. There is no comparable social approbation with regard to renting, perhaps because it is so likely that tenants of one residence are owners of at least one other dwelling.

The most important difference between the role of houses in American and Jordanian identity-making, though, can be addressed at a more fundamental level. Although American dwellings act as core social symbols that represent us, express our identity, and in some sense stand for us, ʿAbbādi homes, not even their concrete homes built in the context of capitalist relations of production, do not serve such a function.[22] ʿAbbādi homes are constituted through the active, embodied movement of those who occupy them. They do not stand apart and therefore cannot *represent* the people who occupy them. The one exception to this nonrepresentational aspect of ʿAbbādi housing is that of sheikhs' houses, but in this case the house or tent represents not only the sheikh but the tribe as a whole.

In chapter 7 we will discuss the implications of the quite-novel use of household items to represent tribal culture in the Jordan Valley; but as of 1982, the dwellings themselves were not being used in a representational fashion.[23] We shall examine further issues of representation when we explore national elections as another context for identity making in the Jordan Valley in chapter 6; but first, let us turn to the ways that tribal culture, or more accurately ideas about tribal culture, have been utilized by the Jordanian government and intelligentsia in culturally constructing (and representing) the nation.

NOTES

1. D. Eickelman (1977) noted the absurdity of treating the Kabyle peasants studied by Bourdieu during the Algerian civil war as being outside the time of complex societies.

2. See Layne (1986) for a fuller discussion of the problems inherent in the assumptions that informed Bourdieu's and Ortner's beliefs about the conservatism of nondiscursive knowledge.

As D. Eickelman (1979) showed, Bourdieu's broader sociological arguments, especially as spelled out in his work on higher education in France, effaced the need for assuming that the distinction between simple and complex societies had contemporary significance.

3. An intriguing example of the decreasing insularity of the home in modern Jordan is the fact that *ḥurmat al-bayt*, the sanctity of the tent, which is protected by special laws in the Bedouin traditional legal code, was ignored by the new jurisdiction on Jordanian Tribal Laws introduced in 1973. Although for many other matters of special importance to Bedouin (such as homicide, impugning of honor including adultery, rape, abduction, and sodomy, and infringement

of guarantees of peaceable conduct by litigants during a truce) the tribal legal practices have been allowed to coexist with civil law, the sanctity of the house is no longer considered valid. This was the only crime of those considered most heinous in the eyes of the Bedouins that was ignored by this law (Oweidi 1982:33, 92).

4. Although it is anthropological tradition to use pseudonyms, with their permission, I have retained their real names. I refer to the al-Ṭālibs by the American equivalents to the terms of respect with which I addressed them in Jordan: for example, Mr. and Mrs. al-Ṭālib instead of Mother and Father of Omar.

In the following descriptions of the al-Ṭālibs' tent and house, I do not use the ethnographic present. The past tense refers to the arrangement during the period of my fieldwork. In the previous chapter I tried to give a sense of the dynamic use of space by the ʿAbbād in their many homes. Although the al-Ṭālib tent and house seemed fairly typical, I do not want to mislead the reader into thinking that the arrangements of furniture are more permanent than they really are by the use of the present tense. I use the present tense only to refer to those aspects that seem to be more constrained by cultural conventions.

5. The two eldest daughters had married men from other tribes in the ʿAbbād confederation and lived with their husbands in other villages. Omar, the eldest son, married a woman from the Ghānānim tribe. During the school year they lived with their three children next door to the al-Ṭālibs in a four-room-and-corridor concrete house.

6. According to his daughter, he made about JD 500 on his tomato crop and about JD 1,000 from the rent of his parcel in 1981.

7. See Lancaster (1981:159, 160) for a brief description of tent repair and the erecting of tents among the Rwala.

8. Simms (1988) notes a number of similarities in a Bdul campsite in southern Jordan.

9. See Musil (1928:66) on the construction of these fireplaces and (1928:100–114) on the preparation of coffee. According to Musil, the placement of the al-Ṭālib fireplace near the front of the tent was the norm for ordinary tribespeople.

10. A similar pattern of use is reported by Centlivres-Demont (1982:139) in the home of a well-to-do family in a northern Afghan village and by Peters (1978:322–23, 331) among Bedouin of Cyrenaica.

11. See Musil (1928:66–72) on the furnishings of the women's section of Rwala tents.

12. These shelters, known as ʿarīsha, are not a native kind of structure but were introduced by Egyptian farm laborers. Normally the sides are open and the roofs are made from plywood and thatched with reeds and palm fronds. The structure provides protection from the sun while packing produce and during tea breaks, and is also used for storing farm implements.

13. This is the room in which I spent most of my time. Because I did not live in this house and because of the increased privacy of the concrete structure, my information on this house is less complete than in the tent where I could observe everyone's activities.

14. In the government-built houses where the rooms do not conform to the

Bedouin principles of equal units, the rooms are referred to by their size—"the big room" (*al-ghurfa al-kabīra*) and "the little room" (*al-ghurfa al-saghīra*).

15. The concepts "multifunctional" and "monofunctional" are relative, based on a continuum. Tents are multifunctional in contrast to urban Jordanian houses, which tend to be more monofunctional in nature. For another relatively monofunctional example, see the Euro-American use of space described by Kent (1984).

16. Abu Jaber (1981) and Hiatt (1981) have discussed the impact of the establishment of the state of Jordan on the Bedouin, but neither explores the implications of their integration into the world capitalist system. Although all sedentarization implies a change in the mode of production, much of the literature on the sedentarization of hunting-and-gathering bands and pastoral nomadic tribes in this century has not adequately dealt with the implications of such a change.

17. Capitalism appears to be the dominant mode of production in the Valley both in terms of percentage of time spent laboring for wages as opposed to production for use and in terms of the percentage of material possessions that are purchased rather than locally produced.

18. Decreasing domestic mobility has been singled out by a number of archaeologists as one of the most important factors influencing changes in the use of domestic space and patterning found in the archaeological record. For example, Kent (1984) suggests that sedentism results in an increase in sex-specific and monofunctional activity areas and sex-specific and monofunctional objects. I believe that sedentism, in and of itself, has little predictive value for changes in a group's use of space and that the consequences of sedentism are conditioned by other factors such as the dominant mode of production and the particularities of the indigenous social organization and system of cultural conventions regarding the use of space.

19. As Beechey (1978) observed, the family is also "involved in the reproduction of the social relations of production which are in capitalist society both class relations and gender relations." This involves "the transmission of property/propertylessness" and "the reproduction of patriarchal ideology" (Beechey 1978:194).

20. Basson and Abuirmeilich's (1980) description of food habits and conservation in northwest Jordan is very similar to that of the ʿAbbād.

21. Although, oddly enough, given his fascinating analysis of the symbolics of Kabyle homes (1977), Bourdieu (1984) does not discuss French houses in terms of social hierarchy. He does analyze French home furnishing as markers of "class," however (1984:2, 77–79).

22. In Amman, however, the palatial architect-designed villas that were built in the 1980s certainly functioned as symbols of both the owners' wealth and their taste.

23. This contrasts with the use of homes in Greece described by Herzfeld (1991) as sites of resistance in the context of state-imposed standards of historic preservation.

CHAPTER 5

National Representations: The Tribalism Debate

IN THE PRECEEDING TWO CHAPTERS we focused on some of the fluid, dynamic identity-making practices of the ʿAbbād tribespeople and on the emergent, nonrepresentational nature of their homes. But as we noted in the introductory chapter, the meaning of tribal identity is also being constructed at the national level.[1] And much like the case explored by Virginia R. Dominguez, this public discourse is a "mechanism of collective objectification" and "the struggle between circles and sectors of the society evident in that discouse—to crystallize certain objectifications and do away with others—lies at the heart of the assumption of peoplehood" (Dominguez 1989:41).

An important context in which the meanings of tribal identity in Jordan have been dialogically constructed was the national debate on tribalism that took place in Jordan throughout the 1980s. During that period the question as to whether Jordanian society was "tribal" and if so whether or not that was a good thing was a matter of public debate in Jordan. Local and international scholars of Jordanian society actively participated in this debate, avidly proposing and evaluating various definitions of "Bedouin" and "tribe" in forums such as the international symposium, Anthropology in Jordan: State of the Art, held in Amman in 1984, and a conference on pastoral nomadism held at Yarmouk University in 1987. Of the nineteen papers on Jordan delivered at the 1984 symposium, eleven concerned Bedouin, including four of the five papers by Jordanian anthropologists. Many of the reasons offered by D. Eickelman (1981) and Abu-Lughod (1989) to account for the fact that in Middle Eastern anthropology Bedouin (by any of the various definitions we have discussed) have been vastly overstudied given their relative numerical insignificance are no doubt relevant here: namely the relative "simplicity" of such communities, anthropologists' need to address "prestige zones" in anthropological theory in order to have their work taken seriously, and the "felicitous correspondence between the views of Arab tribesmen and those of European men" (Abu-Lughod 1989:285). However, only one of the eleven papers on Bedouin addressed segmentation, the topic that Abu-Lughod identifies as "perhaps the most prestigious and enduring zone of anthropological theorizing about the Arab world" (1989:280).[2] Of much more pressing concern was the issue of how to best understand "Bedouin" (and "tribespeople," more generally) in the context not of the classic acephalous societies of segmentary lineage theory but rather in the context of a modern state.

The local news media was another important forum for the debate on "tribalism" (ʿashāʾiriyya). The Jordanian press regularly published articles in both English and Arabic debating the pros and cons of "tribalism" under headlines such as "Jordanian Bedouins Enshrine Arab Virtues," "Can We Afford These Archaic Customs?", and "Detribalisation: Towards the Rule of One Law." Those in favor of "tribalism" portrayed it as the embodiment of a valued past, whereas those against it saw it as outdated and standing in the way of progress.[3]

Whereas in the preceding chapters we have focused on the particularities of the Jordan Valley ʿarabs' sense of time/space, in both the pro and con sides of the Jordanian tribalism debate a Western-styled definition of time and history is prominent. Both positions are based on a unidirectional, segmented, abstract view of time and an associated lineal, multistaged view of progress. (cf. chapter 8).

One example of the antitribalism position is that put forward by newspaper columnist Marwan Muasher. Muasher criticized the government for support of tribal practices that "are followed not only by Bedouins but also by many urbanite, educated Jordanian families" and expressed surprise that "this way of life has survived the modern social transformation Jordan has gone through. . . . These are the eighties, not the twenties, not the fifties, not even the seventies" (Muasher, *Jordan Times*, 19 Jan. 1985). He condemned the focus on the golden age of Arab history in schools suggesting that the curriculum ought to be more forward-looking and modern achievements be given more attention: "One should never lose track of one's history, as long as one does not keep too embedded in it." He also objected to tribal affiliation as a basis for personal pride: "I wish to see people proud because they are part of a professional organization, not because they are members of a big tribe. I wish to see people proud because of their own personal achievements, not those of their cousins. And above all, I wish to see people proud because they are Jordanians, not only because of their surnames" (*Jordan Times*, 19 Jan. 1985).

Another critic, Ahmad al-Anani, bemoaned the fact that "we are unable to extricate ourselves from some outdated nomadic habits" such as the processions and ritual meals held "on occasions of marriage, settlement of blood-feuds, rituals of consolation and congratulation . . . and a long list of similar habits which were extant in Jordan since Pre-Islamic times." In his view, these are empty gestures that may have made sense in the nineteenth century but in 1983 are "harmful conventions" that result in a "vain loss of time, effort or resources" which should be used to make Jordan a better place in which to live in peace and strong enough to defend herself in case of war (al-Anani, *Jerusalem Star*, 1983). This concern with the "squandering" of national resources on "archaic tribal customs" along with the presumed political divisiveness of tribal loyalties led some to cast tribalism as "an obstacle in the path of our national security" (*Jordan Times*, 8 Jan. 1985).

Others were particularly concerned with tribalism as an obstacle to modern bureaucratic administration. Abdallah al-Khatib writes:

> Any student of the tribal concepts within our departments will realize that the unhealthy phenomena in these departments will certainly prevent any reform or modernization of this apparatus. The good organizational framework, the carefully wrought laws and regulations, the incentives, the changes in the cadres, and the various administrative procedures will be canceled by the head of this department if he is unable to get rid of the tribe and subscribe to the administrative concept. . . .
>
> . . . to bypass all the regular steps of appointment for the sake of "our brother," to apply the law to the letter to someone who has no backers in order that another backed person might jump over all kinds of laws and logic . . . will not only hinder the march of our administrative development and abort their goals, but will also ruin the march of the entire country. (*al-Rai*, 24 Jan. 1985, in Satloff 1986:67)

The most consistent criticism of "tribalism" was that it was incompatible with full participation in a modern nation-state. Here we hear echoes of modernization literature where "primordial attachments" were portrayed as being in direct conflict with civil loyalties and therefore as one of the most serious threats to "new states" (Apter and Coleman 1962; Geertz 1973a [1963]). For example, according to Geertz, "It is this crystallization of a direct conflict between primordial and civil sentiments—this 'longing not to belong to any other group'—that gives to the problem variously called tribalism, parochialism, communalism, and so on, a more ominous and deeply threatening quality than most of the other, also very serious and intractable, problems the new states face" (1973a:261).

Like the modernization theorists, Jordanian critics of tribalism assumed that loyalty to a tribe is "automatic," whereas loyalties such as those to class, party, or professional organizations are "pragmatic." For example, Kamel Abu Jaber, a well-known Jordanian political scientist who earned his Ph.D. in the United States in the 1960s, writing in 1982 states: "Surely it is recognized that belonging and loyalty to these and similar groups [such as labor unions, modern business and interest groups, chambers of commerce, teachers' associations] are on more rational bases than the earlier loyalty to family clan or tribe which used to come about automatically" (*Jordan Times*, 4 May 1982). Given this view of tribalism, it is not surprising that Jordanian critics of "tribalism" were particularly vociferous during the period surrounding the 1984 parliamentary by-elections (chapter 6). The elections raised an outcry from a segment of the Jordanian intelligentsia against what they viewed as a resurgence of "tribalism." They were concerned that candidates were running for the wrong reasons and that people would elect representatives for the wrong reasons—that is, for the strength and reputation of the candidate's family/tribe rather than for their individual merit.

For example Mohammed Naji Amairah wrote:

> We are not against extended family ties, nor are we against the family concept, we are not going to be enemies of family relations nor the ties of kinship nor marriage relations. But we are against all of this when it is used as a ladder upon which one can climb to a seat as representative or a way to a national position. As we tour through the towns, villages, and cities we see to our amazement evidence of a strange return to a time before the 1940's. Now in the eighties the times and the people are different . . . (Amairah, *al-Rai*, 9 Mar. 1984)

Another journalist interviewed a number of young voters prior to the election and reported the following complaint: "This is not democracy in the proper sense of the word. All kinds of men are running for elections, and . . . they are not presenting themselves on an individualistic level. And therefore, people would vote for a certain man for his name rather than his personal background, education and actual abilities" (*Jordan Times*, 7 Dec. 1984). Critics were dismayed because they thought that people were placing family ties before all other political allegiances and deemed "tribalism" detrimental to the proper functioning of political life in the context of a modern nation-state. For example, according to Amairah, "'Tribalism' was appropriate and good at the time of no state, it was one of the means for peaceful existence in the absence of a state. But today tribalism is a kind of illness and affliction which eats the fortunes and sustenance of the people" (Amairah, *al-Rai*, 9 Mar. 1984). He likened "tribalism" to the Jahiliyya period before Islam when people followed the precept "Support your brother whether he be aggressor or aggressed against." But, he pointed out, the Prophet Mohammad revolutionized political life when he added "Support him when he is right by supporting his cause but support him when he is wrong by preventing him from committing injustice" (*al-Rai*, 9 Mar. 1984). In his view, "tribalism" is un-Islamic because it perpetuates a blind allegiance toward blood kin regardless of their personal merit or extenuating circumstances.

Islam was also marshaled in support of tribalism. Senator Hayel Srour, the only representative to dissent in a vote in 1985 to eliminate tribal legal practices, is quoted as saying "I believe in the righteous tribal traditions, for God said in his Sacred Book, 'we created you peoples and tribes' not parties and classes." For most of those in favor of tribalism, though, tribalism simply represents a noble heritage and source of national pride.

An excellent example of a more typical pro-tribalism position is provided in a newspaper article by Musa Keilani. There he praised the Bedouin virtues of group solidarity, mutual responsibility, and an affinity for professional military life and claimed proudly [and falsely] that "Jordan is the only Arab country where a visitor gets the chance to feel the real impact of bedouin life on several aspects of a modern society" such as the "modernized version of a bedouin dress" that is worn by the Desert Patrol and by the honor guard that greets heads of state on their arrival at the Amman Airport (Keilani, *Jordan Times*, 13 Feb. 1985). Keilani also expressed his approval of the fact that many Ammanite Jordanians feel proud of their Bedouin origins and asserted his own view that the Bedouin way of life is "an ideal to be emulated" and "a noble moral code to be followed." He analogized the Bedouin virtues of "hospitality, generosity, courage, honour and self-respect" with the Five Pillars of Islam calling them "the five pillars of the bedouin ethos."

> The Arab desert exemplifies the heroic age which sublimated the motivational drives of its inhabitants into deeds of glory and pride . . . the prophet Mohammad was sent as a boy to one of the Bedouin tribes to absorb the best and noblest in the national tradition, manners, customs, and way of live [*sic*]. . . . The Bedouin leads a life which has not changed much since he domesticated the camel in the eleventh century B.C. Moving with his camel, the ship of the desert, the Arab bedouin guarded for us in the 20th century the purity of language, blood and tradition. Even [his attire:] his "thawb," long cloak "abah," "Kufiyya," and "Iqal" did not change since early descriptions of Arabs by Greek historians more than two thousand years ago. (Keilani, *Jordan Times*, 13 Feb. 1985)

Peter Gubser, an American cultural anthropologist who studied the southern Jordanian city of Karak, observed sentiments similar to those expressed by Keilani. According to Gubser, certain social patterns of the Bedouin are

> idealized among the settled people, and often claimed as the origin, or pure form, of what is practiced among the settled people. . . . The commonly held truth—or myth—is that the Bedouin behave as people should, while others' behavior is a pale copy of their practice. . . . It is quite often argued

that the Arabic language as spoken by the Bedouin is the purest and that their poetry is of the highest quality . . . when a villager or a townsman speaks of the Bedouin, he may use the term *badu* or simply say *al-arab*, implying that the Bedouin are the true Arabs, from whom all Arab qualities are derived. (Gubser 1983:26–27)

Both the critics and those in favor of "tribalism" saw tribalism as a repository of an ancient and unchanged way of life. But critics and proponents differed in both their evaluation of the merits of that way of life and in their estimation of the extent to which that way of life still exists in Jordan.[4] While those against tribalism were dismayed by the extent to which tribal customs still inform Jordanian practice, those in favor of tribalism often mourn the passing of that way of life. For example, Seri Nasser, chair of the Sociology Department at the University of Jordan, is quoted in 1982 in an article "Modernation [*sic*] Comes to Jordan's Bedouins" as saying "By and large, I think the traditional Bedouin has disappeared—unfortunately. I think the Bedouin always represented Arab traditions and values and now they are gone" (Earleen F. Tatro, *Jordan Times*, 4 Feb. 1982). This view is strongly reminiscent of the nostalgia for the pastoral documented by Raymond Williams in English literature—"A way of life that has come down to us from the days of Virgil has suddenly ended. . . . A whole culture that had preserved its continuity from earliest time had now received its quietus" (in Williams 1973:9). Just as "the tribe" in Jordanian rhetoric signifies on the one hand backwardness and on the other a noble past, that to which tribe and tribal organization is contrasted—the settled way of life, the modern, the West—is, like Williams's "city," alternatively construed as a corrupting or civilizing force.

TRIBALISM FOR TOURISTS

While the disappearance of the "true Bedouin" is mourned by Jordanians, sumulacra of the Bedouin are being produced for tourist consumption. The government of Jordan and the private-sector tourist industry have commercialized the image of Jordan's noble Bedouin as part of a campaign to attract tourists. During the 1970s and 1980s tourism was actively developed with income from this sector increasing from JD 35.7 million in 1970 to JD 160 million in 1980 and reaching JD 183 million in 1985 (Jordan 1980:136; Jordan 1986:358).[5] Between 1980 and 1984 regional economic stagnation contributed to a slowing of growth in Jordan's tourism sector, but even with the decline in tourism's contribution to the GNP (9.2 percent in 1984 down from 13.1 percent in

1980) the average growth in income from this sector was higher than the overall percentage of growth of the GNP (Jordan 1986:356): income especially important to Jordan given its balance-of-trade deficit, JD 467.3 million in 1979 (Seccombe 1981:16).[6]

Along with Jordan's "natural wonders" like the undersea life of the Red Sea and the ancient cities of Petra and Jerash, the image of the Bedouin is a central ingredient in the making of exotic Jordan. In fact in both government- and privately produced touristic materials Bedouin (usually in full regalia) appear to be the only people of Jordan.[7] For example, the twelve-page brochure *Welcome to Jordan* produced by the Jordan Tourism Authority has seventeen colored photographs. The picture of Petra spanning both front and back covers, like eleven of the other photographs, is totally devoid of people. Two of the four pictures with people in them are of tourists at the seaside resort of Aquaba (e.g., a blond man in a Speedo swimsuit riding a windsurfer). The only Jordanians pictured in the entire brochure appear on pages six and eight. In the first, two men on camels pose in front of the treasury at Petra. In the second, two policemen from the Desert Patrol are seen racing into the distance on their camels in Wadi Rum. Similarly, a packet of twelve Kodak slides available in souvenir shops entitled "Jordan" includes pictures of the Roman Theater in Amman, a "general view" of Aqaba from the sea and an underwater picture of a tropical fish, the map of Jerusalem mosaic in Madaba (reproduced in chapter 1), the court and prison of Petra, the River Jordan, the forum at Jerash, the Dead Sea, and four slides of Wadi Rum—a "general view," a picture of the rest house for tourists, a slide of unidentified "ruins," and, of course, inevitably one of the Desert Patrol with their camels. The Desert Patrol slide is the only one of the twelve that features people. In it we see one man mounted on a kneeling camel and another performing some obscure task, perhaps tightening the saddle. The slide collection "A Souvenir from Jordan" distributed to select guests by the Ministry of Tourism and Antiquities, although more extensive, replicates this pattern. Of the twenty-four slides in this collection, the vast majority are of unpeopled antiquities. Again, two show European tourists in bathing suits (the same windsurfer and a woman reading a newspaper while floating in the Dead Sea), and two slides feature members of the Desert Patrol with their elaborately decorated camels in Wadi Rum. The Bedouin theme is extended with a picture of two riderless camels silhouetted in the sunset.

In addition to these photographic images, flesh-and-blood simulacra of Bedouin play their part in the "staged authenticity" offered to tourists in Jordan.[8] In the lobby of the Intercontinental Hotel a man dressed as a Bedouin sits on cushions preparing bitter coffee, a symbol of Bedouin hospitality. At the first-class hotel that opened in Petra in 1983 "the manager (an Englishman) has contracted with the Bidul to provide a *mansif* (traditional Bedouin feast). . . . They are also paid to provide donkeys to carry wine and beer from the hotel to the site of the *mansif*. . . . Here Bedouin perform traditional dances to entertain the tourists after the [meal]. . . . The hotel has also purchased a large Bedouin tent from a Bidul who erects it and provides 'genuine' Bedouin hospitality to those guests who wish a 'real taste' of Bedouin life" (Shoup 1985:283).[9] Bedouin coffee is offered first-class passengers on Alia, the Jordanian airline by costumed [usually non-Jordanian] stewardesses. For a time, these same passengers were also presented with a pair of painted wooden Bedouin dolls packaged in a bag made from the traditional red-and-white checkered headdress. As mentioned above, camels in and of themselves serve as a metonym for Bedouin, and tourists are offered the chance to ride a camel at many of the tourist sites in Jordan—the Dead Sea, Aqaba, the Roman ruins of Jerash.[10] Such practices construct for the tourist the Oriental Jordan probably best known to them through the film *Lawrence of Arabia*.[11]

TRIBALISM AND JORDANIAN NATIONAL IDENTITY

In addition to contributing to the economy, Jordan's tribal heritage has been expropriated by the state as a symbol of Jordan's distinctive national identity. The other important areas of Jordan's officially constructed collective memory, namely, the Hashemites' role in the revolt against the Ottomans and their descent from the Prophet, highlight links between Jordan and other members of the Arab and Islamic world. Jordan's tribal heritage on the other hand, highlights the distinctiveness of Jordan vis-à-vis its most significant other, Palestine.

Regional politics in the 1980s intensified the need for Jordan to emphasize this distinction. As mentioned in chapter 1, the appointment of Ariel Sharon as Israeli minister of defense in 1981 with his "Jordan is Palestine" platform created a good deal of anxiety in Jordan. In addition to the threat of the "transfer" of a million West Bank Palestinians into Jordan, an ever more extreme worry was that Israel might actively facilitate a Palestinian takeover of Jordan (Bailey 1984:106–7; Shahak 1990).

Thus the pro-tribalism construction of Jordan as a distinctively Bedouin country is directed toward external audience/s (touristic and political). The antitribalism position, too, must be understood in terms of a tacit Western audience. The Jordanians' embarrassment with the retrogressive influence of "tribalism," like their claim to a rich cultural past, reflects a desire to adopt a collective image that is morally respectable according to presumed Western criteria.[12]

But although much of the tribalism debate was directed toward external audiences (Israel in particular; the West in general) and although in many ways the debate about tribalism had little to do with actual tribes, the fact is that many Jordanians still consider themselves to be tribespeople and they listened keenly to what was being said (see Chapter 7). Because the distinction between "tribalism" and "tribes" was not always clear, the King (and perhaps a portion of the tribal population) construed the attack on "tribalism" as an attack against this sector of the population. Furthermore, because of the close association between Jordan's tribes and the King, an attack on tribes could be construed as a veiled attack on the King. Tribespeople have constituted a particularly loyal source of support for the Hashemite rulers of Jordan, and over the years King Hussein has repeatedly expressed his identification with and commitment to protecting Jordan's tribal heritage. For example, in 1976 in an address to the Badiyah Police Headquarters, he said, "We are Arabs and we shall not neglect our worthy customs and lose our distinctive characteristics inherited from our noble ancestors . . . the traditional customs, of which we are justly proud, will continue to be observed" (quoted in Oweidi 1982:86).

A number of events that followed the March 1984 parliamentary by-elections prompted the King to speak out again. In early January 1985 the Upper House of Parliament discussed the issue of "tribalism" and voted to abolish the continuation of tribal legal practices, calling for a single allegiance to the nation governed by a single law (*Jordan Times*, 8 Jan. 1985). (Those people legally considered to be Bedouin had been governed by a set of special laws from 1929 until they were repealed in 1979.) Senator Rifa'i delivered a speech in which he called on the government to abolish tribal laws "on the ground and not only in theory."[13] He said that the "tribal laws were issued half a century ago and that these laws are no longer consistent with the current state of social development in the Kingdom." The minister of the interior, Suleiman Arar, categorically denied that the government encouraged the tribal laws and said that people often misunderstood the use of tribal conciliatory procedures and that is why they had asked the newspapers to refrain from publishing tribal conciliation deeds.

Shortly after this debate in the Senate King Hussein sent a letter to the prime minister objecting to the many attacks on "tribalism" and defending the tribal heritage of Jordan with a request that his letter be published. The minister of information, Mrs. Leila Sharaf, refused to publish it and submitted her resignation. Her resignation was accepted by the King on January 28, and his letter appeared in the local papers that same day.[14] In his letter, the King said that he had noticed that recently a number of journalists had been

> launching attacks on our social institutions and their customs and values. I have not been happy about this attack. . . . Most recently, I have noticed that some writings have been directed against the tribal life, its norms and traditions. This is most regrettable because it harms a dear sector of our society. I would like to repeat to you what I have told a meeting of tribal heads recently that "I am Al-Hussein from Hashem and Quraish the noblest Arab tribe of Mecca which was honoured by God and into which was born the Arab Prophet Mohammad." Therefore, whatever harms our tribes in Jordan is considered harmful to us, as this has been the case all along, and it will continue to be so forever. (*Jordan Times*, 28 Jan. 1985)

As Benedict Anderson (1983) has suggested, nations may best be understood as imagined communities. This chapter has explored the recent historical context in which tribes came to play a central role in the way the Jordanian nation is imagined.

NOTES

1. Earlier versions of portions of this chapter appeared in "Tribalism: National Representations of Tribal Life in Jordan," *Urban Anthropology and Studies of Cultural Systems and World Economic Development* 16, no. 2 (1987):183–203 and "The Dialogics of Tribal Self-Representation in Jordan" *American Ethnologist* 16, no. 1 (1989):24–39.

2. Lancaster (1984) used the concept of "complementary opposition" to discuss the relationship between "nomads v. settlers" in Jordan. Lancaster resembles the segmentary lineage theorists described by Abu-Lughod, who express their admiration of the Bedouin as "real men, free from the emasculating authority of the state and polite society" (Abu-Lughod 1989:286). He asserts that among the Rwala "each man is free, equal and autonomous and will not recognize the legitimacy of *any* claim to political overlordship" (Lancaster 1984:2). He also portrays himself as free "from the projects of domination in which [he] participate[d], directly or indirectly" (Abu-Lughod 1989:285–87), declaring "I . . . had no connection with any government or official body" (Lancaster 1984:5).

3. Caton (1990) and Dresch (1989) report a remarkably similar debate in Yemen. Davis (1991) and Davis and Gavrielides (1991) provide a fascinating comparison of the way tribal heritage has been handled in Iraq and Kuwait. In Iraq, the state has attempted to "eliminate the category of tribe from national political discourse" (Davis 1991:17). Whereas in Kuwait, the Sabahs have tried to channel tribal identites "in directions that it saw as serving its own interests

in promoting a paternalistic modern welfare state" (Davis and Gavrielides 1991:132).

4. See, for example, Kawar's reply, "Tribal Ties Are Still Very Strong in Jordan," (*Jordan Times*, May 1982), to a two-part article on change and development in Jordan by Abu Jaber (*Jordan Times*, 3 and 4 May 1982).

5. During the period from 1970 to 1980, this sector grew at an average annual rate of 35 percent.

6. Jordan's balance-of-payment deficit grew from JD 89.3 million in 1973 to JD 467.3 million in 1979 (Seccombe 1981:16). From 1983 to 1987 the deficit slowly but steadily decreased to JD 406 million in 1987. In order to decrease this deficit even further, the government hoped to increase the income from the tourism sector to JD 232 million by 1990 (Jordan 1986:358).

7. It is interesting that the image of the Bedouin does not appear on Jordanian currency (see chap. 8). In this domain, King Hussein appears to be the only Jordanian. It is likewise striking that the image of the King is not included among those representative images of Jordan provided in the Ministry of Tourism slide packages.

8. The term *staged authenticity* is MacCannel's, quoted in Dumont (1984).

9. Despite the profits that some Bedul are making in this way, the overwhelming effects of tourism have been deleterious, for once Petra was designated as a national park the Jordanian government ordered their relocation (Shoup 1985). See Lavie (1990) for a discussion of similar paradoxes that confront Bedouin in the Sinai.

10. There are several things one can make of the interchangeablity of Bedouin and camels. Both are part of the wonders of the natural world, and by riding a camel one symbolically dominates the animal and that for which it stands.

11. The production at the national level of the romantic Bedouin resembles the invention of the "Indian" in Mexico by the National Indigenist Institute described by Friedlander (1975, 1986). However, in contrast to what Friedlander describes as "the creation of modern Hispanic variations on long-dead indigenous themes," in Jordan practices and objects which are still part of ʿarab daily are being utilized in these ways (see chapter 7.)

12. For a comparable example, see Herzfeld's (1985) discussion of the playing out in Greece of internally conflicting stereotypes that the foreign audience has about Greeks—on the one hand the warm, romantic, undisciplined Mediterranean and on the other the Hellene, the quintessential source of European culture. See also Fernea and Fernea (1987) for an example of the down-playing of the importance of tribes in Jordan for a western audience.

13. See Oweidi (1982) for a history of these laws. According to Oweidi, despite the abolition of the Bedouin Control Law in 1976, tribal law is still powerfully, if unofficially, operative in civil courts. Although state courts do not officially take cognizance of tribal conciliatory procedures, the defendant in disputes, particularly in blood cases, often comes under direct pressure from the police to undertake tribal conciliatory measures which will usually result in the personal charges being dropped, leaving the court to deal only with the public charges. The judge, however, is empowered to exercise his own discretion in

pronouncing sentence regarding public charges, and the sentence is usually minimal if a tribal conciliation has taken place (an interview by Samir Kwar with Col. Ahmad Oweidi Abbadi in the *Jordan Times*, 21 Jan. 1982). Thus, the two systems actually reinforce each other. See also Antoun (1979:124,134).

14. According to one source, Mrs. Sharaf felt that publishing the King's letter would be contrary to the right to a free press. Another source told me that the reason she resigned was because "tribalism" was interfering with her ability to carry out the duties of her position.

CHAPTER 6

The Election of Identity

IN MARCH 1984, by-elections were held in Jordan to fill vacant seats in the lower house of Parliament.[1] These elections drew wide participation. In fact, the level of activity and discussion that the elections generated across the country in both public and private venues leading up to and following the election was striking given the small number of seats being contested (eight out of sixty). Clearly, these elections concerned more than a few seats in the legislature.[2] They became a forum for reexamining the role of tribal political structures in the context of a democratic representational system and a testing ground on which ordinary tribesmen, tribeswomen, and tribal sheikhs renegotiated and reshaped their relationships to one another and the state. Indeed, the participation of the tribespeople of the Jordan Valley in these elections provides another example of the fluid, dynamic, embodied manner by which these *'arabs* constitute their social identities and practice politics. The embodied positioning and repositioning of social/political actors in relation to one another in the context of parliamentary elections illuminates the ways that this social institution, implanted from the West, is being shaped, interpreted, and experienced in terms of indigenous cultural meanings and practices while at the same time providing a vehicle by which these very meanings and practices are being challenged and changed.[3]

TRIBAL IDENTITY AND CITIZENSHIP RECONSIDERED

In 1987 I published an interpretation of the electoral behavior of the tribespeople of the Jordan Valley in the 1984 parliamentary by-elections (Layne 1987a). In my earlier interpretation, I attempted to refute the allegations that had been made in the Jordanian press that tribespeople were somehow incapable of being good citizens and similar arguments that had been made by a number of Western social scientists about African tribespeople (Layne 1987c). I argued that, in fact, "tribesperson" and "citizen" are constructed dialogically, the meanings of each conditioning the other. I suggested, following Clifford (1988), that one of the main reasons that these two sources of identities appeared contradictory was because of the adoption of an organic definition of tribe—that is, a definition that saw "tribes" as coherent, internally closed systems. Because according to such models social development is seen as a unified evolutionary process occurring in a coordinated way like part of a growing body, any element that was not there from the inception (like elections) is considered as alien.

While critically examining the notion of tribe, I took the notion of "citizen" at face value and utilized it in a completely unexamined way. Marx (1967 [1843–44]) not only provides a critical analysis of "citizen," his comparison of Rousseau's "political man" with his own notion of "species-being" also highlights interesting parallels and divergences with the contradiction posited by authors like C. Geertz (1973a) between primordial ties (as in those of a tribe) and civil politics.[4]

In a piece entitled "Primordial Sentiments and Civil Politics in the New States" Geertz describes "the great extent to which peoples' [of the new states] sense of self remains bound up in the gross actualities of blood, race, language. . . . [they] tend to regard the immediate, concrete, . . . as the substantial content of their individuality" (1973a:258). The problem, as Geertz sees it, is that in order to become full participants in the new states, people must "subordinate these specific and familiar identifications in favor of a generalized commitment to an overarching and somewhat alien civil order . . ." (1973a:258). This task requires what Geertz refers to as an "integrative revolution."

Rousseau also posited a revolution as the means by which modern states are to be created, but one of a somewhat different order—"Whoever dares to undertake the founding of a nation must feel himself capable of changing, so to speak, human nature . . ." (quoted in Marx 1967:241). Where Geertz's primordial-ties argument imagines the "before" society as one in which individuals derive their identity from membership in "natural" *groups* based on race, ethnicity, and/or language, Rousseau imagines "each individual [as] in himself a complete but isolated whole [who must be transformed] into a part of something greater than himself" (quoted in Marx 1967:241). In order to accomplish this, Rousseau believed, "man must be deprived of his own powers and given alien powers . . ." (quoted in Marx 1967:241).

Although Marx believed that Rousseau accurately depicted the "abstraction of political man" that came about with the constitution of the political state, he disagreed with Rousseau's chronology. Marx asserts that "a reduction of man to a member of civil society, to an *egoistic independent* individual on the one hand and to a *citizen*, a moral person, on the other . . . is accomplished in *one and the same act* . . . The egoist man is the . . . *given* result of the dissolved society . . ."(1967:241, 240). In other words, according to Marx, "the political revolution" that brought about the modern state is not an "integrative revolution" but rather a disintegrative one that resulted in the creation "egoistic man, man separated from other men and from the community" (1967:240).

While for Geertz the problem is "the tension" between the "'givens' of place, tongue, blood, looks and way-of-life" and the "civil order," (1973a:277) for Marx the problem is the dichotomy itself which is the result of the fragmentation of man into sensuous man and abstract man (citizen): "Man as a member of civil society is regarded . . . as distinct from *citizen*, since he is man in his sensuous, individual, and *most intimate* existence while *political* man [citizen] is only the abstract and artificial man, man as *allegorical moral*, person. Actual man is recognized only in the form of an *egoistic* individual, *authentic* man only in the form of *abstract citizen*" (1967:240).

For Geertz the solution to the dichotomy is for new states to "domesticate" "primordial attachments" "by . . . divesting them of their legitimizing force with respect to governmental authority, . . . and by channeling discontent arising out of their dislocation into properly political rather than parapolitical forms of expression" (1973a:277).

Not surprisingly, Marx has a rather different solution: "Only when the actual, individual man has taken back into himself the abstract citizen and in his everyday life, his individual work, and his individual relationships has become a *species-being*, only when he has recognized and organized his own powers as social powers so that social force is no longer separated from him as *political* power, only then is human emancipation complete" (1967:241).

In my earlier examination of the 1984 elections, I explored the extent to which the tribespeople of the Jordan Valley experienced "primordial ties" as being in tension with their roles as citizens. In the following reexamination of those elections, a number of additional related questions seem pertinent: To what extent do the tribespeople of the Jordan Valley experience citizenship as abstract? To what extent do they experience political power as separate from themselves? Do they experience and or conceive of their sensuous selves as distinct from their political selves? If so, do they situate morality in the allegorical abstract citizen? To what extent do they recognize and organize their powers as social powers? I can provide only preliminary answers to these questions, but they do direct inquiry into the meaning of representation in representational government and call for a more critical and culturally informed approach to the possible meanings of "citizenship."

JORDAN'S PARLIAMENTARY BY-ELECTIONS, MARCH 1984

Since the promulgation of the new constitution in 1946 when Jordan gained its independence, the Kingdom has had a bicameral parliamentary system.[5] The parliament (*Majlis al-Umma*) consists of an upper house (*Majlis al-A'yān*) made up of appointed notables and a lower house (*Majlis al-Nuwwāb*) of representatives elected for four-year terms. Seats in the lower house are allotted in each administrative governorate on a sectarian basis with a certain proportion of seats reserved for Muslims, Christians, Bedouin, and Circassians or Sheeshans and filled by vote by the entire plebiscite within each governorate.

The ninth parliament, elected in April 1967, two months before the Six-Day War with Israel, consisted of sixty seats divided equally between the East and West Banks. This parliament was suspended in November 1974 after an Arab League decision taken in Rabat which declared the Palestine Liberation Organization the "sole and legitimate" representative of the Palestinian people. On January 9, 1984, after a decade of inactivity, the Jordanian parliament was reconvened in response to a royal decree, and a constitutional amendment (Article 73) was approved which allowed for the holding of by-elections to fill the seats of the fourteen legislators who had died during the intervening years.[6] The six vacant seats representing the West Bank were filled by means of an internal election within the parliament while the eight new East Bank members were selected in a general election held in four of the five East Bank governorates on March 12, 1984.

One hundred two candidates competed for the eight East Bank seats and over 50 percent of the 558,581 registered voters cast their ballots.[7] Because elections had not been held for seventeen years, this was the first opportunity that Jordanian women had to exercise the right to vote in a national election since it had been granted them in 1974.[8] It was also the first chance for people twenty to thirty-seven years of age to vote in a national election (the minimum voting age being twenty). Given the young profile of the Jordanian population, this age group represented a rather large segment of the population.[9]

Three of the eight East Bank seats were in the Balqa' Governorate (two Muslim seats and one Christian). Eighteen candidates ran for the two Muslim vacancies in Balqa', and nine candidates competed for the single Christian opening there.

In the Balqa' Governorate, an area that stretches from Amman to the Jordan River and the Dead Sea in the west (fig. 8), 29,597 men and 19,220 women (52 percent) of those who registered voted. These figures represent a heterogenous population including the 'Adwān, 'Abbād, and Mashālkhah *'arab* tribes (including their freed slaves); the Ghawarneh, dark-skinned people popularly considered to be the original inhabitants of the Valley; Palestinians, a small number of whom settled on the East Bank before the creation of Israel in 1948 and large numbers of whom became refugees in 1948 (the Palestinian refugee camp, Moukhaim al-Baq'a, accounted for approximately 15,000 registered voters in the governorate), and still others who became "displaced persons" from the West Bank following the 1967 war; and Saltis (people from the regional capital of Salt) who are themselves socially hetero-genous. Balqa also includes a large proportion of Jordan's small Christian population (an estimated 125,000 on the East Bank [Gubser 1983:19]). They are concentrated in Salt and in the town of Fuhais.

Because of the size and diversity of the governorate, no candidate could hope to win based on support garnered by tribal, ethnic, or sectarian loyalty alone. Because each voter had the right to three votes (two for Muslim candidates and one for a Christian candidate) the electoral process encouraged the forming of alliances across sectarian and tribal lines.

During the election tribesmen and women took on a different set of social roles than the ones that usually shaped their daily lives: namely those of voter and candidate. Candidates were, for the most part, tribal sheikhs, whereas the bulk of the voters were ordinary tribesmen and women. As we shall see, the interests of candidate-sheikhs and voter-tribespersons were not identical.

SHEIKHS AS CANDIDATES

Four candidates from three Jordan Valley tribes competed for the two Muslim seats in the Balqa' Governorate. Faiz Zaidan Hamdan al-Ma-salhah and Jamal Abu Bugar represented the ʿAbbād tribes, Abdl Karim al-Faour represented the Mashālkhah, and ʿAakaf Fahad al-ʿAdwān represented the ʿAdwān.[10] None of these candidates won, but Abu Bugar and al-ʿAdwān came in third and fourth, respectively, close behind the second-place winner.

In accordance with the law, each of these candidates was over thirty years of age; and although the constitution does not stipulate whether or not women may run for office, all candidates from the Valley as throughout the Kingdom were men. In addition, each of the Jordan Valley candidates was a tribal sheikh or the son of a sheikh.

In Jordan as a whole, there has been a striking degree of personal and familial continuity in the holders of high political office, even in the context of drastic changes in the political atmosphere over time (Abu Jaber 1969). In these elections, just as in all previous national elections, representatives were drawn from a small number of leading families.[11] However, in the past, tribal representatives were usually paramount sheikhs (*shaykh al-mashayoukh*: literally, sheikh of sheikhs). Paramount sheikhs were the recognized leaders and spokespersons for a tribe (*qabī-la*) or a tribal confederation. In the last few decades the structural range of tribal authority has been shrinking, and now only sheikhs of smaller tribal units are recognized. As the last generation of paramount sheikhs dies, people are refusing to grant legitimate authority to would-be replacements at the same structural level, that is, at the level of a *qabīla*. Sheikhly authority now rests instead at the unit of an *ʿashīra* (clan). For example, after the death in 1981 of Ahmad al-Naim, the paramount sheikh of the Mashālkhah, Sheikh Ahmad's eldest son, Sālah, replaced him as head of the al-Naim clan, but the other Mashālkhah clans would not recognize him as their sheikh. Each clan is now led by its own sheikh. Meanwhile, the King has taken over the role of "sheikh of sheikhs."

A number of government policies have contributed to the fragmentation of large tribal groupings. For example, the range of responsibility for crimes has gradually been reduced by the state. Although tribes still act corporately in matters of blood vengeance, they do so at a lower structural level. (See Oweidi 1982:27 for details). This process of tribal fragmentation explains, to a large extent, the difficulty the Jordan Valley tribes had in agreeing on a single candidate to represent them and was one of the reasons that none of the tribal candidates won.

The ʿAdwān tribe had difficulty in deciding who would run from their tribe in the election. When I visited the mayor's office in South Shuna the week before the election I learned that the negotiations concerning who would represent the ʿAdwān tribe were still hotly under way. Once the choice was made, the entire tribe did not lend its wholehearted support to the selected candidate. Supporters of the alternate candidate abrogated alliances they had forged for this election with neighboring tribes from the Deir ʿAlla Subdistrict when they learned that their favored candidate was not to run, thus releasing these neighboring tribes from their obligation to vote for the ʿAdwān candidate. In the end the ʿAdwān candidate won a meager twelve votes in the entire Deir ʿAlla Subdistrict.[12]

The ʿAbbādis were also unable to reach a consensus on one candidate to represent them, and ultimately two ran for office.[13] Neither had the full support of the ʿAbbād tribes. The Nuimat and Yasgin tribes supported Jamal Abu Bugar, but the Ghananim tribe refused to support him because they felt that it was their "turn" to have one of their members run for office. These votes were critical, as Abu Bugar missed winning the second seat by only 804 votes. The other ʿAbbādi candidate was hurt by the controversy surrounding his father (see below).

Despite the disagreement about which sheikh (or sheikh's son) should run, there was no mention among tribesmen and women that anyone other than men of sheikhly families should have run. Even though a number of things (such as the inability to agree on a single tribal candidate, sheikhs' inability to deliver votes to other sheikhs with

whom they made alliances, and refusal of tribesmen to replace paramount sheikhs as they pass away) point to a decline in the authority of
tribal sheikhs, they remain powerful symbols of their tribe to their tribe.
Despite the diminishing political power and authority of sheikhs over
members of their tribes and vis-à-vis the state, sheikhs still function as a
public emblem (*wajha*: literally, face) for their tribes and embody values
that the tribe holds dear and by which tribespeople identify themselves
as *ʿarābs*—such as generosity, bravery, and moral uprightness. It is not
surprising, then, that tribespeople still feel that a certain degree of deference should be accorded these figureheads. Although the social role of
sheikhs is being transformed, many of the traditional rules of etiquette
about how one ought to treat a sheikh maintain their moral force.

One episode that occurred in one of the women's polling stations illustrates clearly both the state's challenge to sheikhly authority and the
continuing power of the indigenous system of *awāʿid* concerning
proper behavior by and toward sheikhs. During the morning, the local
sheikh (not one of those running for office) had come to the station and
accused the voting committee of cheating. None of my informants offered an opinion as to the accuracy of his allegation. Of more importance to them was the power struggle that ensued. The head of the committee, that is, a representative of the state, would not suffer such an
accusation and asked the sheikh to leave the premises. The sheikh was
appalled and yelled, "*ana shaykh, ana shaykh!* (I am the sheikh here!)"
Two elements of this event shocked my informants: 1) that anyone
would attempt to evict their sheikh from his own territory; and 2) that
the sheikh felt it necessary to proclaim his status, exceedingly unsheikh-
like behavior. To have one's tribal sheikh publicly disregarded and in-
sulted on what the sheikh considered to be his own tribal territory but
which was on this occasion more convincingly defined as a state-owned
and -operated institution (a classroom in a public school/now polling
station), was unsettling and disturbing to those who looked on. Even
though, as mentioned above, a number of government policies have
worked to reduce the power of sheikhs, this type of direct confrontation
is extremely rare. As discussed in the preceeding chapter, the King has
gone out of his way to avoid such confrontations and personally treats
ʿarab awāʿid with the utmost respect.[14]

TRIBESPEOPLE AS CITIZENS

Sheikhs were not the only local participants in the elections. On March
12, after two months of nationwide preparation and anticipation, the
tribespeople of the Jordan Valley along with the rest of the country cast

their votes to select new parliamentary representatives. From the time the polls opened in the morning until they closed at 7 P.M. tribespeople lined up outside the schoolhouses and civic centers that had been designated as men's or women's polling places—a total of 100 locations in Balqa'. At the woman's polling place in Diyyat a policeman and two leaders of the community (one woman and one man) stood outside the door letting women in three at a time. Once inside voters gave their names and showed their identification cards to a member of the voting committee, who crossed them off the list of voters registered in that district.[15] Voters were then asked to approach one of the three ballot boxes that lined the far wall, consult the list of candidates posted above the boxes, then mark their choice/s on a secret ballot. However, a significant percentage of rural men and an even greater proportion of rural women of voting age (i.e., over twenty) were illiterate.[16] Illiterate voters were asked by the voting committee to state the names of the candidates they wanted; their selection was then repeated out loud by the voting officials and a completed ballot shown to the candidates' representatives. Although the rationale for this procedure was to ensure that votes were not recorded for candidates other than those designated by the voter, voting out loud enabled all present, including me, to hear whom people were choosing.

In Diyyat, a Mashālkhah village, one woman after another voted for the Mashālkhah candidate, Abdl Karim al-Faour. The repetition of his name over and over and over again swelled into a chorus. Although these women were entitled to two other votes (one for another Muslim candidate and one for a Christian candidate) most chose not to use them. Those who made additional choices varied widely in their selection. During the period I was in attendance I heard women vote for the two ʿAbbādi candidates—Fais Zaidan al-Masalhah or Jamal Abu Bugar—Kamal Abdalat, Fawzi Daoud, and Jamal al-Shaʾar. The election results indicate that Mashālkhah men also gave overwhelming support to al-Faour and, according to one source, some men with high-school diplomas pretended that they were illiterate so that they could publicly proclaim their support for the candidate of their choosing. They refused to cast a secret, written ballot, to engage in a politics that separated their selves from their vote. In so doing they maintained the embodied posture of ʿarab politics.

Although most tribespeople in the Valley chose to use one of their votes for a member of their own tribe, tribal membership does not automatically lead to mass support for members of one's agnatic group.[17] There is always the possibility that members of a tribe will feel that their interests will be better served by voting for a candidate not from their group. There are many alternative rationales that can be used to justify not voting for one's kinsmen, all of which present the individual as belonging to a morally superior community (cf. Herzfeld 1985).

An example of this can be seen with the ʿAbbādi candidate Faiz Zaidan. Faiz's father was Zaidan al-Mashālkhah, sheikh of the Mashālkhah tribe of the ʿAbbād confederation. Zaidan's reputation had been tarnished earlier that year in what was popularly referred to as the tomato scandal. Not only was he implicated in a scam to cheat the government; rather than face charges, he had fled to Syria and was reported to be openly criticizing King Hussein from there. For many ʿAbbādis this forced a choice between their loyalty for a member of their tribal confederation and loyalty to their King. The upshot is evident in the election results. Faiz Zaidan finished eleventh out of the eighteen Muslim candidates with a total of 2,827 votes. (As mentioned above, the other ʿAbbād candidate lost ʿAbbādi votes because of a lack of consensus within the confederation about who should represent the confederation in this national election.)

Nor does membership in a tribe preclude support for candidates outside the tribe. In Muʿaddi, a predominantly ʿAbbādi village, the Christian candidate, Jamal al-Shaʾar, received more support than either of the ʿAbbādi candidates. Several women explained to me that they voted for Dr. al-Shaʾar because he had delivered their babies. Their support was a matter of personal choice rather than due to a tribewide agreement.[18]

Another example comes from the village of Krayma in the Irbid Governorate. There—even though a local tribesman, Bashir Ghazawia, was competing for the one open seat in that governorate—when the results were tallied, the "Islamic" candidate had won and Ghazawia came in third.

This last example is unusual in that the winning candidate campaigned with and received support for a specific platform rather than relying on a general identification with local interests. As several critics noted, the 1984 elections were characterized by a striking absence of issues (*Jordan Times*, 13 Mar. 1984). Political parties, with the exception of the Muslim Brotherhood, had been banned since 1954 but had played an important clandestine role in other national elections.[19] The absence of party politics in 1984 signaled a nationwide disillusionment with established Arab political parties, at least among Jordanians of voting age.

As a result, most campaign statements were concerned with issues that the entire electorate was likely to support, such as the liberation of Israeli-occupied Arab land, the enhancement of democratic freedoms, and the development of national industries and agriculture.[20] Because candidates were not readily distinguishable on the basis of their platforms, they needed to garner support in other ways. The predominant means in these elections was alliance making between different candi-dates.[21] In order to win in this way candidates needed 1) the full support of their group and 2) the support of other groups. As we have seen, the tribal candidates from the Valley failed to win the full support of even their own tribes. They were no more successful in forging alliances with other tribes or with nontribal constituencies such as the Christians, Pal-estinians, or Saltis. The problem lay not in candidates' ability to make agreements of mutual support with other candidates but in their ability to speak on behalf of their tribe and ultimately to deliver votes. Three separate incidents illustrate failed efforts to influence voters' behavior.

One sheikh apparently promised the votes of his tribe not to one, but to several opposing candidates. The candidates assumed that he could speak on behalf of his tribe and were purportedly willing to pay for his promise of support. One must assume that the sheikh believed that he could control the votes of his tribe and would be able to direct them to vote for one or two of the several candidates with whom he had made alliances. But on election day it was clear that the people of his tribe were voting for whomever they wished. None of the candidates who had bargained for support from this tribe received the support that had been promised them by the sheikh.

This raises several issues concerning the authority of sheikhs and the high value that ʿarabs place on autonomy. What Abu-Lughod observed for the Awlad ʿAli holds for the ʿAbbād:

> Where individuals value their independence and believe in equality, those who exercise authority over others enjoy a precarious status. . . . They must assert their authority gingerly lest it so compromise their dependents' au-tonomy that it provoke rebellion and be exposed as a sham. . . . Those in authority are . . . expected to respect their dependents' dignity by minimiz-ing open assertion of their power over them. . . . When a superior publicly orders . . . a dependent, he invites the rebellion that would undermine his position (1986:99).

I do not know how this sheikh attempted to direct the votes of his tribespeople, but it would appear that his methods backfired and his au-thority was "exposed as a sham." My informant told me that as a result of his actions this sheikh had been blacklisted and would not be included in any future alliance-making deals.

Sheikhs were not the only ones who misjudged their ability to influ-ence votes. When I arrived at the women's polling station in Muʿaddi I found an ʿAbbādi tribesman, someone who had campaigned vigorously prior to the election for a Christian candidate, standing outside telling women how to vote. Inside, his teenage daughter emulated his behav-ior, directing one woman after another to vote for the three candidates her father supported. This gentleman obviously believed that he had the right to tell the women from his tribe (and perhaps the men, too) how to vote. Not everyone agreed. One of his elder brothers was embarrassed by his behavior, and it was clear that some of the women did not welcome his interference. For example, when a freed slave of the tribe, a schoolteacher, arrived with her mother at the polling station, he instructed them to vote for the two ʿAbbādi candidates and the Christian candidate he supported. The young woman was highly offended at the thought that he would try to tell her how to vote. She told him that she had already made up her mind to vote for two of the candidates he recommended but as for the third, the antiregime candidate from her tribe, she said, "We'll see" in a tone that indicated that she obviously had no intention of voting for him. She told me afterward that she did not vote for him but for someone else.

If tribesmen including tribal sheikhs had limited success in ordering members of their tribe to do their bidding, it is not surprising that outsiders were stymied in their attempts. One of the sisters of a candidate had flown over from Cincinnati to help her brother with the election and was stationed as his representative at the women's voting place in Diyyat. When I visited the polling station, she was busy campaigning—introducing herself and telling the women standing in line waiting to vote for her brother. This approach was not only unsuccessful; it indicated a number of mistaken, though probably not uncommon, cosmopolitan assumptions about tribespeople (perhaps especially tribeswomen) as traditionalist automata who do not have minds of their own but do as they are told (by their sheikhs, by their husbands or fathers). Only a few of these women followed her instructions; most made a public show of their autonmy, voting instead for whom and *only* for whom they chose. The visitor was exasperated that her attempts to drill her brother's name into the women's heads were not more successful. She explained her difficulty to me by the fact that "the women could not remember" her brother's name, concluding that illiterate women should not be allowed to vote. In other words, the failure was viewed not as hers but theirs. In fact, they might have been willing to vote for her brother if they had been approached in a different manner, but for a stranger to approach them in a public place and tell them what to do rather than ask for support was clearly viewed as no way to win votes.

VOTING AS A FORM OF GIFT EXCHANGE

Voting behavior can be interpreted instrumentally and symbolically, and each approach offers a different but not contradictory explanation for the unwillingness of tribespeople to comply with the wishes of a sheikh, fellow tribesman, and outsider. From a pragmatic point of view, the explanation is that the three individuals in question simply went about their task in the wrong way. Votes, like money, are entities whose value and meaning when introduced into a new cultural milieu are multiplex and determined in significant ways by indigenous systems of exchange. In Jordan one of the best-known aspects of the established means for exchanging goods and services is *wasṭa*—literally, go-between. The basic principle of the system is that an individual who has better connections and influence helps someone with less (at least in that domain) to attain his or her goal. As in the case of honor, scholarship on *wasṭa* has focused on the male/formal manifestations of the system. Discussions of *wasṭa* in Jordanian villages by Āmina Farrag (1977) and Richard Antoun (1972; 1979) focus on the roles of pashas (elders of the largest clans chosen by Turkish authorities), clan elders, muktars, and since 1965 mayors and other elected members of the village councils. But as Lawrence Rosen has pointed out for Morocco, "Every relationship implies an obligation. To be related in a particular degree of kinship, to be another's neighbor, to be the client of a merchant in the bazaar carries with it certain expectations of potential recompense" (1984:68). So too, in Jordan, it is not just leaders who participate in such exchanges but ordinary tribespeople, men and women alike.

Votes are clearly valued goods (or, more accurately, services) which ordinary tribesmen and now tribeswomen can offer and that leaders want and need. There are a variety of established means through which Jordanian candidates in the past have attained the votes of their male clients. For example, in the northern Jordanian village Antoun studied, the pasha drew on a "vote bank" which he had developed through good will built up "through more than a half century of the politics of hospitality and successful encounter-through-mediation" as well as with "practical payoffs" (1979:119). Gubser reports that in the southern town of Karak, in preparation for the 1967 parliamentary elections, candidates "visited all the middle-level and many of the low-level leaders from whom they gathered support by various means. Promises to have schools built and roads improved and to secure positions in the bureaucracy and the army for their followers were the most common form of patronage. . . . Direct cash payments for votes were also not uncommon" (1973:170–71).[22] But, as of 1984, these tried-and-true methods were tried only with regard to men. Furthermore, being called upon to support one's sheikh is one thing and being asked to vote for someone else is something else again. From the voters' point of view, the potential benefits of supporting a third party are deflected and diffused.[23] In each of the cases under discussion the person asking for the favor was not the person running for office, and there was no indication that the candidate would ever learn of the favor done on his behalf.

In the cases that I observed firsthand, neither the tribesman nor the candidate's sister approached the voting women in a manner appropriate for exchanges of this type. Neither offered the respect that goes to the giver nor the promise of reciprocity at some later date. In much the the same manner as the holding of the exhibition of tribal culture that will be discussed in chapter 7, ʿarab voters who choose not to make a gift of their votes under these circumstances were engaging in a strategic act of assertion of ownership of valuable resources and of their right to the honor and power that the sharing of those resources engenders.

VOTING AS IDENTITY MAKING: AUTONOMY, DEMOCRACY, AND REPRESENTATION IN CULTURAL CONTEXT

Voting is clearly not simply a pragmatic act but also a symbolic one—a ritual act. Those scholars who have analyzed American elections as rituals have stressed the role that these public political rituals play in affirming the system. Murray Edelman argues that "like all ritual, whether in primitive or modern societies, elections draw attention to common social ties and to the importance and apparent reasonableness of accepting the public policies that are adopted" (1967:3). Dye and Zeigler (1981:208) see elections as a "symbolic exercise in political participation" by which "all political regimes seek to tie the masses to the system" by giving "the ruling regime an aura of legitimacy." This dimension did not escape Jordanian cynics who saw the holding of elections as a clever ploy on the part of the King to keep the populace busy and to provide an acceptable and manageable "outlet" for political dissatisfaction. I do not deny this "social function" (although I do object to the reductionist tendency to interpret Hussein *only* as a Machiavellian caricature. See chapter 8). In addition to whatever function these elections may have served from the point of view of the regime, the elections were utilized by the people of the Valley as a vehicle through which they actively constructed themselves as individuals and as members of a local as well as national community.

Because voting is, among other things, an act of self-definition, tribesmen and women would not allow anyone (not their sheikhs, nor fellow tribesmen, not their husbands, brothers, or fathers, and certainly not an unknown outsider) to tell them how to vote. During the period surrounding the elections, I was told repeatedly by ʿAbāddi men and women that wives would not vote as their husbands did. This was presented to me by both men and women as a source of pride (and amusement). I had encountered a similar attitude during the election of officers for a local club of college graduates called the Alumni Club of the Middle Ghor. During those elections, I met two brothers who supported different candidates (and in so doing different banned political parties), and both boys differed from their father in political preference. Again, all concerned seemed proud of their freedom and independence in this regard.

The *ʿarab* value of personal autonomy and the ideology of democratic elections complemented and reinforced each other. Tribespeople celebrated the *ʿarab* value of autonomy as they exercised their aleatory capacity to move, to position themselves vis-à-vis the candidates and other members of their family and tribe, in potentially new and surprising ways. Indeed, these elections illuminated a number of the new definitions that are emerging about what it means to be a tribesperson in Jordan today. The event occasioned and expressed new relationships between sheikhs and ordinary tribespeople, between tribespeople and the state, and between tribesmen and women.

However, although the *ʿarab* value of autonomy complements the value of personal freedom that we so closely associate with democratic elections, there are some important differences between the meaning of voting in mainstream Amercian culture and that in the Jordan Valley. These differences concern both the issue of representation and the way autonomy is conceived and experienced. Normally when one thinks of representation in the context of democratic elections one thinks of the elected representatives, people who presumably represent their constituencies or at least the interests of their constituencies. (The extent to which elected representatives do actually represent the interests of those who elect them has been the subject of much discussion both among political scientists and voters.) But there is another element of representation in democratic elections that perhaps is less obvious—that of the vote itself.

The secret written ballot that we in the West have come to expect in national elections *represents* our wishes concerning candidates and referendums. By definition, a ballot stands apart from the person it represents.[24] This brings us back to the question of abstractness raised by Marx. Each ballot/vote is separate and equal and represents a citizen who is also separate and equal. Not only are individuals, like the ballots that represent them, construed as fundamentally separated from all others, in the act of casting a secret ballot (i.e., of being a citizen) they also become indistinguishable from others. The abstraction of "citizen" from the sensous self is actualized through the act of representing oneself by means of a written, secret ballot. Here lies the crux of the matter. For among the tribespeople of the Jordan Valley, just as for tribesmen of Northern Yemen described by Paul Dresch (1989), "the equivalence of individual men. . . does not entail identity" (1989:388).[25] To be equal is one thing, to be identical, indistinquishable, is quite another.

The word for "vote" in Arabic (*ṣōt*) literally means voice. In fact, at least in the Jordan Valley, a large proportion of voters literally gave voice to their vote.[26] This occurrence cannot simply be explained by the relatively high illiteracy rates among rural people of voting age. As we saw, a number of those who voted out loud simply feigned illiteracy. It is also important to note in this regard that absentee balloting was not permitted. In order to vote one had to be present, physically present—that is, to have moved to the designated space along with other members of one's community.[27]

Much like the refusal to engage in anonymous gift-giving discussed above, the prominence of oral voting illuminates a number of key features in the practice of politics and identity making in the Jordan Valley and offers some tentative answers to the questions raised at the beginning of the chapter.

As Julian Jaynes has observed, "Sound is a very special modality. We cannot handle it. We cannot push it away. We cannot turn our backs on it. We can close our eyes, hold our noses, withdraw from touch, refuse to taste. We cannot close our ears though we can partly muffle them" (quoted in Schumacher 1989:53).

He suggests that "to listen and understand someone speaking to us [is] in a certain sense . . . to become the other person; or rather, . . . [to] let him become part of us for a brief second. We suspend our own identities, after which we come back to ourselves and accept or reject what he has said . . ." (quoted in Schumacher 1989:52).

In contrast, a major emphasis of literate cultures is "the stress upon the individual" (Goody and Watt 1975:61). Not only are reading and writing normally solitary activities, writing makes possible an abstractness of thought that "disregards the individual's social experience and immediate personal context; and the compartmentalization of knowledge [writing facilitates] similarly restricts the kind of connections which the individual can establish and ratify with the natural and social world" (Goody and Watt 1975:60).[28]

The prominence of oral voting accentuates the importance of performance in the practice of politics among the ʿarabs of the Jordan Valley. Although verbally much less complex than the wedding poems (bālah) of Yemeni tribesmen studied by Stephen C. Caton (1990), voting is also a verbal, although embodied, performance through which tribespeople construct themselves. The act of voting, like that of composing an extemporaneous poem, is anchored in a concrete social context. And although the oral vote is reproduced by officials and then mixed with other anonymous ballots which will be counted by strangers at a different time and place—at the end of the day, at some distant location— "the reception and production" of the performance itself "are immediate and coextensive in time and space" (Caton 1990:258). In other words, these voting practices suggest a unity of political and sensuous selves as well as a recognition of political power as social power—that is, something created by flesh-and-blood human beings, in community, through social action. Of course, in the near future a much larger proportion of the electorate, even in Jordan's most remote areas, will be literate. But the fact that some voters consciously chose to vote out loud may be interpreted as an act of resistance to the fragmentation of political man from sensuous man that so concerned Marx. In this sense, voting orally instead of using the secret, written ballot may be comparable to the intensive use of the corridor, a practice that partially overcomes the increasing fragmentation of domestic social space.

As we saw earlier, 'Abbādi homes are rarely utilized as symbols. Normally homes are not conceived in a way in which they stand apart so as to represent their owners/inhabitants. Similarly, many of the voting practices discussed here seem designed to ensure that people's votes do not stand radically apart from the voter. I am not arguing that the tribespeople of the Jordan Valley are incapable of engaging in acts of representation, for indeed in the following chapter I explore the impact of national representations on tribal self-representations. What I am saying is that in these two quite distinct domains (the home and parliamentary elections) the 'Abbādis construct themselves through embodied performances that do not lend themselves to the abstraction implied by representation in general and citizenship in particular, at least as normally construed by Western scholars. Let us now turn to the contexts in which the 'Abbādis are constructing their identities through acts of self-representation.

NOTES

1. Thanks are due to Dr. A. Sharkas and Governor Khatib (Governor of Balqa' in 1984) for providing me with the election results and for sharing their observations on the election. I am also grateful to Dr. Sharkas for a survey and translation of Arabic language newspaper articles on the subject. All figures on voter registration are from Governor Khatib. Portions of this chapter appeared as "Tribesmen as Citizens: 'Primordial Ties' and Democracy in Rural Jordan," in *Middle East Elections: Implications of Recent Trends*, ed. Layne (Westview Press, Boulder Colo.: 1987), 113–51. See Duclos (1990) for an analysis of the 1989 elections.

2. Several authors argue that this holds true for American elections as well. According to Edelman, despite our commonsense assumptions, issues are only a minor determinate of how people vote, and neither legislative nor administrative behavior depends primarily upon election outcomes (1967:2–3): "Only in a minor degree" does voting entail "participation in policy formation"

(1967:3). Similarly, Dye and Zeigler (1981) concur that elections have a limited role in defining policy but point out that they do serve two other functions: 1) that of choosing personnel to hold public office; and 2) giving the masses an opportunity to express themselves about the conduct of the political officials who have been in power. "Elections do not permit the masses to direct future events but they do permit the masses to render retrospective judgment about *past* political conduct. . . . Elections do not permit masses to decide what should be done in their interests, but they do encourage governing elites to consider the welfare of the masses" because the elected officials know that when it comes time for reelection they are dependent on the support of the masses.

3. See my introduction to *Middle East Elections: Implications of Recent Trends* (1987) and the other essays in that volume for discussion of other examples of this in the region.

4. Schumacher (1989) drew my attention to this essay of Marx's and to many of the issues raised in this chapter.

5. See Abu Jaber (1969) for a description of Jordan's early electoral history.

6. The King explained his decision by saying that he feared that deaths would soon preclude assembly of a quorum of forty. Others saw his reconvening of the parliament, which included representatives of both Banks, as a move designed "to usurp the position of the PLO in peace negotiations with Israel" (Robins 1989:169).

7. According to Governor Khatib the percentage was actually closer to 70 percent. He estimates that if adjustments were made for the people who were registered on family identity cards but were abroad or prohibited from voting because of jobs in the military, security, or police services, 70 to 80 percent of those present and eligible exercised their right to vote.

8. Although Article 6:22 and 23 of the constitution provides for women's political, economic, and social equality, Jordan's Electoral and Municipal Laws denied women the right to vote. The Electoral Law was amended in April 1974 and the Municipal Law in April 1982, making women eligible to vote and run for office in national and municipal elections (*Jordan Times*, 8 Mar. 1984).

9. The proportion of the population under fifteen was 50.7 percent in 1979, up from 45.4 percent in 1961 (Jordan 1986:58).

10. See Layne (1987a) for more detailed election results.

11. Abu Jaber's (1969) survey of the social background of the members of Jordan's parliament and legislative council shows that access to national elected office has been highly restricted. For example, members of only thirty-six families held the approximately eighty seats in the five legislative councils that were elected between 1931 and 1946 and between 1947 and 1967, and the 437 seats competed for in Jordan's nine parliamentary elections were filled by members of only 183 different families (Abu Jaber 1969: 226, 249). Even the leadership of the left-wing parties—Communist, Ba'th, and National-Socialist—has been in the hands of the social, economic, and intellectual elite. (See Gubser (1973:166) for Karaki members of parliament over time.)

The seats allotted to Bedouin have had the least turnover, with representation coming from only five families during the period from 1928 to 1947. For example, Hamd Ibn Jazi, sheikh of sheikhs of the South Jordanian Bedouin tribes was elected to every legislative council from 1928 through 1947 and was elected in the first five parliamentary elections (1950–56). Upon his death, his son Faysal succeeded him (Abu Jaber 1969:237).

12. It is doubtful, even if the alliances had not been abrogated, whether tribespeople from the Deir ʿAlla Subdistrict would have voted for Adwān at their sheikh's bidding. He did profit from an alliance with the victorious Christian candidate, Dr. Fawzi Daoud, however. As a result of this alliance, he won nearly one thousand votes in the Christian town of Fuhais (the largest number of votes for a Muslim candidate there). This alliance differed from the others I learned of in that it was official and public—Adwān and Daoud had appeared together in newspaper advertisements.

The second-place winner, Zouhair al-Zoqan, also received strong support from Fuhais, winning 918 votes there. Apparently, the Christians of Fuhais, unlike the tribespeople of the Jordan Valley, were willing to vote as a group for candidates from tribes with whom their group had made alliances.

13. In principle, because there were two Muslim seats available, it was possible to put two candidates from the same tribe forward—but this hampered alliance-forging.

14. See also, for example, the incident I describe in Layne (1986) in which the King avoided letting ʿAbbādis slaughter a camel for him because of the obligation it would put him under to offer amnesty to the sheikh who had fled to Syria.

15. Each voting station was staffed by an election committee of three made up of locals, nonlocal civil servants, one or two police guards, and representatives of the candidates, all of whom were charged with ensuring that the elections were conducted peacefully and fairly. Each of the candidates had the right to station a representative in each of the polling places to ensure fairness. Most candidates could not recruit enough representatives for each of the voting stations, so at any given station some but not all the candidates would be likely to be represented. In the Deir ʿAlla Subdistrict local girls served as representatives for local candidates and for some of the Christian candidates from Salt in the women's polling stations.

16. Because illiterate voters could not consult the printed list of candidates, they had to have made up their minds before entering the voting station.

Voters were not allowed to cue one another; and if men tried to enter female voting stations to "help" their women vote, they were prevented from doing so by the voting committee.

17. Gubser (1973:171) reports that during the 1967 parliamentary elections one of the Karaki candidates "obtained the votes of only half of his own tribe." Farrag (1977:235) reports that in elections in 1970 for the town council of a village thirty miles north of Amman, although most villagers voted for the candidate from their clan, a number of men from each of the two competing clans (*hamula*) voted for the candidate from the opposing clan. She believes that "in the past it would have been inconceivable for an individual not to support the elder. . . . of his *hamula*" (Farrag 1977:235).

18. By 1984 one of the ʿAbbādi babies he had delivered was a senior in high school. She worked as his representative in Muʿaddi.

19. Members of the Jordan Valley tribes supported Arab political parties in other contexts. Many middle-aged tribesmen told me that they had supported Nasser in the 1950s, and during the period of my research several of the banned political parties had a following among young, educated tribesmen and women in the Jordan Valley. Many members of the Alumni Club of the Middle Ghor were supporters of the Iraqi Ba'th party, the Syrian Ba'th, or the Communist party, in that order of popular support; and the annual club elections were dominated by these parties in 1982 and 1983. Yet during the 1984 parliamentary elections, these same individuals did not organize or participate along party lines. See Antoun (1979:128–29) for a striking contrast in attitude toward party politics even during Jordan's "party period" in the 1950s.

20. Stokes (1985) would call these "valence issues" in contrast to "position issues." With valence issues popular support is sought, not in terms of the position that candidates advocate, but by associating themselves as closely as possible in the public's mind with desirable goals or conditions. Success goes to the contestant who is best able to form these bonds or valences in the public's mind (Stokes 1985:8). Other examples of the valence issues raised by candidates in the 1984 elections are: to uphold justice; to work hard in bringing the voice of the people to the authorities; to support the athletic movement and youth; to support women's rights and the Jordanian countryside; to support the Palestinian people (*Jordan Times*, 13 Mar. 1984). Frequently a single candidate would list a long series of such issues hoping to win support from all sectors of society. (See for example, Khair's campaign flyer in Layne 1987a.)

21. According to Gubser (1973:169) in Karak candidates for parliament normally "enter into agreements with each other to campaign as a group and to exchange various kinds of support. In 1967 the four [three Muslim, one Christian] successful candidates were all united on one ticket."

22. As Huxley noted in Lebanon, votes are sometimes exchanged for money and sometimes for *wasita*, but these two types of exchanges have quite different implications (1978:36).

23. There are obvious risks for the sheikhs as well. For example, Antoun reports that while the Pasha of Kufr al-Ma utilized his supporters' votes for himself during the 1967 parliamentary elections, he refused to form alliances with other politicians outside his own subdistrict when they offered to trade votes—that is, "to encourage their supporters to vote for him if he did likewise." He refused because he felt that this would result in "hard feelings when the leader could not or did not deliver on his promises" (Antoun 1979:120).

24. Caton (1990) has explored the implications of the tape recorder—that is, of the disembodied voices—in terms of the cultural practice of poetry in Yemen. He contrasts the *bālah* poems in which the performative aspect is paramount with *qaṣīda*, which are frequently taped and then bought and sold in markets. It is this latter form that plays an important role in national politics. Although he also mentions poems that are printed in the newspapers, he does not compare the implications of tape-recorded and printed poems.

25. Dresch compares tribal and national notions of history and time in Yemen noting that in marked contrast to tribal imaginations, national discourse

suggests "a serial quality whereby equivalence and indentity are themselves equated" (1989:390).

26. This is certainly one of the most important ways in which the national elections differ for the people of the Valley and for most Americans.

27. For a fascinating comparison, see Davis's account of nonrepresentative direct democracy in Libya (1987:142–53). In the elections he witnessed, there was "no secret ballot, and Libyans voted . . . publicly and in theory were answerable for their actions" (1987:147). Voting was accomplished by moving through the goalposts on a football field or across the stage at a cinema. Also see Herzfeld (1985:105) for a discussion of "secret balloting" in village Crete.

28. Schumacher (1989:61) notes that the verb *to write* originally meant "to tear apart," "to cut," "to split." In addition to the differences entailed between literate and oral cultures, he also sees an important distinction between reading out loud and silent reading in terms of posture.

Constructing Culture and Tradition in the Valley

ALTHOUGH THE TRIBALISM DEBATE and the other national representations discussed in chapter 5 were not primarily directed at Jordanian tribespeople, the tribesmen and women of the Jordan Valley are aware of them and are constructing their own self-images in a dialogic relationship with these objectifications of their culture.[1] In response to the denigration of tribal culture by its critics and the appropriation of tribal culture by the state as a key element of Jordan's national heritage, Jordanian tribespeople are reconceiving and reevaluating what being a tribesperson means. In so doing, they are utilizing some of the same discursive practices as those employed by the state and the Jordanian intelligentsia in constructing tribal representations of Jordan's past. However, these practices do not mean the same thing for local actors as they do for bearers of the dominant discourse. Rather, they provide frameworks that tribesmen and women fill with local content and interpret in terms of indigenous cultural constructions such as *aṣl*, honor, and gift exchange. Two examples—the new meanings associated with the wearing of women's traditional dress and a local exhibition of tribal artifacts—serve to illustrate this process.

WEARING *DILUG*

One example of the dialogic relationship between national and local representations of tribal culture is to be found in the changing meanings of the *dilig* (pl. *dilug*), the traditional embroidered dress, for the tribes of the Jordan Valley. The *dilig* is a black, full-length, long-sleeved, embroidered dress. The machine-embroidered floral or geometric patterns, done in either satin stitch (*ṭara*) or chain stitch (*ṭabʿa*) vary, and no single pattern is identified with a particular tribe.[2] An everyday *dilig* is embroidered with about four to six spools of embroidery thread around the edges of the sleeves, neckline, and hem. Fancier dresses use up to twenty-five spools of thread and cost about JD 45, or $135, in 1981. On these more elaborate dresses multiple vertical bands of embroidery run the length of the dress in addition to a richly embroidered yoke and bands of embroidery around the hem, shoulders, and sleeves. Shelagh Weir (1989:273) suggests that "the expansion of the vertical "branches" on West Bank dresses in the 1980s" is an innovation that "proclaimed and flaunted" the wealth men were earning working in the oil-rich countries of the Gulf. Although few ʿAbbādi tribespeople went to work in the Gulf during the boom years, this form of conspicuous consumption may also have been an innovation in the early 1980s.

Up until the 1930s these dresses were made of hand-woven cotton, linen, or silk, and embroidery thread was home dyed with vegetable and insect dyes (Kawar 1984:41).[3] Around 1930 machine-produced fabrics became available in the markets and mercerized cotton threads replaced silk embroidery threads. By the 1980s tribeswomen were using synthetic fabrics because of their longer durability and easier upkeep. Dress designs and embroidery patterns have also changed. The primary manufacturer of mercerized embroidery thread, Dollfus-Mieg and Cie. (DMC), also produced pattern books which by the 1930s were "circulating among village women, introducing a trail of new European patterns and designs" (Kawar 1984:42). ʿAbbādi women still remember older dress styles such as the long and ample *thūb* still associated with the town of Salt, which they folded over a belt (*shuwayhiyyeh*). They also describe accessories such as the red and black silk Allepo head scarves, which are no longer a part of their wardrobe.

In the 1980s the *dilug* worn by middle-aged and older tribeswomen were loosely cut, ample enough to wear throughout a pregnancy, and the V-neck was low enough in the front to permit nursing. Women wore a long-sleeved dress and pants underneath, which permitted them to lift the *dilig* and tuck it in around their waists to keep it from getting dirty or underfoot while working. These middle-aged and older women usually braided their hair and wore a scarf—solid white, the red or black checked *kufiyya*, or most commonly, a red or black scarf with a bright paisley border—tied around the top of the head with their braids hanging unencumbered from beneath the scarf.

Most younger women usually wore Western clothing. School-aged girls wore the long-sleeved, knee-length brown, blue, or green uniforms of primary, middle, and secondary school while at school and similar dresses or skirts and blouses elsewhere. About half the young women wore a head cover during the period of my research from 1981 to 1982 and 1984. Those who did typically did so as an assertion of their modesty and piety and so wore plain solid-colored scarves which they tied in a variety of ways, all of which completely covered their hair and sometimes also their necks.[4]

Although Western clothing was the typical everyday wear of this generation, young women often chose fancy *dilug* for more formal occasions. For example, during the 1984 parliamentary by-elections the ʿAbbādi girls who served as the local representatives of candidates in the women's polling stations donned *dilug* for the occasion, even though they normally wore Western clothing. *Dilug* were also worn by the senior class from the Deir ʿAlla Secondary School for Girls for their high-school graduation. In addition, *dilug* were frequently chosen by young women for their attire at weddings, or when going to town to shop/be observed by potential husbands, or posing before the anthropologist's camera. These sartorial practices and the meanings given them by the young women and the local community can only be understood in the context of the new meanings accorded these and other elements of folk culture by the national intelligentsia.

The *dilig* has always been subject to innovation as well as changing market and political forces. In recent years one source of change has been the increasing public attention in Jordan and internationally that the *dilig*, along with other "traditional" costumes, has received. Alia, the Jordanian airline, has sponsored a number of fashion shows of women modeling traditional dresses and/or new high-fashion versions of the same. One of the most common types of programs aired on Jordanian television is that of folk dancing performed in colorful folkloric costumes. The extensive private collection of Widad Kawar of Palestinian and Jordanian costumes was the source of photographs used for a set of posters in the late 1970s as well as a calendar put out in 1983 by the Ministry of Tourism and Antiquities. In 1987 a selection of these dresses was exhibited in Cologne under the joint patronage of Queen Noor and Baroness von Weizsacker and later at the Institut du Monde Arabe in Paris. The exhibition was accompanied by an elaborate catalogue with chapters written by anthropologists and historians of Jordan discussing the history and ethnographic contexts of these costumes (Layne 1987b).

The Jerash Festival, an annual cultural festival set in the Roman ruins of Jerash, includes among its many international and local cultural activities groups of young Jordanians who wear "traditional" costumes and perform "folkloric" dances. Queen Noor inaugurated the first Jerash festival in 1981 wearing a beautifully embroidered gown, one that did not represent any single tribe or village but was an exquisitely fine example of the combined traditions of the area; she wore a similar gown for the 1988 Jerash Festival, which she and the King inaugurated together.

Both the King and Queen wear a wide variety of apparel—for example, military uniforms when visiting the various military units and academies, business suits when receiving Western delegations, a cap and gown when presiding over a university graduation. The adoption of these various garbs not only communicates the message that the King and Queen are of the people, but also adds legitimacy to the institutions and practices in question, in this case the wearing of traditional embroidered dresses.

In the Jordan Valley the diversion of *dilug* from their everyday contexts—that is, as the apparel of middle-aged women—and the placing of them in new contexts such as a high-school graduation or a national election, charges these dresses with symbolic value. In concert with the national valorization of tribal culture, the marked wearing of *dilug* by young women has become a symbol of tribal identity and, by extension, of Jordanian identity.

For the women of the ʿAbbād, the wearing of a well-embroidered dress, like a piece of gold jewelry, is a public show of status. But because the *dilug* have become symbols of the ʿAbbādis' tribal heritage, the wearing of a *dilig* by younger women has an additional positive moral valuation. A young woman who wears a *dilig* is referred to as *muḥtarama*. *Muḥtarama* means honored, venerated, esteemed. The gowns worn by unmarried women, although typically cut to be more close fitting than the dresses worn by married women, are looser than most Western clothing. The *dilug*'s respectability is not simply due to the fact that the dresses are relatively loose fitting and a modest choice of garb. In fact, young women with fundamentalist proclivities prefer to wear a plain, coatlike dress that they feel accords with the Koranic injunction that a woman should not draw attention to herself. In contrast, *dilug* are showy and gay, decorated with clusters of flowers and bursting with color. Because *dilug* symbolize ʿ*arab*ness and, by extension, Jordanianness, their selection for wear by young women is a political statement and one that meets with public nods and comments of approval by the local community. The fact that I wore a *dilig* was a repeated source of comments of this kind, and some ʿAbbādis reported with approval that my wearing a *dilig* had increased the popularity of these dresses among local young women. To the extent that this was the case, it reflects the influence of their awareness of Westerners' and the national elite's appreciation of these "folk" aspects of their culture.

Wearing such dresses is deemed an honorable thing to do and, like other honorable acts, the honor it bestows adheres not only to the woman wearing it but to her family and to her tribe at large.[5] In my case, the fact that I showed respect for this respectable element of their culture increased my own respectability, which in turn reflected respect on the ʿAbbādis for hosting me. This mirrorlike multiplication of honor is also evident in the next example of the dialogics of tribal self-representation.

THE EXHIBITION

Another striking expression of the dialogic relation between national and local representations of tribal culture was an exhibition of local culture held in November 1981 at the Krayma Community Center, located in the northern end of the East Jordan Valley. The exhibition consisted of artifacts of tribal life which were displayed in two rooms at the center. The exhibition pieces included objects such as straw mats, carved wooden coffee grinders, embroidered dresses, woven coffee bags, and wooden spindles. Also displayed were ingredients of local cuisine: dishes of spices and herbs and a jar of drained yogurt (*labana*). The objects displayed were not ritual objects, but objects from the tribepeople's daily lives. These items were all handmade but not all were locally produced. The inclusionary criteria appeared to be that they were used locally rather than produced locally.

Although some of the items displayed were becoming less ubiquitous, none were uncommon. For example, by 1981 wooden coffee grinders had been replaced in some homes by electric Molinex grinders or by other innovative substitutes such as Israeli mortar shells. But the only object that I had not already seen during my first two months in the Jordan Valley was the coffee bag, and two such bags were promptly presented to me as gifts when I expressed an interest in this item.

The director of the center was an ʿAbbādi tribesman who had recently completed his B.A. in social science at Yarmouk University in northern Jordan. Under his directorship the center had become a hub of activity in the area. Although I do not know how many people, other than the ʿAbbādi friends who took me, came to the center especially to see the exhibit, people who came for sewing classes, to use the library, to play table tennis, or to bring their children to play on the playground equipment wandered through the exhibit.

The exhibition was clearly directed at a local audience, not at outsiders like me. As an anthropologist in the first stages of research and eager to learn more about tribal culture, I was disappointed that the exhibition was not more interesting. Not only was I already familiar with most of the objects, the captions simply named the objects and did not give any contextual information such as their history, manufacture, or use. Such knowledge was self-evident to the audience.

Unfortunately, because the exhibition was so uninteresting to me in terms of content, I dismissed it quickly as having limited importance to my study. I did not realize the critical importance of the form, the very fact of an exhibition, until I had returned to the United States. As a result, I did not question people as to the purpose of this exhibition, the aims of the exhibitors, or the meaning it held for those who viewed it. Explicit native interpretations would certainly have been desirable, but with this handicap in mind, a number of observations and tentative interpretations can be made.

As noted above, the exhibition was clearly an exhibition of themselves to themselves, a classic collective representation. But this representation was expressed in a new form: a form appropriated from the dominant culture. Mitchell (1988) has described the reaction of Arab visitors to the "Exposition Universelle" held in Paris in 1889 to the bizarre European habit of putting things on exhibit. In his words, "the exhibition . . . epitomiz[es] the strange character of the West, a place where one was continually pressed into service as a spectator by a world ordered so as to represent" (Mitchell 1988:13). Although Mitchell (1988:13) argues convincingly that exhibitions, with their "remarkable claim to certainty . . . the apparent certainty with which everything seems ordered and organized, calculated and rendered unambiguous," were a distinctive and fundamental aspect of the colonial process, this way of knowing is no longer a uniquely Western one.[6]

In recent years exhibitions have become frequent in Amman, often under the sponsorship of foreign cultural centers. According to Jordan's *Five Year Plan*, "Exhibitions became a standard feature of Jordanian life" in the seventies (Jordan 1986:321). Among the most frequent exhibitions are those of local and European art, historic photographs, books, and archeological artifacts. The openings of these events by Jordanian dignitaries, complete with a ritual ribbon-cutting ceremony, are covered on the evening news by the national television station. At a local level, exhibitions of school projects in Jordan's public schools have also become common events.

An exhibition has its own set of characteristics, and the placement of a selection of objects into this structure endows those objects with new meanings. Exhibitions share many of the features of photography. Like photography, putting on or viewing an exhibition "means putting oneself into a certain relation to the world that feels like knowledge—and, therefore, like power" (Sontag 1977:4). And like a photograph, an exhibition of this kind freezes life and disembodies it from its context.

In addition to the media of an exhibition, the content of the Krayma exhibition, that is, "traditional" "products," deserves analysis. Collective representations such as a Balinese cockfight (Geertz 1973c), a Yankee City parade (Warner 1959), or a Gomeran fiesta (Shally 1985) differ in a fundamental way from an exhibition of products. Roy Wagner (1981) argues that because of the division of labor of industrial capitalism, we are obsessed with products rather than producers. "As we produce 'things,' so our concern is with preserving things, products, and the techniques of their production. Our culture is a sum of such things" (1981:26). In contrast, because productivity in tribal societies was part of interpersonal relations and an embodiment of human rather than abstract values, tribal societies were not obsessed with products as such. And yet, like the cargo cults of Melanesia that Wagner describes, the power symbolized by Western things is being laid claim to. However, in the case of the Krayma exhibition it is not Western manufactured goods that are appropriated as cargo but indigenous products that are transformed and endowed with new meanings.

The "invention of tradition" in the Jordan Valley is not a discovery of an obscure past as in the case of the Highland tradition of Scotland (Trevor-Roper 1983), but rather the metaphorization of life into tradition. For Eric Hobsbawm, "the invention of tradition" refers to a process of formalization and ritualization characterized by reference to a historic past that "is largely factitious" (Hobsbawn 1983:2). He asserts that "where the old ways are alive, traditions need be neither revived nor invented" (1983:8). However, the Krayma exhibition, where the objects made "traditional" are neither factitious nor dead suggests that there may be other reasons for inventing tradition.

Why, then, should the tribespeople take items that were still very much in use, bracket them off from their everyday contexts, and set them behind glass for appraisal? At first the display of *labana*, a staple of the Jordanian diet, struck me as comparable to Pop Artist Andy Warhol's painting of a Campbell's Soup can. I do not believe, however, that the sense of irony inherent in Pop Art was present here. Although for some the exhibition may have been a mockery of the many openings in Amman presided over by self-important public figures, I believe that the dominant goal was a celebration of ʿ*arab* life. The primary aim was to valorize the objects of their lives and symbols of their social identity rather than to deflate "high" culture and the activities of national dignitaries. Arjun Appadurai (1986) has described the aesthetics of decontextualization with regard to the display of primitive utilitarian objects in highbrow homes in the West. In a similar fashion, the removing of these objects from their normal realms of use and exchange (or as Appadurai puts it, "the diversion of [such] commodities from their original nexus") serves to accelerate and enhance the value of these everyday items (Appadurai 1986:28). As the illiterate women I observed visiting the exhibition walked in front of the panes reading the exhibition without the aid of the captions, there was a clear tone of self-confirmation. They exclaimed with pleasure and authority their recognition and approval of the objects on display.

I suggest that this exhibition might best be understood as an act of honor.[7] Honor in the Mediterranean has typically been described as "the conferral of public esteem" upon a person as "the reward for successful power maneuvers in which a man's relationship to other men *through women* is the fundamental axis of evaluation" (Gilmore 1987:3–4). However, in recent years, scholars such as Michael Herzfeld (1987) and T. O. Beidelman (1989) have shown how other aspects of honor, such as hospitality, can be used to "englobe" one's opponents and to assert moral superiority over them. And although the sources of honor have typically been certain socially approved modes of interaction, these sources are not static but subject to change. For example, Marisa Escribano (1984) has shown how since the Israeli occupation of the West Bank, land has become a new symbol of honor for West Bankers, and I suggest that in Jordan, "tradition" is now being defined as a source of honor.

There is a tribal precedent for the connection between history and honor. The ʿAbbād tribes of the Jordan Valley think of themselves as *aṣīl* and believe that *aṣīl* tribes have honor and that non-*aṣīl* tribes do not. The word *aṣīl* derives from the root *aṣl* which, as the reader will recall, literally means "origin," "root," or "source." When I asked ʿAbbādis to tell me what distinguished them from another local tribe that they considered to be non-*aṣīl*, they explained that the roots of the tribe in question were not known.[8] In other words, knowledge of one's tribal history is of value in and of itself.

In addition to the tribal genealogies and tales of heroic deeds of the past, material culture and other evidence of "tribal traditions" are now being conceived of as sources of honor by the ʿarabs of the Jordan Valley. All these are elements of *aṣl*, proof of noble tribal ancestry, a revered legacy that one inherits at birth. But *aṣl* is only one element of honor—a prerequisite, if you will. As so many scholars have noted, in order to maintain one's honor one must continually assert it through acts and deeds. Although most Western scholars have focused on the sensational (and male) practices of blood feuds and honor killings,[9] honor also concerns the more mundane matter of compliance with the traditional values of generosity, honesty, deference to one's elders, loyalty to friends, keeping one's word, and generally controlling one's emotions and behavior. Everyday acts such as choice of apparel or the laying out of mattresses are as much a part of honor as vengeance killings. In this sense, honor in the Jordan Valley (like that among the ʿarabs of Egypt's western desert described by Abou-Zeid [1966] and Abu-Lughod [1986]) is "attained, or rather maintained, by simple and sincere conformity to the prevailing social norms" (Abou-Zeid 1966:258). This applies not just to men but to all members of society. As Abu-Lughod has noted, "Exemplary behavior on the part of any individual, of whatever age, level of wealth, or gender, is recognized and rewarded with respect" (1986:92).

One important matrix of exemplary behavior involves the showing of

respect to persons or things worthy of respect. The adjective
muḥtaram(a), meaning respected, honored, esteemed, comes from the
root *ḥaram*, which means holy or sacred. These two concepts are related
not only lexicographically but also in practice. Abu-Lughod (1986) has
described the way that voluntary deference to one's social superiors is
considered an honorable mode of behavior among the Awlad ʿAli
ʿarabs. Her focus was on interpersonal relations. I suggest that this same
logic applies in other contexts as well. Treating things worthy of respect
(the holy places, traditional tribal artifacts, etc.) with the respect they are
due bestows esteem upon the actor whether male or female, young or
old. As we have seen, the young women who wear *dilug* are publicly
asserting respect for the traditions of their tribe (and of their country)
and in so doing are accorded the respect of their community. Similarly,
the exhibition of a selection of everyday artifacts not only defined these
artifacts as a valuable part of tribal heritage, but by venerating them, also
defined both those who designed the exhibition and those who viewed
it as honorable people who value their traditions.

In addition, the exhibition was, I believe, an act of resistance by the
ʿarabs of the Jordan Valley, not to the uses to which their culture and
traditions are being exploited, but to their anonymity in this process.
The Krayma exhibition was a reclamation and relocalization of their culture. It represents not a counterdiscourse to the hegemonic discourse of
the state, but rather, within that same discourse a strategic act of assertion of ownership of valuable resources and rights to the honor and
power that those resources represent. One gains no honor or glory for
a deed if one's name is unknown.

To the extent that the ʿarabs of the Jordan Valley are now conceiving
of their culture as an entity, a possession, the meanings of gift exchange
may also inform the Krayma exhibition. The ʿarabs of the Jordan Valley,
like Homeric aristocrats, view proper exchanges as profoundly personalized (Beidelman 1989). Thus the exhibition may be viewed as an attempt to recast the expropriation of generic tribal culture by the state in
terms of a gift of their personalized tribal culture (ultimately to a state
embodied in the person of the King).

In Jordan, glory accrues to the giver, and to be able to make a gift to
the King, the unquestionable zenith of Jordanian social hierarchy,
would be a glorifying gift indeed. Unlike the queen of England who
never gives anything away (Hayden 1987:102–3), the King is the ultimate Jordanian gift-giver and he accepts very few gifts in return.[10]

In both the Homeric and Jordanian case, people strive to remain autonomous and yet make advantageous alliances between themselves and
other persons of comparable or superior power and dignity through the
prestation of goods. Thus, the ʿAbbādis' gift of tribal culture may be a

way of reinforcing their alliance with the King. Or as Herzfeld has said of hospitality, such gifts enact a moral encompassing of "political asymmetry that allows the client to maintain self-respect" (1987:86).

The Krayma exhibition was one manifestation of the cultural construction of culture and tradition that is taking place at both a local and national level. As Mitchell (1988) has shown, exhibitions are essentially representations—things are collected and arranged to stand for something else, to evoke some larger truth. At the Krayma exhibition, traditional products were brought to serve as a representation of progress and history, honor, and power. And the larger truth to which the exhibition alludes is that these products belong to them and so, too, do any benefits deriving from their use.

THE DIALOGICS OF TRIBAL SELF-REPRESENTATION

The issues explored in this chapter complement the recent work of Marxist historians (The Popular Memory Group [1982]; Bommes and Wright [1982]) on the power and persuasiveness of historical representations, their connections with dominant institutions, and the part they play in winning consent and building alliances in the processes of formal politics. But whereas the Marxist framework has tended to focus on either compliance or resistance to "hegemonic discourse," the examples explored in this chapter provide a more nuanced view of the way local communities participate in the constitution of such discourse by their simultaneous compliance and resistance.

M. M. Bakhtin's concept of dialogism illuminates this process. He describes how a word "enters a dialogically agitated and tension-filled environment of alien words, value judgments and accents, weaves in and out of complex interrelationships, merges with some, recoils from others, intersects with yet a third group . . ." (Bakhtin 1981:276). This dialogic process pertains to symbolic systems more broadly. As we have seen, the tribespeople of the Jordan Valley define themselves in an environment full of others' definitions and variously evaluating commentary, and the tribepeople's views are entangled with these discourses (cf. Bakhtin 1981:276–77). The meanings that the ʿarabs of the Jordan Valley give to their lives "harmoniz[e] with some of the elements in this environment, strik[e] a dissonance with others, . . . [and] in this dialogized process," they shape their own "style" (Bakhtin 1981:277).

The two specific areas explored in this chapter—the public display of "tribal" objects and the changing meanings associated with the *diliǧ*—also illustrate the changing roles that possessions are playing in defining individuals and groups. In the past, possessions provided props for the dynamic flow of social interaction in pastoral nomadic societies such as the one described here. Livestock was stolen and defended, bought and sold, consumed and reproduced, given and received (Meeker 1979). In such a context individual possessions mattered little for, at least in some spheres, there was a kind of interchangeability of possessions. (As we have seen, tents—and now houses—are more or less alike.) Rather it was one's relative position in an elite group of actors who were constantly testing their ability to obtain and retain such possessions that distinguished people. In chapter 3 we examined another example of the importance of objects as social props in the way that portable furnishings are continuously moved to define and negotiate social relations. This use of possessions is quite different from the use of things as emblems or symbols that we have been investigating here. The examples drawn out in this chapter document an increasing referentiality of things in the Jordan Valley.

The use of things as symbols of group identity is also evident at the national level. Handler has noted the centrality of possessive individualism to nationalist ideologies: "Thus the nation and its members 'have' a culture, the existence of which both follows from and proves the existence of the nation itself" (Handler 1988:51). Others have noted that over the last two hundred years there has been a progressive concretization of history, whereby history is increasingly identified with property rather than with knowledge and culture (Bommes and Wright 1982). A striking instance of this occurred recently when, following his brush with cancer, King Hussein was proclaimed a "national treasure" (Fineman 1992).

This chapter has illustrated the way that tribal artifacts are playing an increasingly important role in representing Jordan's "national heritage."[11] While for all nations the possession of a heritage, of culture, is considered crucial proof of national existence, "an outsider's denial of national existence" (such as that of Sharon) is a challenge that prompts nationalists to "claim and specify the nation's possessions" in an effort to "construct an account of the unique culture and history that attaches to and emanates from the people who occupy it" (Handler 1988:154). It is in such a context that tribes came to play such an dominant role in the symbolization of Jordan's national identity.

The symbolization of tribes has been facilitated by the Jordanian government's policy over the last several decades to unify and integrate individual tribal identities into one broad tribal identity, that is, to promote tribalism in a general way rather than encouraging each tribe to maintain and develop its own individual identity. Oweidi (1982) has described a number of legal steps directed toward this end. Another vehicle for the transformation of the plurality of tribal identities into a shared source of national pride and common heritage has been the use of symbols drawn from the tribes' material culture.

This is accomplished through a set of "folkloric" frameworks (not unlike the conceptual pigeonholes discussed in chapter 1) into which the cultural heritage of different groups is placed and displayed. But there are significant differences depending upon one's point of view and the sphere in which these frameworks are utilized. Local communities such as the one described in this chapter are appropriating frameworks from the dominant culture, while state apparatuses are appropriating local artifacts and symbols with which to fill such frameworks. This process enables local communities to personalize these frameworks at the local level but results in the anonymity at the national level that the ʿarabs of the Jordan Valley are struggling against.

In this chapter we have seen how the frameworks of an "exhibition" and "traditional costume" are being filled by members of local groups. It is important to note, however, that in both of the cases explored here, the objects in question did not "represent" a single tribe. The exhibition was a regional one that displayed objects which would be likely to be found among any of tribes of the area. Nor are *dilug* tribally specific. In the Jordan Valley, distinct political groups are being merged through the display of shared culture.[12]

In contrast, at the national level, a single political unit (the Kingdom) is represented through the display of a diversity of cultures. For example, at the Jerash festival, youth groups from each region and from distinctive ethnic groups such as the Circassians, wear folk costumes and perform folk dances. Similarly, at the national costume museum the traditional costumes of each region are displayed side by side. In both cases, slots (time slots in the program or exhibition cases in the museum) are filled with a range of Jordan's cultural diversity.

In the 1980s this included Palestinian folk culture as well. For example, the 1983 calendar put out by the Ministry of Tourism entitled "Jordan" included dresses from Transjordanian, the West Bank, *and* pre-1948 Palestine. The cover photo is not of a regionally identifiable dress but a close-up of several brightly colored bands of embroidery, and the first picture after that of the King and Queen is of two women—one in a Transjordanian dress and the other in a Palestinian dress. The caption for this photo is "Jordan and Palestine." The photographs that accompany all the other months are of a single woman and the captions give a more localized provenance, for example, Ramallah, Maʿan. Similarly, the exhibition in Cologne and Paris included examples from both Palestine and Jordan.

At the national level such practices sometimes result in what I call the mix-and-match method of Jordanian cultural representation. One example of this would be the Algerian flight attendant wearing a Palestinian village dress who served me ʿarab coffee on my most recent trip to Jordan. Also of this genre are the collections of folk objects displayed in the living rooms of many bourgeois families in Amman.[13]

There are other differences between the national and local levels. Whereas, at the national level, "heritage" is inscribed within a framework that distinguishes it from everyday life, at the local level "heritage" tends to spill over and merge more closely with the everyday and in so doing historicizes the familiar. The Krayma exhibition of the artifacts of everyday life is a clear example of this process.

The focus of this chapter has been on the way tribal self-representations are dialogically related to national representations of tribal life in Jordan. The changing meanings associated with the wearing of the *dilig* and the exhibition of "traditional tribal artifacts" both reflect and contribute to the process of folklorization of tribal culture in the Jordan Valley. In their reification of their culture, the tribesmen and women of the valley are employing the same discursive practices as the national intelligentsia and the state. However, it would be rash to assume that this discourse is the dominant one. It is only one of many discourses that they employ.

The transformation of objects from their everyday contexts into symbols of traditional culture has wide-ranging implications for social life in the Jordan Valley. To the extent that the Krayma exhibition and the marked wearing of the *dilig* indicate a "sense of detachment, both physical and conceptual, of the self from an object world" (Mitchell 1988), it signals a fundamental change in the way life and labor will be experienced in rural Jordan. The metaphorization of life into culture cannot leave life unchanged. But, as I have shown, the construction of "culture" in the Jordan Valley is taking place within the framework of the indigenous cultural constructions of *aṣl* and honor. The two cases explored in this chapter are examples of the dynamism of these constructs and of the way the ʿarabs of the Jordan Valley are making themselves into the future.

NOTES

1. An earlier version of this chapter appeared as "The Dialogics of Tribal Self-Representation in Jordan," *American Ethnologist* 16, no. 1 (1989):24–39.

2. Hand embroidery which is associated with Palestinian village dresses is distinguished by the tribespeople of the Valley from their own machine embroidery as *taṭriz falāḥīn*, peasant embroidery. For more on the making of these dresses, see Layne (1987b).

3. See Weir (1989) for more on the history of dress materials.

4. Cf. Beck's (1992) description of Qashqaʿi schoolgirls' attire in postrevolutionary Iran.

5. Both J. Anderson (1982) and Abu-Lughod (1986) have insightfully interpreted another element of women's apparel, the veil, in terms of broader cultural patterns of deference.

6. For interesting comparative examples in the region see Dominguez's (1989) insightful discussion of exhibitions by the Department of Jewish Ethnography of the Israel Museum of the "material culture" of "non-Ashkenazi Jewish communities"; Slyomovics (1989) on a living museum in Egypt where tourists can experience a "hyperreal" Pharonic village; and al-Najjar (1991) and Davis and Gavrielides (1991) on nationalism and the growing interest in "folklore" in the Gulf.

7. I follow Friedrich and Abu-Lughod here and use *honor* in a broad sense to refer to "'a code for both interpretation and action: in other words, with both cognitive and pragmatic components.' In its first aspect it is 'a system of symbols, values, and definitions in terms of which phenomena are conceptualized and interpreted.' In the second, honor guides and motivates acts 'organized in terms of categories, rules, and processes that are, to a significant degree, specific to a given culture. . . .'" (Friedrich quoted in Abu-Lughod 1986:86).

8. As Rosen has pointed out, knowledge of a person's origin also can be an important resource for "arranging a marriage, a political alliance, an economic network, or acting as a knowledgeable go-between facilitating such arrangements for others" because a person's origin is thought to influence the way he/she will act (1984:25).

9. Ginat's (1987) book *Blood Disputes among Bedouin and Rural Arabs in Israel* is a recent example.

10. Although Jordanian royal iconography owes a great deal to British symbols and rituals of monarchy (Jordan was, after all, part of the British Mandate, and King Hussein was schooled at Sandhurst), this is one of the important differences in the meanings associated with the monarchies of these two nations.

11. The great interest throughout the 1980s in Jordan's "national heritage" parallels similar interest throughout the Arab world. Al-Najjar (1991) correlates interest in popular culture in the Arab Gulf with the introduction of oil wealth: "Nationalists argued that [popular culture] had to be nurtured in order to repair the damage resulting from the tremendous material and cultural change that had affected Arab Gulf inhabitants." The Gulf states directed sizable resources to the study, preservation, and exhibition of popular culture and to the institutionalization of folklore as a field (al-Najjar 1991:182–83).

12. One would like to know whether this merging is taking place with regard to other groups or whether this is particularly prevalent among Jordan's tribal population. For example, are the Circassians and Sheeshans accentuating their shared cultural traditions or emphasizing their differences in folkloric contexts?

13. The construction of a national Jordanian culture has a number of parallels with the emergence of a national Indian cuisine described by Appadurai (1988). He describes the proliferation of cookbooks in the last two decades that reflect the twin processes of regional and ethnic specialization, on the one hand,

and the development of overarching, crosscutting national cuisines. These cookbooks are organized according to a set of structural devices that provide a framework which is filled with items from different regional or ethnic traditions. Just as these cookbooks cater to an urban middle-class audience, the use of Jordanian folk objects as decor in middle-class homes in Amman is part of the process of the construction of a complex public culture involving media and travel. During the last decade there has been a significant rise in the number of domestic tourists in Jordan (Jordan 1986:356). As mentioned above, the government plans "to develop and diversify traditional trades and handicraft industries as a means of increasing purchases by tourists as well as by the public" (Jordan 1986:358).

CHAPTER 8

Monarchal Posture

THROUGHOUT THIS BOOK I have explored the dialogic construction of tribal and national identities in Jordan. In this final chapter I focus on several structural similarities in the way that collective identity is conceived and constituted at the local and national level and argue that these similarities derive from similar approaches to space and time. In the following discussion I tack back and forth between local and national contexts, drawing analogies between practices I observed among tribespeople in the Jordan Valley and those of Jordan's King and compare these two Jordanian examples with Western models of nationalism. I want not only to highlight differences between the ways that nations are culturally constructed in different parts of the world, that is, across space, but also to acknowledge and explore how these cultural constructions have changed over time. I hope to show how in this postmodern era, Western views of space, at least with regard to the boundaries of social groups, are becoming a bit more like the Jordanians', while the Jordanians' conception of time and of social groups therein is becoming, in some ways, more like "modern" Western ones.

Despite a rich anthropological literature on kingship, Jordan's kings have not been the subject of anthropological inquiry.[1] Yet, as we noted in chapter 1, "the concept of 'Jordan'" is so closely linked with King Hussein some "find it difficult to conceive of Jordan without Hussein" (Jureidini and McLaurin 1984:68). Most treatments of Hussein have interpreted him as a Machiavellian prince, that is, in terms of a narrowly defined, universalistic set of criteria. A more cultural approach is needed to move beyond such Machiavellian interpretations to a point where we can appreciate what Clifford (1978) has referred to as the "plenitude" or "numerousness" of a person's life, even a king's. By understanding the way the self, in this case that of Jordan's King, is socially constituted in space and time, we will better understand how other social identities such as those of "tribesperson" or "Jordanian" are constructed and construed.

As discussed in chapter 1, King Hussein, although not originally from Jordan, is so closely linked with the country he has ruled for more than half of its exisitence, he serves as a key symbol of the Jordanian nation. To the extent to which he embodies cultural notions of history, tradi-

tion, and peoplehood shared by the people of Jordan he is also a metonym for the country. In this sense Hussein resembles more the Han-
overian monarchs than the Tudors in that though clearly "head of the
social pyramid," he differs "from his peers in degree, not in kind"
(Starkey 1977:217). As Clifford Geertz so nicely put it, it is such "a
deep, intimate involvement . . . in the master fictions by which [an]
order lives" that makes political leaders numinous (Geertz 1983:146).

Yet, it is perhaps this very numinousity that leads Benedict Anderson
to assert that "'serious' monarchy lies transverse to all modern conceptions of political life" (B. Anderson 1983:25).[2] Richard Rose and Dennis Kavenagh (1976) concur with Anderson's assessment of modern
monarchies, asserting that "the survival of a monarchy depends on the
readiness of the reigning family to withdraw from a politically active role
. . . and the repudiation of a monarchy results from the continuation or
adoption by the monarchy of an active political role . . ." (1976:567).[3]
Yet Hussein, one of the Middle East's longest-ruling monarchs, must
certainly be considered a serious king.[4] As Shinn describes it:

> The monarchy remains the most important institution in the country. The
> king appoints the prime minister, the president and members of the Senate,
> judges, and other senior government and military functionaries. He com-
> mands the armed forces, approves and promulgates laws, declares war, con-
> cludes peace, and signs treaties. . . . The king convenes, opens, adjourns,
> suspends, or dissolves the legislature; he also orders and may postpone the
> holding of elections. He has veto power that can only be overriden by a
> two-thirds vote of each house. . . . The king, as head of state, is immune
> from all liability. (Shinn 1980:160)

Analysis of such a king should throw into relief some of the taken-for-
granted assumptions underlying concepts like "nationality" and "modernity" while at the same time illuminating a culturally nuanced understanding of Jordanian statecraft.

THE SPACE OF "NATION"

In the last decade a number of anthropological analyses of nationalism
have appeared. Although differing in some respects concerning the
causes and conditions for the emergence of nations, these works tend to
be in agreement about the characteristics of national identity once nations emerged toward the end of the eighteenth century. This agreement
is not so surprising if one accepts Anderson's (1983:14) depiction of nationality, of nationness, as "modular." He asserts that modern nationalism is a cultural artifact that "once created, . . . became 'modular,' capable of being transplanted . . . to a great variety of social terrains . . . "

One of the ways in which nations differ from the forms of social organization and sovereignty that preceded them is the way they are imagined to exist in space. One of the most striking characteristics of nations is the rigidness and absoluteness with which their boundaries are conceived and constituted. Anderson contrasts nations with the two important cultural systems, the religious community and the dynastic realm, out of which and against which nations emerged. In the former forms of social organization, "the fundamental conceptions about social groups were centripetal and hierarchical" (B. Anderson 1983:22), and "states were defined by centres, borders were porous and indistinct, and sovereignties faded imperceptibly into one another" (B. Anderson 1983:26). In contrast, nations are "boundary-oriented and horizontal" (1983:22), "state sovereignty is fully, flatly, and evenly operative over each square centimetre of a legally demarcated territory" (B. Anderson 1983:26).

In a similar vein, Handler defines nationalism as "a variety of Western individualism, the dominant, encompassing ideology of modern societies. A living individual is one, precisely delineated with reference to a spatial and temporal environment. In other words, it is bounded in space, continuous in time, and homogeneous within those spatiotemporal boundaries" (Handler 1988:50).

This notion of space forms a marked contrast with that of the ʿAbbād tribespeople of the Jordan Valley. As we have seen, rather than utilizing an abstract, essentialist, homogeneous sense of space, the ʿAbbādis constitute space (and social identity) through movement: an active, personal, embodied, positioning and repositioning of the self vis-à-vis other social actors and the material world. In chapters 3 and 4 I described a number of aspects of ʿAbbādi posture: the way the ʿAbbādis arrange their bodies when sitting or reclining on a mattress, or when entering a tent or house; how they position themselves vis-à-vis other social actors by moving their residences and by rearranging themselves and their furniture within their houses. I argued that together these practices constitute posture in the third sense of the term, a state of being, and in chapter 5 I tried to show how such postures informed the ʿarabs' participation in national political processes.

Here I take the argument further as I show how the principles and practices examined above inform the monarchical posture as well. Like the nineteenth-century king of Morocco described by Geertz (1983), the Hashemites' rule of Jordan has been one "founded on motion." According to Wilson (1987:61), "Throughout his reign Abdullah lived a peripatetic existence. In the early years, before his palace was built in Amman, he lived in various places in the Balqaʿ," in the homes of local dignitaries or in his tents. Even after his palace was built, he engaged in a kind of transhumance, moving from Amman in the summer to South Shuna in the Jordan Valley in the winter (Wilson 1987:62).[5]

King Hussein also rules through movement. Like the nineteenth-century kings of Morocco, the current King regularly engages in royal progresses (*ziyāra shaᶜbiyya*) throughout country.[6] In 1983 Hussein visited every region of the country, touching base with various constituencies and displaying to the entire country, thanks to national television coverage, the measure of his realm. But whereas the nineteenth-century Moroccan kings accomplished sovereignty on such progresses by traveling with their armies and collecting tribute, Hussein travels with bureaucrats and dispenses the fruits of economic development.

His visit to the Jordan Valley began in the government-built, government-run central marketing center in the northern reaches of the Valley. The events of the day began with a ceremony and a lunch hosted by the King. The luncheon ceremony was attended by close to a thousand local notables—mostly tribal sheikhs and civil servants posted in the region. As we noted in chapter 7, the King is the ultimate Jordanian gift-giver.[7] In offering a meal in the Valley, he made the Valley his home and reenforced ties of debt with all those who accepted his hospitality. In addition, by organizing events of the day in this way, the sheikhs had to come to him before he went to them.

Although the ceremony did not begin until noon, sheikhs and their entourages arrived throughout the morning, positioning themselves in the rows of folding chairs as close to centerstage as possible. Despite the Western-style seating arrangement—rows of identical folding chairs arranged in regular rows facing the front—the local dignitaries arranged and rearranged themselves in these throughout the morning as other delegations arrived, much as they might have in the course of an evening of visiting in a tribesperson's tent or house. The group I was with was one of the first to arrive and during the course of the morning changed seats four times. While we waited, the army band played and pamphlets documenting the achievements the government had made in developing the Valley were distributed to the guests.

Finally the King arrived. The assembled crowd rose as he entered and did not resume their seats until after the King sat down in the centermost seat on the stage. Members of his cabinet, government officials, and foreign ambassadors representing the countries that had contributed to the development projects[8] took clearly prearranged seats on either side of him. The national anthem was played, and a blessing was offered. Then the King made a speech which not only included quotations from the holy Koran and from classical Arabic poetry but also contained facts and figures, a bureaucratic accounting of the government's accomplishments in the Valley over the previous decade: how many dunums of land brought under cultivation, how many schools and health clinics built, how many parcels of land redistributed.

When the ceremony was over, the King rose, his guests immediately following suit. He then descended from the stage and walked alone, at a deliberate pace, down the center aisle through the assembled crowd to the luncheon area at the rear of the hall. For any head of state to walk like this, unprotected by bodyguards, is surely a dramatic declaration of legitimacy. And given the number of times that there have been attempts on the King's life, it was also a public act of courage—one of the King's personal characteristics that is much admired by the tribespeople of Jordan. By adopting this posture, alone, and at the center of the assembled notables with no intervening presence, the King constituted himself literally and figuratively as close to these individuals. One of the sheikhs I was with who had strategically placed himself in an aisle seat managed to kiss the King as he passed by.

When the King finished traversing the room, a *mansaf* (an ʿarab specialty of rice and lamb), which has come to be known as Jordan's national dish, was served. The guests arranged themselves around the tables that had been set up at the rear of the hall. The meal was eaten standing up, about twelve to a table. It was a hasty affair, as most of those present needed to hurry back to their villages in order to be there to receive the King. This was not unseemly, though, for although *mansaf* is typically served in the course of an extended, slow-paced occasion, the meal itself is often consumed with dispatch.

After the lunch the King progressed by car from north to south, the entire length of the Valley. Whereas in the past, tribal rugs had been hung out for royal progresses, on this trip the route had been decorated with the Jordanian national flag. Local shop owners had done a brisk business for several days prior to the royal visit selling film, banners, and flags (large flags sold for JD 1.500, smaller ones for JD. 800) to local inhabitants. Village councils, private corporations, and the local offices of some federal agencies had had banners made that welcomed the King on their behalf. Their messages were prominently displayed on scaffoldings decorated with oleander branches under which the royal motorcade passed.

The King stopped along the way in each village to greet people, receive petitions, unveil monuments commemorating various development projects, and to hand out the remaining property deeds of the land-redistribution program. At each stop he was welcomed by village dignitaries, ushered into a black goat-hair tent, and offered the bitter coffee that is the traditional sign of tribal hospitality. Crowds of younger men, women, and children pressed forward hoping to see and be seen by the King.

Whereas at the invitation-only lunch the King had walked with no obstructions between himself and his subjects, at these village stops he was buffered from the crowd by members of his entourage and representatives of the local welcoming committees. Nevertheless, at least at the stop at which I was present, the King made a show of overcoming this human barrier (as if it were not his wish that it be there) in order to reach his people. Scenes like these are familiar to American television viewers who have seen American presidents on campaign tours (and the visiting Gorbachev) reach across policemen to shake hands and kiss babies. But the Jordanian case differs in one crucial respect: when the King reached beyond his guards to the crowd, more often than not it was to accept a petition that was being held out toward him. Although touching is certainly an important element of such moments in Jordan, the preponderant feature of these interactions is the act of asking (or, as importantly, having the opportunity to ask but not asking).

There is a widespread belief in Jordan, at all levels of society, that the King cannot and will not refuse a request. Much of palace protocol is designed to preserve this myth by protecting the King from overly onerous requests. Petitions from those who have no other route of access (and are therefore by definition in some sense "poor," *miskīn*) are accepted daily at the street-level office of Bassman palace, and it is my understanding that such requests are as a rule fulfilled. The myth of noblesse oblige is so powerful, if a request was not fulfilled, the supplicant would probably assume that the petition had not been delivered to the King.

Occasions such as the progress through the Valley that bring people face-to-face with the King are therefore especially important as they present a valuable opportunity to make a request directly.[9] But such moments are also important because they afford the chance of making a public display of one's honor by *not* making use of such an opportunity. During my stay in Jordan I repeatedly heard apocryphal tales of persons to whom the King was, in one way or another, indebted (for example, of people who had been hurt in an automobile accident involving a member of the royal family). The stories invariably told of people who, having been invited to make a request of the King in recompense for some wrong, requested simply a photograph of him. Such individuals, like those who were near enough to the King during his visit to the Valley to make a request but instead simply kissed his hand, construct themselves as honorable in a number of ways through this act. First, in behaving in this manner they present themselves as people who do not need anything, that is, who are not dependent on others. Such acts also construct them as loyal subjects, people to whom a royal picture or a kiss means more than any pecuniary reward.

Although the royal visit afforded tribespeople the opportunity to refrain publicly from making a request of the King, by stressing the development projects on this trip, the King in a sense created debtors of all, even of those who did not make personal requests. This is reminiscent of a sheikh in the Valley who had refused to let the government bring electricity to his village or to construct a public school there during his lifetime. Young people of his tribe explained to me that in following this course the sheikh was attempting both to preserve his hold over the members of his tribe and to preserve his independence from the King.[10]

In other words, both the King and the tribespeople of the Jordan Valley utilized the royal visit to construct themselves, dialogically, together. Through such progresses the King reterritorializes his reign by revitalizing his interpersonal links with his subjects. By moving across the landscape, positioning himself vis-à-vis his subjects (at the top of the social hierarchy and at the same time near his people), he articulates the same political philosophy as that expressed through the household practices of the tribespeople he came to visit. Because spaces, whether domestic or national, are defined by people and not by places, they are not permanent or fixed. It is the social action of individuals that makes both house and homeland. The King, and the ʿAbbādi tribespeople, endow the world with a particularly aleatory quality, always keeping clearly before themselves the possibility of reordering and reconstituting their social world (cf. Schumacher 1989). In this way, contemporary Jordan resembles traditional Morocco, where, according to Geertz, "the continuity of the social order lay less in any durability of the arrangements composing it or the groups embodying it, . . . than in the constancy of the processes by which, incessantly reworking those arrangements and redefining those groups, it formed, reformed, and re-reformed itself" (Geertz 1973b:246).

I do not mean to imply that the place itself is not important. The traces of social action mark the land. In the Jordan Valley, for example, one finds the tomb of Abu Obeida, a companion of the Prophet, as well as a monument in memory of those who died defending the village of Karama from an Israeli attack. Furthermore, one of the three main sources of Hashemite legitimacy is their historical role as defenders of Islamic holy places. The King reminded everyone of this role in his speech announcing his plans to relinquish sovereignty over the West Bank: "It has been our belief, since the Israeli aggression of June 1967, that our first priority should be to liberate the land and holy places from Israeli occupation. Accordingly, as is well known, we have concentrated all our efforts during the twenty-one years since the occupation toward this goal" (*Jordan Times*, 1 Aug. 1988). King Hussein also highlighted this dimension of Hashemite kingship while inaugurating the King Abdullah Mosque, noting that "the late King Abdullah has fought hard in defence of the Arab homeland and fell as a martyr while defending the Arab and Islamic nations' rights in the Holy City of Jerusalem where he is buried alongside his father, Sharif Hussein Ibn Ali near the Aqsa Mosque" (*Jordan Times*, 6 Apr. 1989:1). Nevertheless, this conception of space/place differs from that normally associated with nationalism.[11] Perhaps this conceptualization of sacred and other spaces might be accurately portrayed in the terms Dale F. Eickelman used to describe Moroccan tribal timekeeping "as discontinuous islands, meaningful primarily as landmarks of concrete experience. . . . They mark but do not measure . . ." (Eickelman 1977:43).

Progresses are not the only way that this political cosmology is manifest. I first became cognizant of this aspect of Jordanian statecraft in the course of attempting a cultural analysis of Jordan's 1988 disengagement from the West Bank (Layne 1990a). At first I interpreted Hussein's decision to relinquish claims to the West Bank as an effort to produce a Jordanian nation that conformed more closely to the outlines of a modern, Western nation-state, "an irreducible, homogeneous unit, securely in control of its borders, self-contained, autonomous, and complete, asserting itself against a world of similar entities" (Handler 1988:194). As I mentioned in chapter 1, my initial prediction following the disengagement that, given the Jordanian government's efforts to clarify the boundaries of its collective Self as distinct from a Palestinian Other, the tribal dimension of Jordanian national identity would be accentuated proved to incorrect.[12] As we saw, no sooner had the King clarified the ambiguity concerning the extent of his sovereignty vis-à-vis the West Bank, than he reintroduced a measure of ambiguity by publicly reaffirming his commitment to the ideals of Arab nationalism. Rather than welcoming the clarification of limits of the Jordanian nation-state, the King took immediate steps to compensate for this new level of clarity by accentuating the tentativeness of his borders (and those of his neighbors) when seen in the light of Arab nationalism.

Throughout this book we have focused on the ways Jordanian tribespeople and the King construct the spaces and boundaries of their homes and their homeland. Many of the space- and identity-making practices we have examined produce spaces (and identities) that bear a striking resemblance to "the fluid, irregular shapes of [postmodern] landscapes, shapes which characterize international capital" and are complementary to the postmodern or poststructuralist view that sees cultural forms as "fundamentally fractal, that is as possessing no Euclidean boundaries" (Appadurai 1990:7, 20).

MODERN TIMES AND ROYAL PROGRESS

If the Jordanians' approach to space (whether household or national) bears certain resemblances to those that we now associate with postmodernism, their approach to time is, at least in some contexts, strikingly modern. This modern view of time, characterized by B. Anderson as "'homogenous, empty time,' . . . measured by clock and calendar" (B. Anderson 1983:30) replaced a medieval conception of time as "a simultaneity of past and future in an instantaneous present" (B. Anderson 1983:30). Fredric Jameson describes this alteration as "the bourgeois cultural revolution" which brought about the transition from feudalism and the ancien régime to industrial capitalism and contemporary science, creating in place of "a whole world of qualities . . . the grey world of quantity and extension, of the purely measurable—together with the substitution of the older forms of ritual, sacred or cyclical time by the new physical and measurable temporality of the clock and the routine, of the working day" (Jameson 1985:374). This transformation from premodern to modern temporality brought with it a new sense of history, a linear one in which the past is "cumulative and forever growing" (as opposed to an ahistoric past that "remain[s] constant in size") (Eickelman 1977:50). This understanding of history complemented the idea of territorial nationalism.[13] According to B. Anderson, "the idea of a sociological organism moving calendrically through homogenous, empty time is a precise analogue of the idea of the nation, which also is conceived as a solid community moving steadily down (or up) history" (B. Anderson 1983:31).

Now this portrayal of the transition from premodern to modern times, although cast in universalistic terms, is based on Western (mostly European) history. We know surprisingly little about Arab temporal categories, how these are related to social structure, and how they may have changed over time. In one of the only anthropological accounts of time reckoning in the Arab world,[14] Eickelman documents several different modes employed simultaneously, although differentially. Townspeople and leaders tended to think of time more frequently in terms similar to those outlined above, whereas most of the Bni Battu tribespeople employed a system of temporal concepts that were "nonabstract and tied closely to other aspects of local society" in most areas of their lives (1977:41). Neither the succession of the seasons, recurrent social events such as the cycle of weekly markets, the obligatory five daily prayers, nor the Julian solar calendar nor the Muslim lunar calendar were "used to provide measured intervals of duration" (1977:45). Although "calendar time and clock time are known by tribesmen to be important in some contexts, . . . the remembrance of things past depends only marginally upon measured, linear patterns of time-reckoning" (1977:45). Instead, the Bni Battu "conceive events temporally in terms of sequences of ir-regular, island-like concrete experiences" (1977:46).

We have no comparable account of time reckoning in Jordan, but during the period of my research (1980–82, 1984), it was clear that the language of social evolution and modernization theory had been adopted by a large proportion of Jordan's highly educated population and informed animated discussions about what kind of a country Jordan was and how it ought to be (see chapter 5). Critics who condemned tribalism as a retrogressive barrier to development, those who championed it as the rich source of Jordan's national heritage, and Jordanian tribespeople who in response (to the denigration of tribal culture by its critics and the appropriation of tribal culture by the state) began reconceiving and reevaluating their culture each articulated their views in the terms of the modern Western metanarrative of history and progress (Layne 1990b).[15]

The Hashemites, too, are now telling their history in these terms.[16] In Hussein's forword to the supplement of his grandfather's memoirs (*al-Takmilah*) published in 1978, he describes his grandfather King Abdullah. This is a fascinating document in that it can be read as a self-portrait of Hussein himself. I focus here, however, only on those passages that place Abdullah in history and in so doing portray a particular view of history. I quote at length:

> As a son of the Hijaz and of the Arabian Peninsula, he was to a degree a traditionalist, deeply imbued with the morals, mores and values of Arab society, in their unadulterated form. But he was equally a product of the modern world, having obtained his higher education and later, having lived and served in Istanbul as elected deputy of Mecca in the Ottoman Mabuthan (parliament). . . .
>
> King Abdallah's character and experience constituted a unique admixture and a confluence of the two streams, the traditionalist and the modern. In his private life, he was devoutly attached to his early traditionalist upbringing, with its stable norms, its poetry, its simplicity and its genuineness. His nostalgia for that form of life was never diluted or undermined by his extensive encounters with the intricacies and the fundamental forces of modern civilization. My hunch is that he would have preferred the former, at least emotionally. But my grandfather was too shrewd, too farsighted and pragmatic a man not to perceive that the old ways, in a forbidding, ever-changing, and shrinking world, were a thing of the past, which could no longer be sustained and were doomed to an irretrievable fading away.

Hence, his public career, whether in statecraft, war or diplomacy, was predominantly forward-looking, open and modern. In a world where only the
fittest survive, a continual surging forward was the only avenue to survival.
(Hussein Ibn Talal 1978:v–vi)

This text does more than simply adopt a Western view of development where only the fittest nations and kings survive;[17] it positions the
Hashemites pivotally in a way that makes them uniquely capable of
bridging the past and the future. In this they are transcendent figures. But perhaps *transcendent* is the wrong word; for neither Hussein
nor Abdullah are outside or above the dual opposition traditional/
modern but rather are, or at least seek to be, active mediators of these
categories.

I see two possible interpretations of Hussein's self-positioning in history. The first sees Hussein as casting himself (and his predecessors) as
agents of change. Unlike the African kings studied by A. I. Richards
(1960, 1968), King Hussein is not normally considered to be divine.
His "health, sickness, anger, sorrow, . . . dreams, misdemeanors" are
not thought to affect his territory and yet, in a sense, as chief engineer
of economic development he may be thought of as possessing "animating powers" (Richards 1968:26, 29).[18] The power to change the landscape dramatically, to make the Valley bloom, to transform Jordan into
a modern country: such were the powers that were being displayed during the King's visit to the Jordan Valley in 1983. This interpretation
which sees Hussein constructing himself as transformer of the "traditional" to the "modern" leaves intact the assumptions underlying Western versions of "history" and "progress."

My second interpretation is derived from another source of royal symbolism, Jordanian currency. Like the Queen of England, the King has
his portrait on each of the Jordanian bills and coins. But whereas the
Queen's image is stable and static, the King's image is a kind of trompe
l'oeil. On the front of each bill he is pictured on the left-hand side
dressed in a suit and tie, the modern, forward-looking pragmatic per-
sona, one who is fluent in Western ways. But if one holds the bill up to
the light, the King dressed in a checkered *kufiyya*, the traditional tribal
head scarf, emerges from the watermark on the right-hand side.[19] The
traditionalist, bearer of noble heritage and authenticity, faces his alter
ego.[20] What one sees depends on how one holds the bill. In other words,
we have returned again to the realm of posture. The shape and meaning
of the King, or of his image on a bill, like the shape and meaning of
Jordan itself depend very much on how one is positioned vis-à-vis the
King, a dinar bill, or the country.

In other words, the employment by Hussein and the people of Jordan

FIG. 8 A Jordanian dinar bill

of a classically modernist linear narrative to describe King and country may mark an important shift in the way that Jordanians are constructing themselves. This shift, however, may not be as straightforward as it might first appear. Rather than stabilizing the dynamic dimensions of their identity-making practices, they may in fact be destabilizing, agitating, challenging the certainties, the all-or-nothingness, of an essentially essentializing discourse.

CONSTRUCTING COLLECTIVITY IN POSTMODERN JORDAN

The preceding discussion has illuminated a number of important differences between the ways Jordanians and Westerners conceive and constitute "nation." One such difference regards the relationship between local- and state-level modes of constituting collectivities. According to Herzfeld (1986), in Greece (as in other European nation-states) state ideologies are characterized by an absolutist logic that is in striking contrast to the theoretical underpinnings of popular discourse: "Even in the most centralized nation-states . . . it seems that everyday usage continues to reflect the relativism of ordinary discourse rather than the absolutism of the state . . . [This] suggests that people continue to use a theory of meaning that conflicts with the lexicographical rigidity endorsed by the state" (Herzfeld 1986:82). In contrast, the Jordanian example explored here illustrates a fundamental complementarity between the way the people of Jordan and their King construct themselves and their nation.

The importance of the King in Jordanian affairs of state perhaps accounts for the complementarity of local- and state-level modes. But, of course, the King is not the sum total of Jordanian government. The kingdom has a well-developed bureaucracy, reputed to be "one of the most functional and least corrupt in the Arab world" (quoted in Shinn 1980:163). In the early 1980s the civil service consisted of twenty-two separate ministries, which in turn were organized into a variety of departments. Together the civil and military services employed almost half of the total employed and represented nearly 60 percent of nonfarm employment (Eglin 1980:111–12). Nevertheless, there is no reason to assume that Jordanian civil servants conceptualize space and time in ways identical to their bureaucratic counterparts in the West. Indeed, the subject of Jordanian bureaucratic culture is a fascinating but, as far as I know, as-yet unexplored topic of research.

One tantalizing glimpse of the possible findings of such a study comes from Jordan's Department of Libraries, Documentation and National Archives (DLFNA). This department was established in the late 1970s in the Ministry of Culture. Its first director, His Excellency Dr. Ahmad Sharkas, instituted as one of the department's programs a reading tent. Sharkas had earned an M.A. in library science at a State University of New York campus before completing a Ph.D. in Islamic Intellectual History at Harvard. His idea of the reading tent was consciously modeled on the American bookmobiles that he had become acquainted with while in the United States. The reading tents were a success and fulfilled many of the same objectives of the bookmobiles on which they were modeled. The tents were popular among the populous and no doubt encouraged reading in rural areas, but the reading tents differed from their American prototypes in one important respect: the tents were immobile! A tent was set up at the beginning of the summer in a selected community and remained there for the duration of the summer. The following summer, another community would be selected.

Another important set of differences between Western and Jordanian approaches to "nation" derives from different constructions of space and time and the related construction of nature. Herzfeld has described what he calls the paradox of nationalism whereby "the 'nation'. . . , that most cultural of entities, ultimately derives its legitimacy from its foundation in 'nature'" (1986:76).[21] According to Herzfeld, "the unity of the state . . . generates unitary definitions. Since they are unitary they are also absolute; and, being absolute, they acquire the culturally attributed characteristics of the natural" (Herzfeld 1986:90). But nature, too, is a cultural construct, endowed in different places and times with quite different characteristics and qualities (Merchant 1980; Haraway 1991). The correlation of nature with absolutism is surely as European and as "modern" as the ideologies of nation-states that they have come to be associated with.

This raises a number of interesting questions: Is the notion of nation always, by definition, associated with nature? Is the Jordanian conception of nation so associated and if so what in the Jordanian worldview does nature represent? Based on the material presented here, one must posit a more dynamic and relational view of nature. In recent years, as Western "natural" scientists are "discovering" a much less absolute nature, one that has less to do with masses and laws than with relationships, tendencies, and movement (Capra 1982; Beyerchen 1989), postmodern social scientists are conceptualizing collectivities in space and time in more free-floating, less rigidly defined terms and in so doing are moving closer to a Jordan-styled construction of the world. That these three spheres of knowledge are becoming related in this way is perhaps not coincidental. A primary impetus for rethinking anthropological approaches comes in large part from the failure of our conceptual frameworks to make sense of (some would say to contain) the cultural economy of the current global system. Social constructivists of science might make similar claims about the emergence of new approaches in the natural sciences.

Despite these provocative similarities a word of caution is due, for this similitude is by no means complete. For one thing, some of the dimensions of postmoderism that resonate with the Jordanian case are also characteristics of the premodern world (e.g., the porousness of borders). Furthermore, there are many aspects of postmodernism, such as the depthlessness described by Jameson (1984a) that do not apply to the Jordanian social world. And just as Western social scientific models of collectivities in space are becoming more dynamic, King Hussein and the people of Jordan are adopting classically "modern" Western narrative devices to describe their history (albeit transforming and reworking these narratives in the process).

The Jordanian example provides a useful sounding board through comparison with which the particularities of Western notions of nation-state become more apparent. The fluid, embodied, aleatory manner in which the ʿAbbād ʿarabs of the Jordan Valley constitute themselves through movement as ʿarabs and as Jordanians and the like manner in which the King constitutes his realm illuminate some central features of Jordanian national politics. In addition, these Jordanian identity-making practices may also prove illustrative of more adequate anthropological approaches and models with which to proceed in these postmodern times.

NOTES

1. There are no studies of Jordanian kingship or political culture comparable to the many fine analyses of Morocco's monarchy (Waterbury 1970, Geertz 1983 [1977], Leveau 1985, Combs-Schilling 1989).

2. I assume B. Anderson (1983) means to distinguish serious monarchies from constitutional ones like that of Britain. Anderson places the demise of dynastic systems during the seventeenth century but notes that "as late as 1914, dynastic states made up the majority of the membership of the world political system." In 1966, according to Huntington about "15 of the world's 120 sovereign entities [were] ruling or oligarchical monarchies" (Huntington 1966:765), and Huntington believed that "the future of the existing traditional monarchies [was] bleak" (1966:785). Despite these predictions, monarchy remains one of the most important forms of rule in the Arab world. As L. Anderson has noted, monarchs "rule more than a third of the countries of the Arab League. Taken together, the kings in Morocco, Saudi Arabia, Jordan, the sultan of Oman, and the amirs of the smaller Gulf states—Kuwait, Bahrain, Qatar, and the United Arab Emirates—have almost forty million subjects" (L. Anderson 1991a:1).

3. Hayden (1987), on the other hand, argues that the powerlessness of the Bristish queen is a myth, albeit a myth on which the continuity of the monarchy depends.

4. Indeed, all the monarchs of the region must qualify as "serious." L. Anderson (1991a:3) argues that the prevalence of this type of regime can be accounted for by "an affinity between monarchy as a regime type and the projects of nation building and state formation."

5. The current King owns a number of houses in Amman, but his movement between them has less to do with ruling than it does with domestic matters (Day 1986:7). His visits to his home/s abroad may be closer to the mobility of his grandfather's with respect to governing.

6. Of course, in addition to such movement within the country, like any head of state, King Hussein exchanges visits with allies on a regular basis.

7. On this trip to the Valley he refused to accept the gift of a camel because of the obligation it would put him under to offer amnesty to a certain individual (Layne 1986:117–18).

8. The ambassadors in attendance were those of the USA, West Germany, and Korea. The USA and West Germany had funded most of the projects, and Korean firms had won the contracts for most of the construction projects.

9. However, the King immediately—that is, in full view of the petitioners—passed the written requests to an associate. Thus, presumably, the same rationale could be used to explain a unfulfilled request.

10. The rationale that he gave the King, apparently, was that the money should be spent to free Jerusalem instead.

11. In a rather elusive passage, K. L. Brown (1976:204–5) suggests that an idea of "territorial nationalism" was not successful in mobilizing support in

Morocco for a protest movement against French colonial occupation. Instead the "values and emblems of Islam" were more effective.

12. Perhaps the tribal segment of the Jordanian population expected the same. It is striking that the April price riots were concentrated in southern Jordan, a particularly tribal area and traditional bastion of support for the regime. Reports indicate that following the King's announcement of the disengagement, East Bank Palestinians and Jordanians took refuge in a certain level of chauvinism (*New York Times*, 18 Oct. 1988). As far as I know, the King refrained from making public Jordanian chauvinistic remarks. However, upon the King's return from the United States following the riots, the first press-release photos of him to appear showed him wearing a *kufiyya*.

13. See Boyarin (1990b:1, 2) for a discussion of the way that the Enlightenment belief that modernity is the "progressive unfolding of Reason" and "the nationalist belief that individual identity is properly realized in wholehearted participation in the territorially-defined nation-state" were linked in Hegel's philosophy of history and in Zionism.

14. In D. Eickelman's (1989) extensive survey of anthropological studies of the Middle East, he lists only this article and an excerpt from his *Moroccan Islam* as dealing with Middle Eastern notions of time. (He does mention the work of Michael Marcus (1986) on cultural conceptions of history.)

15. In contrast, postmodernism has been characterized by "a dissolution of linear narrative" (Jameson 1984b:54) and its replacement with an "open, fragmented story line" (Traube quoted in Moffat 1990:367).

16. For a comparison with contemporary history-making practices in other Middle Eastern countries see L. Anderson (1991b) and Dessouki (1991) on historiography in Libya and the Arab Gulf.

17. This text also reproduces several other dichotomies often associated with modernism: private and public, emotional and rational.

18. As an anonymous reviewer pointed out, Hussein's animating powers are similar to those of American presidents as evidenced, for example, in the behavior of the American stock market in response to the report of President Bush's thyroid condition.

19. The profile of the King also appears on each coin—the 10, 25, 50, and 100 fils pieces. As the relief stops at his neck, it is difficult to be certain what he is wearing; but he is bareheaded (without *kufiyya*), and on the ten fils coins it looks as though he may be wearing a tie and dress-shirt collar.

A scene of Jordan appears on the back of each bill. The Dome of the Rock in Jerusalem is on the back of the one-dinar bill, which is green, the color of Islam; the rose red city of Petra is on the red five-JD bill, the sandy-colored Roman ruins of Jerash on the brown half-dinar bill; and the Palace of Culture in Amman is juxtaposed (actually positioned over) with the Roman amphitheater in Amman on the ten-JD bill.

Whereas the Queen of England represents continuity, the image of a famous personage, like Sir Issac Newton on the one-pound note, has the same transformative effect as that of Hussein, appearing both on the back of the British bills and in the watermarks.

An interesting comparison might be made with the two-sidedness of the British royal seal on which an image "of the king enthroned in majesty, full-face, and equipped with the emblems of royalty" appears on one side, and "on the other, an image of the king armed and on horseback . . . [portraying] the king as judge [and the king] as warrior-defender of his people" (Starkey 1977:189).

20. The king frequently combines these two sartorial traditions and wears a *kufiyya* with a Western suit.

21. Even for the Romantic nationalists of the early nineteenth century for whom nationhood was conceived of as "explicitly *cultural*," the "claims to the eternal validity" of nationhood, according to Herzfeld, "rested on the authority of a culturalized *nature*" (1986:77).

References

Abou-Zeid, Ahmed
  1966 "Honour and Shame among the Bedouins of Egypt." In *Honour and Shame: The Values of Mediterranean Society*, edited by J.G. Peristiany, 243–59. Chicago: University of Chicago Press.
Abu Hassan, Mohammad
  1984 "Bedouin in Jordan: Study in Terminology and Legal Anthropology." Delivered at the Symposium on Anthropology in Jordan: State of the Art, Amman.
Abu Jaber, Kamel S.
  1969 "The Legislature of the Hashemite Kingdom of Jordan: A Study in Political Development." *The Muslim World* 59(1):220–50.
  1980 *The Jordanians and the People of Jordan*. Amman: Royal Scientific Society Press.
Abu Jaber, Kamel S., and Fawzi A. Gharaibeh
  1981 "Bedouin Settlement, Organizational, Legal, and Administrative Structure in Jordan." In *The Future of Pastoral Peoples: Proceedings of a Conference Held in Nairobi Kenya, 4–8 August 1980*, edited by John G. Galaty, Dan Aronson, Philip Carl Salzman, and Amy Chouinard, 294–302.
Abu Jaber, K., F. Gharaideh, S. Khawasmeh, and A. Hill
  1978 *Bedouin of Jordan: A People in Transition*. Amman: Royal Scientific Society Press.
Abu-Lughod, Lila
  1986 *Veiled Sentiments: Honor and Poetry in a Bedouin Society*. Berkeley: University of California Press.
  1989 "Zones of Theory in the Anthropology of the Arab World." *Annual Reveiw of Anthropology* 18:267–306.
Abu Shaikha, Ahmad
  1971 *Land Tenure in Jordan: A Case Study of the Bani-Hasan Area*. M.S. thesis, American University of Beirut.
al-Najjar, Muhammad Rajab
  1991 "Contemporary Trends in the Study of Folklore in the Arab Gulf States." In *Statecraft in the Middle East: Oil, Historical Memory, and Popular Culture*, edited by Eric Davis and Nicolas Gavrielides, 176–201. Miami: Florida International University Press.
Al-Tall, Ahmed
  1979 *Education in Jordan: Being a Survey of the Political, Economic and Social Conditions Affecting the Development of the System of Education in Jordan 1921–1977*. Islamabad: National Book Foundation.
Altorki, Soraya, and Donald P. Cole
  1989 *Arabian Oasis City: The Transformation of 'Unayzah*. Austin: University of Texas Press.

Anderson, Benedict
  1983 *Imagined Communities: Reflections on the Origin and Spread of Nationalism.* London: Verso.
Anderson, Jon
  1982 "Social Structure and the Veil: Comportment and the Composition of Interaction in Afghanistan." *Anthropos* 77:397–420.
Anderson, Lisa
  1991a "Absolutism and the Resilience of Monarchy in the Middle East." *Political Science Quarterly* 106(1):1–15.
  1991b "Legitimacy, Identity, and the Writing of History in Libya." In *Statecraft in the Middle East: Oil, Historical Memory, and Popular Culture,* edited by Eric Davis and Nicolas Gavrielides, 71–91. Miami: Florida International University Press.
Andoni, Lamis
  1988 "Hussein Throws Out a Multiple Challenge." *Middle East International* 331:3–4.
  1992 "Jordan and Saudi Arabia: Tussle over Jerusalem." *Middle East International* 29 (May):10–11.
Antoun, Richard T.
  1972 *Arab Village: A Social Structural Study of a Transjordanian Peasant Village.* Bloomington: Indiana University Press.
  1979 *Low-Key Politics: Local-Level Leadership and Change in the Middle East.* Albany: State University of New York Press.
Appadurai, Arjun
  1986 "Introduction: Commodities and the Politics of Value." In *The Social Life of Things,* edited by Appadurai, 3–63. Cambridge: Cambridge University Press.
  1988 "How to Make a National Cuisine: Cookbooks in Contemporary India." *Comparative Studies in Society and History* 30(1):3–24.
  1990 "Disjuncture and Difference in the Global Cultural Economy." *Public Culture* 2(2):1–24.
Apter, David E., and James S. Coleman
  1962 *Pan-Africanism Reconsidered.* American Society of Pan-African Culture, Berkeley: University of California Press.
Aramco World
  1983 "The Greening of the Arab East." *Aramco World Magazine* 34(5): 1–40.
Axelrod, Lawrence
  1978 "Tribesmen in Uniform: The Demise of the Fidaiyyun in Jordan, 1970–71." *The Muslim World* 68(1): 25–45.
Azoy, Whitney G.
  1982 *Buzkashi: Game and Power in Afghanistan.* Philadelphia: University of Pennsylvania Press.
Bailey, Clinton
  1984 *Jordan's Palestinian Challenge 1948–1983: A Political History.* Boulder: Westview Press.
Bakhtin, M. M.
  1981 "Discourse in the Novel." In *The Dialogic Imagination: Four Essays by*

M. M. Bakhtin, edited by Michael Holquist, 259–423. Austin: University of Texas Press.

Barth, Fredrik
1961   *Nomads of South Persia: The Basseri Tribe of the Khamseh Confederacy.* Boston: Little, Brown.

Basson, Priscilla, and Naji Abuirmeileh
1980   "Food Conservation in North-West Jordan." United Nations, Food and Agriculture Organization Report.

Beck, Lois
1986   *The Qashqa'i of Iran.* New Haven: Yale University Press.
1992   "Qashqa'i Nomads and the Islamic Republic." *Middle East Report* 177:37–41.

Beechey, Veronica
1978   "Women and Production: a Critical Analysis of Some Sociological Theories of Women's Work." In *Feminism and Materialism: Women and Modes of Production*, edited by Annette Kuhn and AnnMarie Wolpe, 155–98. London: Routledge and Kegan Paul.

Beidelman, T. O.
1989   "Agonistic Exchange: Homeric Reciprocity and the Heritage of Simmel and Mauss." *Cultural Anthropology* 4(3):227–59.

Beyerchen, Alan D.
1989   "Nonlinear Science and the Unfolding of a New Intellectual Vision." *Papers in Comarative Studies* 6:25–49. Center for Comparative Studies in the Humanities, Ohio State University.

Bocco, Riccardo
1984   "The Bedouin of Jordan: A People Without History?" Paper given at the Symposium on Anthropology in Jordan: State of the Art: Amman.
1985   "La Notion de Dirah chez les Tribus Bédouines en Jordanie: Le Cas des Bani Sakhr." *Terroirs et sociétés* collection etudes sur le monde Arabe, edited by B. Cannon (2):193–214. Lyon: Presses Universitaires de Lyon, Maison de l'Orient.
1986   "Petite Villes et citadinite en Jordanie: Quelque Pistes de réflexion sur l'urbanisation en zone pastorale." In *Petites Villes et villes moyennes dans le monde Arabe*, edited by P. Signoles, 167–83. Tours: URBAMA.
1989a "Espaces étatiques et espaces tribaux dans le Sud jordanien: Législation foncière et redéfinition des liens sociaux." *Magreb/Mashrek* 123:144–62.
1989b "L'Etat producteur d'identites locales: lois electorales et tribus bédouines en Jordanie." Actes de la Table-Ronde "Le Nomade, L'Oasis et la Ville" Tenue a Tours. Fascicule de Recherches n2. Centre d'Etudes et de Recherches Urbanisation du Monde Arabe.

Bommes, Michael, and Patrick Wright
1982   "'Charms of Residence': the public and the past." In *Making Histories: Studies in History-Writing and Politics*, edited by Richard Johnson et al., 253–302. Minneapolis: University of Minnesota Press.

Bourdieu, Pierre
1977   *Outline of a Theory of Practice.* Cambridge: Cambridge University Press.
1984   *Distinction: A Social Critique of the Judgment of Taste.* Cambridge, Mass.: Harvard University Press.

Boyarin, Jonathan
1990a   "Palestine and Jewish History." *The Working Paper Series,* no. 92. New York: Center for Studies of Social Change, New School for Social Research.
1990b   "Hegel's Zionism?" *The Working Paper Series,* no. 95. New York: Center for Studies of Social Change, New School for Social Research.

Brand, Lauri
1988   *Palestinians in the Arab World: Institution Building and the Search for State.* New York: Columbia University Press.

Brown, Kenneth L.
1976   *People of Sale: Tradition and Change in a Moroccan City 1830–1930.* Cambridge, Mass: Harvard University Press.

Brown, L. Dean
1982   *The Land of Palestine: West Bank Not East Bank.* Middle East Institute Problem Paper, no. 23.

Burckhardt, John Lewis
1822   *Travels in Syria and the Holy Land.* London: John Murray.

Capra, Fritjof
1982   *The Turning Point: Science, Society, and the Rising Culture.* Toronto: Bantam Books.

Caton, Steven C.
1986   "Salam Tahiyah: Greetings from the Highlands of Yemen" *American Ethnologist* 12(2):290–308.
1990   *"Peaks of Yemen I Summon": Poetry as Cultural Practice in a North Yemeni Tribe.* Berkeley: University of California Press.

Centlivres-Demont, Micheline
1982   "Espace construit, espace social, espace symbolique: Esquisse d'une maison du Nord Afghan" *Afghanistan Journal* 9(4):137–40.

Chatty, Dawn
1980   "The Pastoral Family and the Truck." In *When Nomads Settle: Processes of Sedentarization as Adaptation and Response,* edited by Philip Carl Salzman, 80–93. New York: Praeger.
1986   *From Camel to Truck: The Bedouin in the Modern World.* New York: Vangage Press.

Clifford, James
1978   "'Hanging Up Looking Glasses at Odd Corners': Ethnobiographical Prospects" In *Studies in Biography,* edited by Daniel Aaron, 41–56. Cambridge: Harvard University Press.
1988   "Identity in Mashpee." In *The Predicament of Culture: Twentieth-Century Ethnography, Literature, and Art,* 277–346. Cambridge: Harvard University Press.

Cole, Donald Powell
  1975 *Nomads of the Nomads: The Al Murrah Bedouin of the Empty Quarter.* Chicago: Aldine Publishing Company.
Combs-Schilling, M. E.
  1989 *Sacred Performances: Islam, Sexuality and Sacrifice.* New York: Columbia University Press.
Conder, Claude Reignier
  1892 *Heth and Moab: Explorations in Syria in 1881 and 1882.* London: Alexander P. Watt.
Coon, Carleton S.
  1951 *Caravan: The Story of the Middle East.* New York: Holt, Rinehart and Winston.
Dajani, Jarir S., Jared Hazleton, Richard Rhoda, and David Sharry
  1980 *An Interim Evaluation of the Jordan Valley Development Effort: 1973–1980.* U.S. Agency for International Development.
Dann, Uriel
  1984 *Studies in the History of Transjordan, 1920–1949: The Making of a State.* Boulder: Westview Press.
Davis, Eric
  1991 Theorizing Statecraft and Social Change in Arab Oil-Producing Countries. In *Statecraft in the Middle East: Oil, Historical Memory, and Popular Culture*, edited by Davis and Nicolas Gavrielides, 1–35. Miami: Florida International University Press.
Davis, Eric, and Nicolas Gavrielides
  1991 "Statecraft, Historical Memory and Popular Culture in Iraq and Kuwait." In *Statecraft in the Middle East: Oil, Historical Memory, and Popular Culture*, edited by Davis and Gavrielides, 116–48. Miami: Florida International University Press.
Davis, John
  1987 *Libyan Politics: Tribe and Revolution.* Berkeley: University of California Press.
Day, Arthur R.
  1986 *East Bank/West Bank: Jordan and the Prospects for Peace.* New York: Council on Foreign Relations.
de Bretteville, Sheila Levrant
  1979 "The 'Parlorization' of Our Homes and Ourselves." *Chrysalis* 9:33–45.
Dessouki, Assem
  1991 "Social and Political Dimensions of the Historiography of the Arab Gulf." In *Statecraft in the Middle East: Oil, Historical Memory, and Popular Culture*, edited by Eric Davis and Nicolas Gavrielides, 92–115. Miami: Florida International University Press.
Diab, Henry, and Lars Wahlin
  1983 "Geography of Education in Syria in 1882. With a translation of 'Education in Syria' by Shakim Makarius, 1883." *Geografiska annaler* 65 B:2,105–28.

Dickson, H.R.P.
1949 *The Arab of the Desert: A Glimpse into Badawin Life in Kuwait and Sauᶜdi Arabia.* London: George Allen & Unwin.

Dominguez, Virginia R.
1989 *People as Subject, People as Object: Selfhood and Peoplehood in Contemporary Israel.* Madison: University of Wisconsin Press.
1992 "Invoking Culture: The Messy Side of 'Cultural Politics'" *South Atlantic Quarterly* 91(1):19–42.

Dresch, Paul
1986 "The Significance of the Course Events Take in Segmentary Systems." *American Ethnologist* 13(2):309–24.
1989 *Tribes, Government, and History in Yemen.* Oxford: Clarendon Press.

Duclos, Louis-Jean
1990 Les Elections législative en Jordanie. *Magreb/Machrek* 129:47–75.

Dumont, Jean-Paul
1984 "A Matter of Touristic 'Indifferance'" *American Ethnologist* 11:139–51.

Dye, Thomas R., and L. Harman Zeigler
1981 *The Irony of Democracy: An Uncommon Introduction to American Politics.* 5th ed. Monterey, Calif.: Duxbury Press.

Edelman, Murray
1967 *The Symbolic Uses of Politics.* Urbana: University of Illinois Press.

Eglin, Darrel R.
1980 "The Economy." In *Jordan, A Country Study*, edited by Richard F. Nyrop; pp. 105–53. Washington: American University Press.

Eickelman, Christine
1984 *Women and Community in Oman.* New York: New York University Press.

Eickelman, Dale F.
1976 *Moroccan Islam: Tradition and Society in a Pilgrimage Center.* Austin: University of Texas Press.
1977 "Time in a Complex Society: A Moroccan Example." *Ethnology* 16(1):39–55.
1979 "The Political Economy of Meaning." *American Ethnologist* 6(2):386–93.
1981 *The Middle East: An Anthropological Approach.* 1st ed. Englewood Cliffs, N.J.: Prentice-Hall.
1989 *The Middle East: An Anthropological Approach.* 2nd ed. Englewood Cliffs, N.J.: Prentice-Hall.

Eickelman, Dale F., and James Piscatori
1990 "Social Theory in the Study of Muslim Societies." In *Muslim Travellers: Pilgrimage, Migration and the Religious Imagination*, edited by Eickelman and Piscatori, 3–25. Berkeley: University of California Press.

El-Edroos, S. A. Brigadier
1980 *The Hashemite Arab Army 1908–1979: An Appreciation and Analysis of Military Operations.* Amman: The Publishing Committee.

Escribano, Marisa
   1984 "Honor, Authority and Social Organization in Two West Bank Vil-
          lages." Paper delivered at the symposium Anthropology in Jordan:
          State of the Art, Amman.
Farrag, Amina
   1977 "The Wastah among Jordanian Villagers." In *Patrons and Clients in
          Medditeranean Societies*, edited by Ernest Gellner and John Water-
          bury, 225–38. London: Duckworth and Co.
Favret, Jeanne
   1972 "Traditionalism through Ultra-modernism." In *Arabs and Berbers:
          From Tribe to Nation in North Africa*, edited by Ernest Gellner and
          Charles Micaud, 307–24. Lexington, Mass.: Lexington Books.
Fernandez, James
   1986 "The Dark at the Bottom of the Stairs." In *Persuasions and Perfor-
          mances: The Play of Tropes in Culture*, 214–38. Bloomington: Indiana
          University Press.
Fernea, Elizabeth Warnock, and Robert A. Fernea
   1987 *The Arab World: Personal Encounters*. Garden City, N.Y.: Anchor
          Books.
Fineman, Mark
   1992 "Jordanians Confront Monarch's Mortality" *Los Angeles Times*, A-4.
Foster, Robert J.
   1991 "Making National Cultures in the Global Ecumene." *Annual Reviews
          in Anthropology* 20:235–60.
Foucault, Michel
   1979 *Discipline and Punish: The Birth of the Prison*. New York: Vintage
          Books.
Franken, H. J.
   1969 *Excavations at Tell Deir Alla I*. Leiden.
Friedlander, Judith
   1975 *Being Indian in Hueyapan: A Study of Forced Identity in Contempo-
          rary Mexico*. New York: St. Martin's Press.
   1986 "The National Indigenist Institute of Mexico Reinvents the Indian:
          the Pame Example." *American Ethnologist* 13(2):363–67.
Friedman, Thomas L.
   1988 "The King's Move: Hussein Cuts Off West Bank, Spites Arafat; Stay
          Tuned." *New York Times*, 7 August.
Fussel, Paul
   1983 *Class: A Guide through the American Status System*. New York: Sum-
          mit Books.
Geertz, Clifford
   1973a "The Integrative Revolution: Primordial Sentiments and Civil Poli-
          tics in the New States." In *The Interpretation of Cultures: Selected
          Essays by Clifford Geertz*, 255–310. New York: Basic Books.
   1973b "After the Revolution: The Fate of Nationalism in the New States."
          In *The Interpretation of Cultures: Selected Essays by Clifford Geertz*,
          234–54. New York: Basic Books.

Gertz, Clifford
1973c "Deep Play: Notes on the Balinese Cockfight." In *The Interpretation of Cultures: Selected Essays by Clifford Geertz*, 412–54. New York: Basic Books.
1983 "Centers, Kings, and Charisma: Reflections on the Symbolics of Power." In *Local Knowledge*, 121–46. New York: Basic Books.
Geertz, Hildred
1979 "The Meanings of Family Ties." In *Meaning and Order in Moroccan Society: Three Essays in Cultural Analysis*, 315–79. Cambridge: Cambridge University Press.
Gellner, Ernest
1969 *Saints of the Atlas.* Chicago: University of Chicago Press.
Gilmore, David D.
1987 "Introduction: The Shame of Dishonor." In *Honor and Shame and the Unity of the Mediterranean*, edited by Gilmore, 2–22. Washington, D.C.: American Anthropological Association.
Gilsenan, Michael
1982 *Recognizing Islam: Religion and Society in the Modern Arab World.* New York: Pantheon Books.
1990 "Very Like a Camel: The Appearance of an Anthropologist's Middle East." In *Localizing Strategies: Regional Traditions of Ethnographic Writing*, edited by Richard Fardon, 222–39. Edinburgh: Scottish Academic Press and Smithsonian Institution Press.
Ginat, Joseph
1987 *Blood Disputes among Bedouin and Rural Arabs in Israel: Revenge, Mediation, Outcasting and Family Honor.* Pittsburgh: University of Pittsburgh Press.
Glassie, Henry
1975 *Folk Housing in Middle Virginia: A Structural Analysis of Historic Artifacts.* Knoxville: University of Tennessee Press.
Glubb, Major John B.
1938 "The Economic Situation of the Trans-Jordan Tribes." *Journal of Central Asian Studies* 25:448–59.
Glueck, Nelson
1951 *Explorations in Eastern Palestine, IV. Annual of American Schools of Oriental Research*, 25–28.
Godelier, Maurice
1977 *Perspectives in Marxist Anthropology.* Cambridge: Cambridge University Press.
Goody, Jack, and Ian Watt
1975 "The Consequences of Literacy." In *Literacy in Traditional Societies*, edited by Jack Goody, 27–68. Cambridge: Cambridge University Press.
Greenwood, Davydd J.
1976 *Unrewarding Wealth: The Commercialization and Collapse of Agriculture in a Spanish Basque Town.* Cambridge: Cambridge University Press.

1985 "Castilians, Basques, and Andalusians: An Historical Comparison of Nationalism, 'True' Ethnicity and 'False' Ethnicity." In *Ethnic Groups and the State*, edited by Paul Brass, 202–27. London: Croom Helm.

Gubser, Peter
1973 *Politics and Change in al-Karak, Jordan: A Study of a Small Arab Town and its District.* London: Oxford University Press.
1983 *Jordan: Crossroads of Middle Eastern Events.* Boulder: Westview Press.

Haidar, Aziz
1988 "The Different Levels of Palestinian Ethnicity." In *Ethnicity, Pluralism, and the State in the Middle East*, edited by Milton J. Esman and Itamar Rabinovich, 95–120. Ithaca: Cornell University Press.

Handler, Richard
1988 *Nationalism and the Politics of Culture in Quebec.* Madison: University of Wisconsin Press.

Haraway, Donna J.
1991 *Simians, Cyborgs, and Women: The Reinvention of Nature.* New York: Routledge.

Harik, Iliya
1981 "The Political Elite as a Strategic Minority." In *Leadership and Development in Arab Society*, edited by Fuad I. Khuri, 62–91. Beirut: American University of Beirut.

Harkabi, Yehoshafat
1988 "Hussein's West Bank Shock Strategy." *The Washington Report on Middle East Affairs* (September):40.

Harris, George L.
1958 *Jordan: Its People, Its Society, Its Culture.* New Haven: HRAF Press.

Hassan, bin Talal (Crown Prince of Jordan)
1981 *Palestinian Self-Determination: A Study of the West Bank and Gaza Strip.* London: Quartet Books.

Hayden, Ilse
1987 *Symbol and Privilege: The Ritual Context of British Royalty.* Tucson: The University of Arizona Press.

Henry, Donald O.
1984 "Patterns of Transhumance in Southern Jordan: Ethnographic and Archaeologic Analogs." Paper delivered at the Symposium on Anthropology in Jordan: State of the Art: Amman.

Herzberg, Arthur
1988 "This Time, Hussein Isn't Being Coy" *New York Times*, 9 August.

Herzfeld, Michael
1985 *The Poetics of Manhood: Contest and Identity in a Cretan Mountain Village.* Princeton: Princeton University Press.

Herzfeld, Michael
1986 "Of Definitions and Boundaries: The Status of Culture in the Culture of the State." In *Discourse and the Social Life of Meaning*, edited by Phyllis Pease Chock and June R. Wyman, 75–94. Washington, D.C.: Smithsonian Institution Press.

Herzfeld, Michael
  1987 "'As in Your Own House': Hospitality, Ethnography and the Stereo-
         type of Mediterranean Society." *Honor and Shame and the Unity of the
         Mediterranean,* edited by David Gilmore, 75–89. Washington, D.C.:
         American Anthropological Association.
  1991 *A Place in History: Social and Monumental Time in a Cretan Town.*
         Princeton: Princeton University Press.
Hiatt, Joseph Merrill
  1981 *Between Desert and Town: A Case Study of Encapsulation and Seden-
         tarization Among Jordanian Bedouin.* Ph.D. diss., University of
         Pennsylvania.
Hirschon, Renee
  1989 *Heirs of the Greek Catastrophe: The Social Life of Asia Minor Refugees
         in Piraeus.* Oxford: Clarendon Press.
Hobsbawm, Eric
  1983 Introduction: "Inventing Traditions." In *The Invention of Tradition,*
         edited by Eric Hobsbawm and Terence Ranger, 1–14. Cambridge:
         Cambridge University Press.
Huntington, Samuel P.
  1966 "The Political Modernization of Traditional Monarchies" *Daedalus*
         95(3):763–88.
Hussein ibn Talal, King of Jordan
  1978 Forword to *My Memoirs Completed (al-Takmilah).* Abudullah bin
         Hussein, v–xvii. London: Longman Group.
Huxley, Frederick Charles
  1978 *Wasita in a Lebanese Context: Social Exchange Among Villagers and
         Outsiders.* Ann Arbor: Musuem of Anthropology, Univeristy of Mich-
         igan Press.
Ibrahim, Youssef M.
  1988 "Jordan's West Bank Move Upsetting Daily Life." *New York Times,*
         18 October.
Jackson, Jean
  1989 "Is There a Way to Talk About Making Culture Without Making Ene-
         mies?" *Dialectical Anthropology* 14(2):127–43.
Jameson, Fredric
  1984a "Postmodernism, or the Cultural Logic of Late Capitalism." *New
         Left Review* 146:53–92.
  1984b "The Politics of Theory: Ideological Positions in the Postmodernism
         Debate." *New German Critique* 33 (Fall 1984):53–65.
  1985 "The Realist Floor-Plan." In *On Signs,* edited by Marshall Blonsky,
         373–83. Baltimore: Johns Hopkins University Press.
Jarvenpa, Robert
  1992 "Commoditization versus Cultural Integration: Tourism and Image
         Building in the Klondike." Paper presented on the panel "Empire
         and Desire: The Commodification of the Exotic in Postcolonial Con-
         texts" at the American Ethnological Society's Annual Meeting,
         Memphis.

Jordan, The Hashemite Kingdom of
  1971 *Climatic Atlas of Jordan.* Amman: Meterological Department.
  1972 *Rehabilitation and Development Plan of the Jordan Valley (East Bank) 1973–1975.* Amman: Jordan Valley Commission.
  1978 *Population and Housing Census Pretest.* Amman: Department of Statistics. Unpublished preliminary results provided by the Jordan Valley Authority.
  1980 *Five Year Plan for Economic and Social Development 1981–1985.* Amman: National Planning Council.
  1981 *Results of The Agricultural Census in Jordan Valley 1978.* Amman: Department of Statistics Press.
  1986 *Five Year Plan for Economic and Social Development 1986–1990.* Amman: Ministry of Planning.
Joseph, Suad
  1988 "Feminization, Familism, Self, and Politics: Research as a Mughtaribi" In *Arab Women in the Field: Studying Your Own Society*, edited by Soraya Altorki and Camillia Fawzi El-Solh, 25–47. Syracuse: Syracuse University Press.
Jureidini, Paul A., and R. D. McLaurin
  1984 *Jordan: The Impact of Social Change on the Role of the Tribes.* The Washington Papers/108, vol. 12. Washington: The Center for Strategic and International Studies.
Kaplan, Irving
  1980 "The Society and Its Environment," In *Jordan: A Country Study.* 3d. ed., edited by Richard F. Nyrop, 51–104. Washington, D.C.: American University Press.
Karpat, Kemal H.
  1974 "Ottoman Immigration Policies and Settlement in Palestine." In *Settler Regimes in Africa and the Arab World: The Illusion of Endurance*, edited by Ibrahim Abu-Lughod, Baha Abu-Laban, 57–72. Wilmette, Illinois: Medina University Press International.
Kawar, Widad
  1984 "Traditional Costumes of Jordan and Palestine." *Arts* 2(1):41–42. Special issue on the arts of Jordan.
Keeley, Charles B., and Bassam Saket
  1984 "Jordanian Migrant Workers in the Arab Region: A Case Study of Consequences for Labor Supplying Countries." *The Middle East Journal* 38(4):685–98.
Kent, Susan
  1984 *Analyzing Activity Areas: An Ethnoarchaeological Study of the Use of Space.* Albuquerque: University of New Mexico Press.
Khalaf, 'Abd al-Hadi
  1987 "The Elusive Quest for Gulf Security" *MERIP Report* 148:19–22, 32–33.
Khalidi, Rashid
  1991 "Arab Nationalism: Historical Problems in the Literature" *American Historical Review* 96(5):1363–73.

Khammash, Ammar
  1986   *Notes on Village Architecture in Jordan.* Lafayette: University of Southwestern Louisiana.
Khouri, Rami G.
  1981   *The Jordan Valley: Life and Society below Sea Level.* London: Longman.
Kirkbride, Sir Alec Seath
  1956   *A Crackle of Thorns: Experiences in the Middle East.* London: John Murray.
Klat, Paul J.
  1955   Whither Land Tenure in the Arab World. *Middle East Economic Papers*, 47–61.
LaBianca, Oystein
  1983   "The Return of the Nomad: An Analysis of the Process of Bedouinization in Jordan." Paper delivered at the American Anthropological Association's Annual Meeting, Chicago.
Lancaster, William
  1981   *The Rwala Bedouin Today.* Cambridge: Cambridge University Press.
  1984   "The Relations Between the Nomadic and Settled People of Jordan: The Case of the Rwalla Bedouin." Paper delivered at the Symposium on Anthropology in Jordan: State of the Art: Amman.
Laroui, Abdallah
  1977   "Sands and Dreams." In *Arab and American Cultures*, edited by George N. Atiyeh, 3–14. Washington, D.C.: American Enterprise Institute for Public Policy Research.
Lavie, Smadar
  1990   *The Poetics of Military Occupation: Mzeina Allegories of Bedouin Identity Under Israeli and Egyptian Rule.* Berkeley: University of California Press.
Layne, Linda L.
  1984a "The Use of Space Among Settled Bedouin in the Jordan Valley." Paper delivered at the symposium on Anthropology in Jordan: State of the Art: Amman.
  1984b "The Muʿaddi Iskan: An Evaluative Case Study of the Government Housing Projects in the Jordan Valley." Paper delivered at the Western Social Science Association's Annual Meeting, San Diego.
  1985   "On Being Bedouin: The Construction of Tribal Identity in Jordan." Paper delivered at the Middle East Studies Association's Annual Meeting, New Orleans.
  1986   "The Production and Reproduction of Tribal Identity in Jordan." Ph.D. diss., Princeton University.
  1987a "Tribesmen as Citizens: Primordial Ties and Democracy in Rural Jordan." In *Middle East Elections: Implications of Recent Trends*, edited by Linda L. Layne, 113–51. Boulder: Westview Press.
  1987b "Das dilig der Beduinen in Jordanien—Seine Bedeutung im heutigen Nationalstaat." In *Pracht und Geheimnis: Kleidung und Schmuck*

aus Palastina und Jordanian, edited by Karin Welck, 168–71. Cologne: Rautenstrauch-Joest-Museum für Volkerkunde.

1987c   "Tribalism: National Representation of Tribal Life in Jordan." *Urban Anthropology and Studies of Cultural Systems and World Economic Development* 16(2):183–203.

1989   "The Dialogics of Tribal Self-representation in Jordan." *American Ethnologist* 16(1):24–39.

1990a   "Jordan's Happy Family: State Ideologies of Jordanian Nationalism." Paper presented at SUNY Binghamton's Southwest Asian and North African Studies Program.

1990b   "King Hussein: Pre-Modern, Modern, or Post-Modern Figure?" Paper delivered at the Middle East Studies Association's Annual Meeting, San Antonio.

Leveau, Remy
1985   *Le Fellah Morocain: Défenseur du trone.* 2d. ed. Paris: Presses de la Fondation Nationale des Sciences Politiques.

Lerner, Daniel
1958   *The Passing of Traditional Society: Modernizing the Middle East.* New York: The Free Press.

Lewis, Norman
1987   *Nomads and Settlers in Syria and Jordan, 1800–1980.* Cambridge: Cambridge University Press.

Ma'oz, Moshe
1968   *Ottoman Reform in Syria and Palestine 1840–1861: The Impact of the Tanzimat on Politics and Society.* Oxford: Clarendon Press.

Marcus, Michael
1986   "'Horsemen Are the Fence of the Land': Honor and History among the Ghigata of Eastern Morocco." In *Honor and Shame and the Unity of the Mediterranean,* edited by David D. Gilmore, 49–60. Washington, D.C.: American Anthropological Association.

Martin, Emily
1992   "Ethnography of the Body and Work." Paper presented at the Department of Science and Technology Studies, Rensselaer Polytechnic Institute.

Marx, Karl
1967   "On the Jewish Question." In *Writings of the young Marx on Philosphy and Society,* translated and edited by Loyd D. Easton and Kurt H. Guddat, 216–48. New York: Anchor Books.

Mazur, Michael P.
1979   *Economic Growth and Development in Jordan.* London: Croom Helm.

Meeker, Michael E.
1979   *Literature and Violence in North Arabia.* Cambridge: Cambridge University Press.

Merchant, Carolyn
1980   *The Death of Nature: Women, Ecology and the Scientific Revolution.* New York: Harper and Row.

Mitchell, Timothy
1988   *Colonizing Egypt.* Cambridge: Cambridge University Press.

Moffat, Michael
  1990 "Do we really need 'Post Modernism' to understand *Ferris Bueller's Day Off*? A comment on Traube." *Cultural Anthropology* 5(4):367–73.
Moore, Sally Falk
  1989 "The Production of Pluralism as a Process." *Public Culture* 1(2):26–48.
Musil, Alois
  1928 *The Manners and Customs of the Rwala Bedouins.* New York: The American Geographical Society.
Muslih, Muhammad Y.
  1988 *The Origins of Palestinian Nationalism.* New York: Columbia University Press.
Naval Intelligence Division
  1943 *Palestine and Transjordan.* Geographical Handbook Series.
Nyrop, Richard F.
  1980 *Jordan: A Country Study.* 3d. ed. Washington, D.C.: American University Press.
Oppenheim, Max Von
  1943 *Die Beduinen. Vol. 2, Die Beduinenstarme in Palestina, Transjordanien, Sinai, Hejaz.* Leipzig: Otto Hanasowitz.
Oren, Michael B.
  1990 "A Winter of Discontent: Britain's Crisis in Jordan, December 1955–March 1956." *International Journal of Middle East Studies* 22(2):171–84.
Ortner, Sherry B.
  1984 "Theory in Anthropology since the Sixties." *Comparative Studies in Society and History* 26(1):126–61.
Oweidi, Ahmad Saleh Suleiman
  1982 *Bedouin Justice in Jordan (The Customary Legal System of the Tribes and its Integration into the Framework of State Polity from 1921 Onwards).* Ph.D. diss., Cambridge University.
Patai, Raphael
  1971 *Society, Culture, and Change in the Middle East.* Philadelphia: University of Pennsylvania Press.
Peake, Frederick G.
  1958 *A History of Jordan and its Tribes.* Coral Gables, Florida: University of Miami Press.
Perin, Constance
  1977 *Everything in Its Place: Social Order and Land Use in America.* Princeton: Princeton University Press.
Peters, Emrys L.
  1978 "The Status of Women in Four Middle East Communities." In *Women in the Muslim World*, edited by Lois Beck and Nikki Keddie, 311–50. Cambridge: Harvard University Press.
Popular Memory Group
  1982 "Popular Memory: Theory, Politics, Method." In *Making Histories:*

Studies in History-Writing and Politics, edited by Richard Johnson et al., 205–52. Minneapolis: University of Minnesota Press.

Richards, A. I.
  1960 "African Kings and Their Royal Relatives." *The Journal of the Royal Anthropological Institute of Great Britain and Ireland* 22:135–50.
  1968 "Keeping the King Divine." *The Royal Anthropological Institute of Great Britain and Ireland. Proceedings* 22:23–35.

Rinehart, Robert
  1980 "Historical Setting." In *Jordan: A Country Study*. 3d. ed., edited by Richard F. Nyrop, 1–50. Washington, D.C.: American University Press.

Robins, Philip
  1989 "Shedding Half a Kingdom: Jordan's Dismantling of Ties with the West Bank." *British Society for Middle Eastern Studies Bulletin* 16(2):162–76.

Rose, Richard, and Dennis Kavanagh
  1976 "The Monarchy in Contemporary Political Culture." *Comparative Politics* 8:548–76.

Rosen, Lawrence
  1979 "Social Identity and Points of Attachment; Approaches to Social Organization." In *Meaning and Order in Moroccan Society: Three Essays in Cultural Analysis*, 19–112. Cambridge: Cambridge University Press.

Rosen, Lawrence
  1984 *Bargaining for Reality: The Construction of Social Relations in a Muslim Community*. Chicago: University of Chicago Press.

Ryan, Sheila, and Muhammad Hallaj
  1983 *Palestine Is, But Not in Jordan*. Belmont, Mass.: The Association of Arab-American University Graduates Press.

Sahlins, Marshall D.
  1968 *Tribesmen*. Englewood Cliffs, N.J.: Prentice-Hall.

Satloff, Robert B.
  1986 "Troubles on the East Bank: Challenges to the Domestic Stability of Jordan." *The Washington Papers/123*. Washington, D.C.: The Center for Strategic and International Studies.

Schumacher, John
  1989 *Human Posture: The Nature of Inquiry*. Albany: State University of New York Press.

Seccombe, Ian J.
  1981 *Manpower and Migration: The Effects of International Labour Migration on Agricultural Development in the East Jordan Valley 1973–1980*. Centre for Middle Eastern and Islamic Studies Occasional Papers Series, no. 11. Durham: University of Durham.

Shadid, Mohammed, and Rick Seltzer
  1988 "Political Attitudes of Palestinians in the West Bank and Gaza Strip" *Middle East Journal* 42(1):16–32.

Shahak, Israel
   1990   "Preparing the Israelis for War?" *Middle East International* 381:15–16.

Shally, Beth
   1985   "Living One's Stories of 'To Be Gomero': Dynamic Processes of Identification in the Gomeran Fiesta." Ph.D. diss., Princeton University.

Shinn, R. S.
   1980   "Government and Policies." In *Jordan, A Country Study*, edited by Richard F. Nyrop, 155–90. Washington: American University Press.

Shoup, John A.
   1981   "Hima: The Bedouin Land Use System." A research proposal to the Social Science Research Council.
   1984   "Nomads in Jordan and Syria." *Cultural Survival Quarterly* 8(1):11–13.
   1985   "Bedouin of Petra." *The Middle East Journal* 39(2):277–91.
   1990   "Middle East Sheep Pastoralism and the Hima System." In *The World of Pastoralism*, edited by Galaty and D. L. Johnson, 195–215. London: Guilford Press.

Simms, Steven R.
   1988   "The Archaeological Structure of a Bedouin Camp." *Journal of Archaeological Science* 15:197–211.

Sinai, Anne, and Allen Pollack, eds.
   1977   *The Hashemite Kingdom of Jordan and the West Bank: A Handbook.* New York: American Academic Association for Peace in the Middle East.

Slyomovics, Susan
   1989   "Cross-Cultural Dress and Tourist Performance in Egypt" *Performing Arts Journal* 33/34:139–48.

Sontag, Susan
   1977   *On Photography.* New York: Dell.

Starkey, David
   1977   "Representation Through Intimacy." In *Symbols and Sentiments*, edited by I. Lewis, 187–224. London: Academic Press.

Stewart, Frank H.
   1987   "Tribal Law in the Arab World: A Review of the Literature." *International Journal of Middle East Studies* 19:473–90.

Stokes, Donald E.
   1985   "The Paradox of Campaign Appeals and Election Mandates." *Proceedings of the American Philosophical Society* 129(1):20–25.

Strathern, Marilyn
   1972   *Women in Between: Female roles in a Male World, Mount Hagen, New Guinea.* London: Seminar Press.

Street, Brian
   1990   "Orientalist Discourses in the Anthropology of Iran, Afghanistan and Pakistan. In *Localizing Strategies: Regional Traditions of Ethnographic Writing*, edited by Richard Fardon, 240–59. Edinburgh: Scottish Academic Press and Smithsonian Institution Press.

Tapper, Richard
1979   *Pasture and Politics: Economics, Conflict and Ritual among Shahsevan Nomads of Northwestern Iran.* London: Academic Press.
Trevor-Roper, Hugh
1983   "The Invention of Tradition: The Highland Tradition of Scotland." In *The Invention of Tradition,* edited by Eric Hobsbawm and Terence Ranger, 15–41. Cambridge: Cambridge University Press.
Vatikiotis, P. J.
1967   *Politics and the Military in Jordan: A Study of the Arab Legion 1921– 1957.* New York: Praeger Publishers.
Wagner, Roy
1981   *The Invention of Culture.* Chicago: University of Chicago Press.
Wahlin, Lars
1982   *Education as Something New: The Introduction of Village Schools and a Study of Two Student Cohorts 1948–1980.* Stockholm: University of Stockholm, Department of Human Geography.
1988a   "Occurrence of Mushaᶜ in Transjordan." *Geografiska Annaler* 70B(3):375–79.
1988b   "Land Ownership Pattern Around as-Salt in the 1940s as Record of Nineteenth Century Land Allocation." Paper presented at the BRISMES Conference, University of Leeds.
1991a   "The Opening of Transjordan to Modern Means of Transport." Working paper from the Enviornment and Development Studies Unit, no 10. School of Geography, Stockholm University.
1991b   Stability of Village Territories in Transjordan. Paper presented at the BRISMES Conference, University of London.
1992   *Back to Settled Life?: An Historical Geographical Study of Changing Living Conditions in the Allān Area of Jordan, 1867–1980.* Preliminary manuscript version for a seminar on 26 November 1992. Department of Human Geography, Stockholm University.
Walpole, G. F.
1948   "Land Problems in Transjordan." *Journal of the Royal Central Asia Society,* 35(1):52–65.
Warner, W. Lloyd
1959   *The Family of God: A Symbolic Study of Christian Life in America.* New Haven: Yale University Press.
Waterbury, John
1970   *The Commander of the Faithful: The Moroccan Political Elite—A Study in Segmented Politics.* New York: Columbia University Press.
Weiner, Annette B.
1976   *Women of Value, Men of Renown: New Perspectives in Trobriand Exchange.* Austin: University of Texas Press.
Weir, Shelagh
1976   *The Bedouin: Aspects of the Material Culture of the Bedouin of Jordan.* London: World of Islam Festival Publishing Company.
1989   *Palestinian Costume.* Austin: University of Texas Press.

Wilkinson, J. C.
  1977   *Water and Tribal Settlement in South-East Arabia: A Study of the Aflaj of Oman.* Oxford: Clarendon Press.
Williams, Raymond
  1973   *The Country and the City.* New York: Oxford University Press.
Wilson, Mary
  1987   *King Abdullah, Britain and the Making of Jordan.* Cambridge: Cambridge University Press.
Wolf, Eric
  1988   "Inventing Society." *American Ethnologist* 15(4):752–61.
Wright, Susan
  1981   "Place and Face: Of Women in Doshman Ziari, Iran." In *Women and Space: Ground Rules and Social Maps,* edited by Shirley Ardener, 136–56. London: Croom Helm.
Yorke, Valerie
  1988a   "Jordan Is Not Palestine: The Demographic Factor." *Middle East International* April 16:16–17.
  1988b   "Domestic Politics and the Prospects for an Arab-Israeli Peace." *Journal of Palestine Studies* 17(4):3–25.
Zenner, Walter P.
  1972   "Aqiili Agha: The Strongman in the Ethnic Relations of the Ottoman Galilee." *Comparative Studies in Society and History* 14(2):169–88.

Index

ʿAbbad-ʿAdwān war, 40–41
ʿAbbādi tribes: agricultural practices of, 38,
40, 43–45; *aṣl* concept within, 53–54,
74n.4; confederation structure, 38,
48n.2; dispersal of political authority in,
41–42; domestic mobility of, 64–67; furnishings and social identity-making, 67–
72; household organization and practices, 29, 55–59; links with King Hussein, 144–50; occupational survey of,
46–47; parliamentary candidates from,
113–14; pastoralism among, 38–40, 43–
46; terminology for groups within,
49n.10; use of space by, 52–73, 80–
93
Abdalat, Kamal, 115
Abdul Hamid II, 21
Abdullah bin Hussein (King): domestic
mobility of, 145 formation of Jordan
and, 11–12, 21–22, 32n.18; memoirs
(*al-Takmilah*), 152–53; modern narratives of progress, 153; pan-Arabism and,
22; portrayal of, as Bedouin, 12, 32n.18
Abou-Zeid, Ahmed, 135
absentee balloting, Jordan prohibition
against, 122
Abu Bugar, Jamal, as political candidate,
112–15
Abu Hassan, Mohammad, 14, 22, 33n.23
Abu Jaber, Kamel, 20, 95n.16, 98–99,
112, 124n.11
Abu Obeidah, tomb of, 149
Abu-Lughod, Lila; on Bedouin Middle
Eastern anthropology, 96, 105n.2; research on cultural aspects of honor, 135–
36, 141nn.5, 7; on residence styles, 63;
on tribal and national identities, 9, 17;
on voting patterns, 117
ʿAdwān tribe, electoral politics and, 113
ʿAdwān, Aakaf Fahad al-, 112–14, 125n.12
agnatic groups, voting patterns and, 115–
16
agricultural economy: in Jordan Valley, 42–
46, 49n.17, 50n.18; of ʿAbbādis, 23–24,
38, 40–46, 49n.17, 50nn.18. *See also*
economic development
Ali bin Hussein, 21

alliance-building, in Jordanian elections,
112, 117–18, 125nn.12–13, 126n.21;
women's role in, 117–20. *See also* coali-
tion politics
Alumni Club (Middle Ghor), 120, 126n.19
Amairah, Mohammed Naji, 99
Anani, Ahmad al-, 97–98
Anderson, Benedict, 8, 20–21, 32n.9, 105,
141n.5, 144–45, 151, 157n.2
anthropology, overresearch of Bedouins in,
9–10, 96–101; relative absence of Mid-
dle East studies in, xi
Anthropology of Jordan, State of the Art
Symposium, 96
antitribalism: Jordanian formulations of,
97–99; Western context of, 103–4
Antoun, Richard T., 57, 119, 126n.20
Appadurai, Arjun, 28, 134, 150
Apter, David E., 98
Arab Army of Jordan, 32nn.10–11
Arab Cooperation Council, 27
Arab Legion, in Jordan, 10, 32n.10
Arab nationalism: comparison with western
models of, 20–21, 35n.41; cultural symbolism and, 141n.11; economic benefit
of, for Jordan, 36n.53; importance of
Jordanian nationalist rhetoric, xv, 26–28,
36n.53, 150, 158n.12; scholarly neglect
of, 20. *See also* nationalism
ʿarabs: Arab nation, existence of, 20; Arab
nationhood, relationship with member-
state nations, 20; autonomy and voting
patterns, cultural context, 120–23; concept of posture among, 54 55; Jordanian
nationhood, Palestinian context, 21;
patrilineal descent of, 38; terminology
regarding, 15–17, 33nn.23–25,
34n.29
aṣl: constitution of, 53–54, 74nn.3–4,
135–37; cultural heritage and, 140;
awaʿid (code of conduct), and non-discursive knowledge, 53–55; research on, 53;
values promoted by, 74n.5
Arar, Suleiman, 104
artifacts of tribal life: exhibition of, 132–37;
as symbol of national heritage, 102–3,
138–40;

autonomy: of ʿarab tribes, housing styles and, 62–64; cultural context of, in voting patterns, 117–18, 120–23
Axelrod, Lawrence, 11
Azoy, Whitney G., 71

badiya, defined, 33n.20
Bakhtin, M. M., 137
Balqaʾ, King Abdullah in, 145; transhumance in, 38–40
Bālqaʾ Governorate, Jordanian parliamentary elections and, 111–14
Barth, Fredrik, 62
Basque farm families, comparisons with ʿAbbādi changes in mode of production, 50n.23
Baʾth party, support for, 126n.19
bayt, multiple definitions of, 55
Bedouin Control Laws (1924, 1929, 1936), 17, 104, 106n.13
Bedouin tribes: anthropological focus on, 9–10, 96–97, 105n.2; "authenticity" of, 12–17; camels as symbol of, 102–3, 106n.10; characteristics of, 9–12, 33–34nn.21–28; definitions of, 13–17; designated seats in parliament, 77n.32, 111, 124n.11; ethical and social characteristics attributed to, 100–101; impact of capitalism on, 95n.16; Jordanian national identity and, 27–28; and King Hussein, 11, 104–5; laws of, in conflict with Jordanian civil law, 66, 77n.32; legal definition of, 17, 106n.10; problems with population statistics on, 13; role of, in Jordanian army, 10–12, 32nn.11–14; simulacra of, 101–3; as tourist attraction, 101–3; use of space by, 52–54
Beechey, Veronica, 90, 95n.19
behavior, honor linked with, 135–37
Beidelman, T. O., 135–36
Beni Sakhr tribe, 40
Beyerchen, Alan D., 8, 156
Bni Battu tribespeople, temporal concepts of, 151–52
Bocco, Riccardo, 11, 17, 34nn.26, 30–31, 34, 46–47, 51n.27, 52
bodyguards, Hussein's lack of, 147
Bommes, Michael, 137–38
Bordieu, Pierre, 7, 54, 79, 93nn.1–3, 95n.21
boundaries, clarity or ambiguity of, 21, 28, 35n.43, 150

Boyarin, Jonathan, 158n.13
Brand, Lauri, 4, 19
bride-wealth payments, modern patterns in, 67–68
British Palestine Mandate, Department of Land and Surveys, 42
Brown, K. L., 157n.11
Burckhardt, John, 61
bureaucracy: Jordanian culture of, 155–56; tribalism as obstacle to, 98–99

camels, as symbol of Bedouin, 102–3, 106n.10
capitalism: as dominant production mode in Jordan Valley, 95n.17; politics of space and, 79–93
Capra, Fritjof, 6, 8, 156
Caton, Steven C., 105n.3, 122, 126n.24
Centilivres-Demont, Micheline, 94n.10
Circassians, 3, 111, 141n.12
citizenship: cultural context of, in Jordan, 114–23; alternative meanings of, 108–10, 114–18
class structure, housing as symbol of, 92;
Clifford, James, 9, 14–15, 29, 33n.25, 108, 143
clothing, 130, 100, 139–40; dilug worn by women as, 128–31; of King and Queen, 130–31, 158n.12; and pigeon-hole approach to collective identity, 3
coalition politics, in Jordanian elections, 112, 117–18, 125n.12, 126n.21
Cole, Donald Powell, 10
Coleman, James S., 98
collective identity: border ambiguities and, 8, 21, 25–31, 35n.43, 150; Jordanian nationalism and, 9–12, 21–23, 25–31, 96–105; modularity of, 8; monarchal posture and, 143–56; mosaic vs. segmentary images of, 3–6, 31nn.1–3; pigeon-hole model of, 3, 6–8, 13, 20, 139; postmodern construction of, 28–31, 150, 154–55; real/not real Bedouin distinction, 15–16; "true" Jordanians, confusion regarding, 18–24
colonialism, social contract models of collective identity in context of, and scientific revolution, 7
Communist party, support for, 126n.19
"complementary opposition," prominence of, in Middle East anthropological studies, 105n.2
concrete housing: innovations in design of,

53–59; introduction of, 44, 56; typical floor plans of, 56–59; use of space in case study of, 86–89

Conder, Claude Reignier, 13–14, 40

construction. *See also* housing

construction industry, oil boom, remittances and, xi

cookbooks, as symbols of cultural identity, 141n.13

Coon, Carleton, 3–6

corridor: in comparison with Omani houses, 75n.18, as new concept in ʿAbbādi house plans, 58–60, 75n.17, 88

courts, tribals laws within, 104, 106n.13

cultural identity: Arab nationalism and, 141n.11; *dilug* as symbol of, 128–31; local exhibitions as symbol of, 132–37; as symbol of national heritage, 138–40; voting patterns and, 120–23

"cultural wholeness" concept, 13, 15, 33n.25, 108

currency (Jordanian): comparison with British currency iconography, 158n.19; King Hussein's image on, 106n.7, 153–54, 158n.19

Dajani, Jarir S., 43, 46, 49n.16

Daoud, Fawzi, 115, 125n.12

Davis, Eric, 105n.3

Day, Arthur R., 11–12, 14

decor, of middle-class Jordanian homes, 140, 141n.13

democracy: Jordanian cultural context regarding, 112–23; Libya compared with, 127n.27; U.S. compared with, 127n.26; Yemen compared with, 126nn.24–25

Desert Mobil Force, 10, 33n.21, 42

Desert Patrol, as tourist attraction, 100, 102

dilug (embroidered dress): comparison with Palestinian village dresses, 140n.2; dialogics of tribal self-representation and, 137–40; wearing of as identity-making practice, 128–31; as worn by Queen Noor, 130

domestic mobility: ʿAbbādi preference for, 62–67, 76n.27; capitalism and, 95n.18; of King Hussein, 155n.6

Dominguez, Virginia R., 9, 31n.1, 96, 141n.6

Dresch, Paul, 6, 105n.3, 121, 126n.25

Dye, Thomas, R., 120, 124n.2

East Ghor Canal Project, impact of, xi-xii, 43–47

economic development: mixed economy in Jordan Valley, 46–47; of Jordan Valley and, 43–45, 49n.16; remittances and, xi; royal progresses (*zibrah shaʾbiyya*) and, 146–50; tourism as aid to, 101–3, 106n.6

Edelman, Murray, 120, 123n.2

education: ʿAbbādi participation in service sector and, 46; capitalism and, 90–91; sedentarization and, 43

Eglin, Darrel R., 155

Eickelman, Christine, 71, 75nn.18, 22, 77n.40

Eickelman, Dale, xv, 4, 6–9, 32nn.4, 8, 96, 150; on Bedouin in Middle Eastern anthropology, 96; on temporal concepts, 151–54, 158n.14; on tribal identity, 9

elections: American and Jordanian comparisons, 120–23, 123n.2; antitribalism during, 99–101; as identity-making practice, 120–23; Jordanian parliamentary elections, history of, 110–11, 124n.11; oral voting at, 115, 121–23, 125n.16; polling place procedures and, 115, 125n.15; sheiks as candidates in, 112–14, 116, 124n.11; tribal identity and, 108–27. Women's participation in, 111–12, 115, 117–20, 124n.8. *See also* politics; voting

Electoral and Municipal Laws, 124n.8

El Edroos, S. A. Brigadier, 32n.11

elites, dominance of, in parliamentary elections, 112–13, 124n.11

embroidery: of *dilug*, xiii, 128–29; hand vs. machine embroidery, 140n.2

employment, level of, in Jordan, xi, xv; in Jordan Valley, 45–46, 50n.24, 51n.25; patterns among "abbadis," 46

Escribano, Marisa, 135

ethnic groups: changing cultural construction of, 141n.12; parliamentary representation, 111–12; portrayal of, in guidebooks of Jordan, 18–19, 34n.32. *See also* Palestinian Jordans; specific tribes

Evans-Pritchard, E. E., 4, 6

exhibitions: as act of resistance, 136–37; cultural implications of, 132–37; dialogics of tribal self-representation and, 137–40

Faisal bin Hussein, 21, 32n.17

Faour, Abdl Karim al-, 112, 115

farash (large mattresses), 69
Farrag, Amina, 119, 125n.17
Favret, Jeanne, 31n.3
Fawaz Toqan, 20
Fernandez, James, 9
Fineman, Mark, 138
fireplaces (*nafila* and *ladaya*), ʿAbbādi construction and use of, 82–83, 85; in concrete houses, 88–89
fodder crops, decline in, in Jordan Valley, 45, 50n.21
folklore, xiii, 141n.12; as natural resource, 139, 141n.11
food imports, Jordanian economy and, 50n.17
food production and processing, 140, 141n.13; decreased household participation in, 91; symbolic aspects of, 102, 125n.14, 132, 134, 147, 157n.7
Foucault, Michel, 7–8
Friedlander, 106n.11
Friedman, Thomas L., assessment of Hussein, 12, 27
furniture: importance of, in identity-making practices, 67–73, 138; Western and traditional styles of, in ʿAbbādi homes, 67–68, 77n.36; as women's wealth, 67–70
funerals, furniture and, 71
Fussell, Paul, 92

Geertz, Clifford, 32n.4, 98, 109–10, 133, 144–45, 149
Gellner, Earnest, 6
Germany, Palestinian emigration to, 49n.14
Ghawarna (original valley inhabitants), relations with ʿAbbādis, xiv, 111
Ghazawia, Basheer, 116
Ghazawis, 18
Ghunmi, Nada Abu, xi
gift exchange: comparison with Homeric exchange, 136; exhibition as form of, 136–37; voting as form of, 118–20, 122; with King Hussein, 136–37, 146–49
Gilmore, David D., 135
Gilsenan, Michael, xi, 7, 66, 77n.33
Glassie, Henry, 59
Glubb, John Bagot, 10, 33n.21, 42
Glueck, Nelson, 48n.4, 55–56
Goody, Jack, 122

government housing projects: ownership patterns in, 76nn.29–31; as resource for domestic mobility, 63–64, 76n.27
Great Arab Revolt: formation of Jordan and, 21, 42; role of, in Jordanian nationalist rhetoric, 26–28, 36n.53
Greece: comparison of gift exchange in, 137; refugees, comparisons with Jordanian Palestinians, 35n.38; state ideologies in, 37n.57, 154–55; stereotypes concerning, 106n.12
greeting rituals, among ʿAbbādis, 71–72
Greenwood, Davydd J., 50n.23,
Gubser, Peter, 10, 13–14, 18–20, 42, 100–101, 112, 119, 125n.17, 126n.21

Haidar, Aziz, 23
handicrafts, 141n.13. *See also* folklore
Handler, Richard, 20, 28, 138, 145, 150
Haraway, Donna J., 156
Harik, Ilya, 11, 32n.16
Harris, George L., 18
Hashemite Kingdom: ambiguity of borders in, 21, 25–31, 35n.43, 156; concepts of history in, 152–53; cultural constructions of, 10–12; evolution of, 18; Great Arab Revolt and, 27, 36n.50, 103; independence from Britain, 42; monarchal posture and, 149–50; "natural wonders" of, 102–3; Palestinian support for, 20–29, 35n.46, 130, 139–40; West Bank annexed by, 22–24
Hayden, Ilse, 136, 157n.3
heritage, 138–40, 141nn.6,11
Herzfeld, Michael, 106n.12, 116, 135–37, 154–56, 159n.21
Hiatt, Joseph Merrill, 95n.16
Hirschon, Rence, 35n.38
history: honor linked with, 135; Jordanian concepts of, 97, 151–53, 158n.16; progressive concretization of, 138–40; tribal and national notions of, 126n.25
Hobsbawm, Eric, 21, 134
Holquist, Michael, 9
honor: definitions for, 141n.7; *dilug* as sign of, 130–31; everyday practices and, 135; exhibitions as acts of, 134–37; and history, 135; requests to King Hussein linked with, 148–50; study of by western scholars, 135. *See also* asiil; asl
hospitality, xii-xiv, 53–54, 131, 137
house, inviolability of (*hurmat al-bayt*), ac-

cording to customary law, 54, 74n.8, 93n.3

housing: ʿAbbādi construction techniques, 56–59, 86–89; changing locus of production and, 90–91; concrete houses as supplement to tents, 61–64; increased construction of, in Jordan Valley, 43–44, 55–56; nomenclature of domestic space by ʿAbbādis, 65–66; of sheikhs, 59–60; traditional floor plans in nontraditional structures, 55–59; transhumance patterns and, 61–64; U.S.-Jordanian comparisons in, 91–93

hurmat al-bayt (sanctity of the home), 93n.3; ʿAbbādi concept of, 54, 74n.8

Hussein bin Talal (King Hussein): as agent of change, 146–47, 153; attempts on life of, 147; attire of, 130–31; comparison with African kings, 153; comparison with British Queen, 136, 141n.10, 153, 158n.19; disengagement from West Bank by, 26–28, 150, 158n.12; domestic mobility of, 157n.5; as gift giver, 136, 148–49, 157n.9; health status of, 12, 35n.48, 153, 158n.18; on history, 152–53; identification with tribes, 11–12, 104–5; images of, on currency, 153–54, 158n.19; Iraqi invasion of Kuwait and, 37n.53; Machiavellian interpretations of, 27–28, 37n.54, 120, 124n.6, 143–44; as national symbol, 59, 138, 143–56; Palestinian support for, 18–19, 25–26, 35n.48; powers of, 144; royal progresses (*zibrah shaʾbiyya*) of, 146–50, 157n.6; as "sheikh of sheiks," 113

Hussein ibn Ali, Sharif, 37n.53, 150

Ibn Saud, 32n.18

illiterate voters, oral voting by, 115–18, 122, 125n.16

India, national culture and, 141n.13

Indian (indigenous) cultures, authenticity of Bedouin tribes compared with, 14–15, 29, 106n.11

intermarriage, among Jordan Valley tribes, 74n.3

"invention of tradition" in Jordan, 12–14, 97–103, 134–40

Iran/Iraq war, xv

Iraq, invasion of Kuwait, 37n.53; tribalism in, 105n.3

Islam: allocation of parliamentary seats, 111; celebration of religious holidays, 81, 85; proportion of Sunnis and Shias in Jordan, 18; role of, in Jordan, xv; tribalism linked with, 99–101; and women's attire, 129, 131

Israel: bonds with, 35n.43, 37n.53; campaign issue in Jordanian elections, 116; collective identity, comparisons with, 31n.1, 35n.42, 96, 141n.6; creation of, impact on Jordanian population, 18–19, 22–23; Jordanian national identity and, 25–27, 35n.48, 103–4, 149–50; Six Day War with, 43–44, 111–12

issue-oriented politics, absence of, in Jordanian elections, 116–17, 123n.2, 126n.20; in Jordanian nationalist rhetoric, 26–27, 149–50; and 1984 parliamentary bi-elections, 116

Jackson, Jean, 14

Jameson, Fredric, 151, 156, 158n.15

Jarvenpa, Robert, 14

Jaynes, Julian, 122

Jazi, Hamd Ibn, 126n.11

Jerash, as tourist attraction, 102

Jerash Festival, collective identity-making at, 130, 139

Jerusalem, in Jordanian nationalist rhetoric, 27, 150

Jordan. *See* Hashemite Kingdom

Jordan Valley, climate and topography of, 38–40

Jordanians and the People of Jordan, The, 20

Jureidini, Paul, 10–12, 42, 143

Kahane, Meir (Rabbi), 35n.48

Kaplan, Irving, 4, 11, 14, 18–19, 31n.2

Karpat, Kemal H., 41

Kavenagh, Dennis, 144

Kawar, Widad, 129–30

Keeley, Charles B., 47,

Keilani, Musa, 100

Kent, Susan, 95nn.15, 18

Khalidi, Rashid, 21

kharbush tents, 57–58

Khatib, Abdallah al-, 98

Khouri, Rami G., 19, 43–44

khuwa payments, 48n.6

King Abdullah Mosque, 150

kinship charts, xiii

kitchen, in ʿAbbādi concrete houses, 88

Klat, Paul J. 41, 48n.7

Krayma Community Center exhibition, as new form of tribal identity-making, 132–37, 140

kufiyya: and collective identity, 3; wearing of, by King Hussein, 153, 158nn.12,19–20; as worn by women, 129

Kuwait, tribalism in, 105n.3

Lancaster, William, 10, 40, 63, 74n.8, 76n.26, 105n.2

land settlement laws, 42

land surveys, impact on agricultural practices, 42

land tenure: *hima*, 38, 40, 48n.5, 49n.7; *musha*, 40–43, 48n.7; "tribal territory" concepts of, 52

Laroui, Abdallah, 35n.41

Lawrence of Arabia, 12, 32n.17, 103

Lawrence, T. E., 21

Layne, Linda L., 4, 108, 150, 152–53

Lerner, Daniel, 19, 35n.37

Libya, example of non-representative democracy, 127n.27

livestock census, Jordan Valley, 45, 50n.21

McLaurin, R. D., 10–12, 42, 143

Majali family, 18

mansaf (national dish), 85, 103, 147

Ma'oz, Moshe, 41

marriage: intermarriage between noble and common tribes, lack of, 74n.3; multiple marriages, 59–60

Martin, Emily, 8–9, 28–29

Marwan al-Kasim, 26

Marx, Karl: on citizenship, 109–10, 121; dialogics of tribal self-representation and, 137–38;

Mashalkha tribes: field work among, xiv; housing plans of, 60; terminology among, 49n.10

Mashalkhah, Zaidan al-, 116

Mashpee Indians, import of an organic model of culture for, 14–15, 29

material culture: changing means of, xiii, 133–40; honor linked with, 134–37; increasing referentiality of, 138

mattresses, dimensions of, 69; rituals for arrangement of, 70–72, 78n.43; role of, in 'Abbadi women's social identity, 68–71, 77n.36; and honor, 68, 70–73, 135;

Sheik's use of, 71; storage and placement of, 58, 65–67, 69; terminology surrounding, 68–70

matwa, for mattress storage, 70–72, 82

Meeker, Michael E., 138

Merchant, Carolyn, 156

migration and oil, xv, 23, 47

military forces of Jordan: 'Abbadi participation in, 46–47; association of Bedouin and, 10, 32nn.10–14, 100; and changing authority of tribal leaders, 42

Mitchell, Timothy, 7, 133

modernity: royal progresses and, 151–54, 158n.13; tribalism seen as barrier to, 98–101. See also postmodernism

monarchy: Bedouin tribal support of, 11; comparison with Moroccan, 145–46, 149, 157n.1; cultural construction of, in Jordan, 11–12, 143–56; dynastic vs. constitutional forms of, 157n.2; importance of, in Arab world, 157nn.2,4; Jordanian-British cultural comparisons of, 136–37, 141n.10, 157n.3158n.19; posturing of, in Jordan, 143–56

Moore, Sally Falk, xi, 9

mosaic as image of collective identity, 3–6, 31nn.1–2; as model for science, 31n.6

Moukhaim al-Baqa'a (Palestinian refugee camp), 81, 111–12

Muasher, Marwan, 97–99

muhtarama (honorable): cultural concepts and, 136; *dilug* linked with, 131

music, as national heritage, xiii

Musil, Alois, 15–16

Muslim Brotherhood, xv, 116

Naim, Ahmad al-, 113

Naim, Salah al-, 113

Nasser, Gamel Abdul, Jordanian support for, 126n.19

Nasser, Seri, 101

nation, models of, 8, 20

National Broadcast Service, xiii

national heritage, comparison with other Arab nations, 141n.11

national treasure, King Hussein as, 138

nationalism: Arab vs. country-specific nationalism, 20–22; Jordanian-Palestinian nationhood, relationship between, 21–23; nature and, 155–56; Palestinian changes in, 25; possessive individualism

and, 138–40; space and, 8, 144–50; vs. tribal identities, 9–12, 96–105. *See also* Arab nationalism; collective identity
nature, Jordanian nationalism and, 155–56, 159n.21
Naval Intelligence Division, 18
news media, tribalism debate within, 97–99
Newton, Isaac, 6
Nomads of the Nomads, 10
Noor al-Hussein (Queen Noor), 130–31
Nyrop, Richard F., 18, 144

objects, increased referentiality of, in Jordan, 137–40
occupational patterns, capitalism and changes in, 45–47, 90–91
oil boom, impact on Jordan Valley, 47
Oppenheim, Max Von, 40
oral voting: cultural context of, 121–23; prevalence of, in elections, 115–18
organic model of culture and nation, Bedouin tribes and, 13–15, 28, 108–9
Ortner, Sherry B., 79–80
Ottoman Empire: Jordanian tribes and, 41–42; King Abdullah and, 152; origins of Jordan and, 21, 42
Ottoman Land Code of 1858, 40
Oweidi, Ahmad, 53, 63, 66, 74n.8, 75n.19, 104, 106n.13, 113, 138

Palestine, Jordan's relations with, 21–22, 25–26, 36n.51
Palestine Exploration Fund, 40
Palestine Liberation Organization (PLO): Arab League recognition of, 111; popularity of, among West Bank Palestinians, 25–26, 124n.6
Palestinian Declaration of Independence, 25
Palestinian Jordanians: classification of, 18–20, 34n.36; East Bank/West Bank populations, differences in, 19; folk culture of, as Jordanian national heritage, 139–40; influx of refugees from Israel, 23, 42–43, 49n.14; participation in parliamentary elections, 111–12; support for King Hussein among, 18–19, 25–26
paramount sheiks, as political candidates, 112–13
parliamentary structure in Jordan, 110–11
pastoral nomads, demographics of, 9–12

pastoralism, 38–40, 43–46. *See also* agricultural economy
Peake, Frederick, 10
Perin, Constance, 92
petitions to the king, and identity-making, 148–50, 157n.9
Petra, as tourist attraction, 102
pigeonhole model of collective identity, 3, 6–8, 13, 20, 139
pillows: construction and use of, 69, 77n.38; role of, in social identity-making, 68–72
Piscatori, James, 7–8
poetry, oral voting compared with, 122–23, 126n.24
political parties, banning of, in Jordan, 116–18; Jordanian support for pan-Arab parties, 126n.19
politics: ʿAbbādi tribalism and, 41–42, 49n.10; oral voting patterns and, 122–23; regionalism, and Jordanian national identity, 103–5; tribalism during elections and, 99–101, 108–27. *See also* elections
Pollack, Allen, 18
polling places: *dilug* worn by women at, 130; procedures described, 115–18, 125n.15
Popular Memory Group, 137
postmodernism: as dissolution of narrative and, 158n.15; models of collective identity, 28–31, 143, 150, 156
posture, concept of, 54–55; in ʿAbbādi household, 55–59, 61–73, 80–91; Jordanian monarchy and, 145–56
primordial ties, citizenship and, 98–99, 109
privacy: new attitudes towards, among ʿAbbādis, 63, 84; oral voting and, 121–23; social construction of, 66–67, 77n.33
progress, Hashemite narratives of, 152–53

quilts: construction of, 70; as part of marriage settlement, 69

rabʾa (women's quarters): ʿAbbādi use of, 83–84, comparisons with women's rooms in concrete houses, 87–88; furnishings in, 82; location of, 65–66; men and, 83–84; seating arrangements in, 71; social privacy in, 66–67; structure of, 58

Ramadan, ʿAbbādi practices concerning, 85

Rashrash, Hussein, xii

reading tent, blend of tribal and bureaucratic cultures, 155

Red Sea, as tourist attraction, 102

religious minorities, in Jordan, 18–24, 34n.32

representation, in electoral politics, 121; houses and, 92–93; material culture and, 132–40

residence patterns, Bedouin, 13–17; houses and, 92–93; material culture and, 132–40

resistance, to hegemonic discourse, 29, 136–37

Richards, A. I., 153

rites of passage, tents and, 61

Rose, Richard, 144

Rosen, Lawrence, 32n.4, 119

Rousseau, Jean-Jacques, 109

royal progresses (*zigrah shaʾbiyya*), tribal and national identity-making and, 146–50

rugs, and ʿAbbādi space-making, 69

Rwala tribes, compared with ʿAbbādis, 40, 66, 76n.26

Saket, Bassam, 47

San Remo Conference, 21

Saudi Arabia, Jordanian border with, 35n.43

Schumacher, John, 122, 124n.4, 127n.28, 149

science, models of identity, 156

scientific revolution: and colonial domination, 7; influence on social identity models, 6–7, 151

seating arrangements, social identity and, 70–72, 77n.40

Seccombe, Ian J., 45

secret balloting: cultural context of, in Jordan, 121–23; vs. oral voting in Jordanian elections, 115–18

segmentary linkage systems: Middle East anthropological research and, 96, 105n.2; models of collective identity and, 3–6, 8, 31n.3, 5

Seltzer, Rick, 26

Shadid, Mohammed, 26

Sharaf, Leila, 104–5, 107n.14

Sharif Hussein: leader of Great Arab Revolt, 21; self-comparison of King Hussein with, 37n.53

Sharkas, Ahmad, 123n.1, 155

Sharon, Ariel, 25

Sharr, Jamal al-, 115–16

Shasha, Najwa, xii

Sheeshans, 111, 141n.12

shiag (men's quarters): ʿAbbādi use of by men and women, 83–84; comparable space in concrete houses, 86–87; location of, 65–66; seating arrangements in, 71; social practices as definition of space within, 66–67; structure of, 58

sheikhs: attempts at voter influence by, 117–18, 126n.23; authority of, in ʿAbbādi tribes, 41–42, 114; furniture and, 71; housing size and social relationships, 56–57, 59; as political candidates, 112–14; relationships with King Hussein, 125n.14, 146–47, 149, 157n.10; tent and housing styles of, 59–60, 75n.22

Shinn, R. S., 155

Shoup, John A., 42, 48nn.5–7

Sinai, Anne, 18

slavery, abolition of, 51n.29

Slyomovics, Susan, 141n.6

Smith, Robertson, 4

social masses, models of collective identity and, 6, 8

social services, Jordan Valley economic development and, 44–45, 49n.16

sovereignty, monarchal posture and, 10–12, 21–29, 103–5, 130–36, 143–54

space: ʿAbbādi concept of, 53–73, 80–93, 145–50; sheikh's tents and houses, 59–60; capitalist use of domestic space, 89–91; concrete house case study, 86–89; constitution of tribal territory, 40, 52–53; monarchal posture and, 143–50; nationhood and, 144–50; nondiscursivity and change regarding, 79–80; politics of, 79–93; privatization of, 59, 63, 84, 87, 89–91; social relationships as definition of, 65–67, 145–50, 153; tent as case study of, 80–85; traditional floor plans in non-traditional structures, 55–59; transhumant practices and, 61–64; women's wealth and social identity linked with, 67–73

Srour, Hayel, 100

"staged authenticity," Jordanian tourism and, 102–3, 106n.8

State of the Art symposium. *See* Anthropology of Jordan, State of the Art Symposium

statistics, use of, in Jordanian nationalist rhetoric, 23, 35n.46

Stokes, Donald E., 126n.20

Strathern, Marilyn, 77n.34

Street, Brian, 17

Tatro, Earleen F., 101

tents: ʿAbbādi construction and use of, 55–59; al-Talib case study and, 81–85; ceremonial uses for, 60, 75n.19; erection of, 81–82; as locus of political and productive activity, 53–54; multifunctionality of space, 65–67; nomenclature for, 57–58, 76n.15; of sheikhs, 59–60; stacking of mattresses in, 69–70; as supplement to permanent housing, 61–64

"territorial nationalism," 151, 157n.11, 158n.13

time, monarchal posture and, 151–54, 158n.14. *See also* history; space; modernity

tourism: folkloric costume as promotion for, 130; importance to Jordanian economy, 101–2, 106nn.5–6, negative effects of, 106n.9; tribalism as attraction for, 101–3, 106n.6

tradition, as source of honor, 135

transhumance: ʿAbbādi practice of, 38, 40, 48n.3, 61; housing and, 61–64

Transjordan: definition of, 18; historical origins of, 21–22; social composition of, 10–12. *See also* East Bank; Hashemite Kingdom; West Bank

transport, ʿAbbādi employment in, 46, 51n.26

Trevor-Roper, Hugh, 134

tribal laws, abolishment of, 104–5, 106n.13. *See also* Bedouin Control Laws

tribalism, national debate concerning, 96–101; anthropological participation in, 96–97; Israel anda, 103–4; regional

comparisons with, 105n.3; regional politics of, 103; territory, constitution of, 40–53; tribespeople's response to, 128–40; tourism and, 101–3; western audiences and, 103–4. *See also* antitribalism

unmarried tribesmen, housing patterns among, 76nn.30–31

urban migration, lack of, in Jordan Valley, 47

"valence issues" in Jordanian politics, 126n.20

von Weizsacker, Baronness, 130

voting patterns: as form of gift exchange, 118–20, 126n.22; as identity-making act, 120–23; participation rates in Jordanian elections, 111–12, 124n.7, tribal loyalties and, 17, 112–18, 125nn.12, women's participation in, 111–12, 115, 117–19, 124n.8. *See also* elections; politics

Wagner, Roy, 133–34

Wahabism, 22

Wahlin, Lars, 34n.28, 40, 46, 50n.26

wajha (face), sheikhs as emblem of tribe, 114

Walpole, G. F., 42, 48n.7

wasta (go-between): in electoral politics, 119–20, 126n.22

water storage, ʿAbbādi practices concerning, 82

Watt, Ian, 122

wedding poems (*balah*), oral voting compared with, 122–23, 126n.24

weddings, use of mattresses and pillows at, 72

Weiner, Annette B., 77n.34

Weir, Shelagh, 129

Welcome to Jordan (brochure), 102

West Bank: Israeli occupation of, and changing meaning of honor, 135; Jordanian annexation of, 22–23, 42; Jordanian disengagement from, xv, 25–29, 35n.47, 36n.49, 150, 158n.12; Jordanian parliamentary elections and, 111

Wilkinson, J. C., 17, 34n.29

Williams, Raymond, 101

Wilson, Mary, 10, 12, 21–22, 32n.18, 34n.34, 35n.44, 42, 145

Wolf, Eric, 9

women: autonomy of voting patterns among, 115–22, 124n.8, 125n.16; *awa'id* (code of conduct) and, 53–54, 73n.7; *dilug* as cultural symbol among, 128–31; labor force participation by, xii, 45, 50n.24, 51n.25, 90–91; voting patterns and, 115–18, 125n.15; wealth of linked with social identity, 67–73, 77nn.34–35

wool, as mattress material, 68–70

Wright, Patrick, 137–38

Wright, Susan, 33n.24

Yemen: concepts of history in, 126n.25; oral performances in, 122–23, 126n.24; tribalism in, 105n.3

Yorke, Valerie, 19, 23, 26

Young Turks, 21

Zaidan al-Masalhah, Faiz Hamdan, 112, 115

Zeigler, L. Harman, 120, 124n.2

Zoqan, Zouhar al-, 125n.12